Non-Performing Loans, Non-Performing People

Non-Performing Loans, Non-Performing People

LIFE AND STRUGGLE WITH MORTGAGE DEBT IN SPAIN

MELISSA GARCÍA-LAMARCA

THE UNIVERSITY OF GEORGIA PRESS
Athens

© 2022 by the University of Georgia Press
Athens, Georgia 30602
www.ugapress.org
All rights reserved

Set in 10.25/13.5 Minion 3 Regular

Most University of Georgia Press titles are
available from popular e-book vendors.

Printed digitally

Library of Congress Cataloging-in-Publication Data

Names: García-Lamarca, Melissa, author.
Title: Non-performing loans, non-performing people : life and struggle with mortgage debt in
    Spain / Melissa García-Lamarca.
Description: Athens : The University of Georgia Press, [2022] | Series: Geographies of justice and
    social transformation | Includes bibliographical references and index.
Identifiers: LCCN 2022021568 | ISBN 9780820362991 (hardback) | ISBN 9780820363004 (paperback)
    | ISBN 9780820363011 (ebook)
Subjects: LCSH: Mortgage loans—Spain. | Debt—Spain.
Classification: LCC HG2040.5.S7 G37 2022 | DDC 332.7/20946—dc23/eng/20220525
LC record available at https://lccn.loc.gov/2022021568

To Chelo, who didn't get to finish the fight for her home.
Whose life, and that of her husband José Luis, was taken by the bank.
Her love and warmth will always be in our hearts.

CONTENTS

BOXES, TABLES, AND FIGURES

ABBREVIATIONS AND COMMONLY USED TERMS

Barracas: Shacks or shantytowns, widespread in Spanish cities from the 1920s to the 1970s

Caixa (Catalan) or *caja* (Spanish): Colloquial term for savings bank (*caixa d'estalvis* or *caja de ahorros*)

Compañeras: Female companions or comrades

Compañeros: Male companions or comrades

Compañerxs: Gender-neutral term for companions or comrades

Dación en pago: Mortgage debt cancellation in exchange for the bank taking possession of the home

EMF: European Mortgage Federation

EU: European Union

FROB: Spanish Fund for Orderly Bank Restructuring (Fondo de Reestructuración Ordenada Bancaria)

FTA: Asset Securitization Funds (Fondo de Titularización de Activos)

ILP: Popular Legislative Initiative (Iniciativa Legislativa Popular)

INE: National Institute of Statistics (Instituto Nacional de Estadística)

LAU: Urban Letting Act (Ley de Arrendamientos Urbanos)

MoU: Memorandum of understanding

PAH: Platform for Mortgage-Affected People (Plataforma de Afectados por la Hipoteca)

REIT: Real estate investment trust

RMBS: Residential mortgage-backed security

SAREB: Management Company for Assets Arising from Bank Reorganization (Sociedad de Gestión de Activos Precedentes de la Reestructuración Bancaria)

SOCIMIs: Sociedades Anónimas Cotizadas de Inversión Inmobiliaria (Spanish REITs)

TAIFA: Grassroots critical economy group based in Barcelona

VPO: State-subsidized housing (*vivienda de protección oficial*)

ACKNOWLEDGMENTS

This book would not have come to fruition without the support, encouragement, and inspiration of countless people. I shaped its core ideas in my doctoral thesis at the University of Manchester, where Erik Swyngedouw and Maria Kaika were outstanding mentors, providing me with the perfect balance of support, autonomy, and intellectual stimulation. Their thoughtful and thought-provoking comments on my work from incipient ideas to consolidated chapters were invaluable. I am also grateful to my examiners Susanne Soederberg and Stefan Bouzarovski, who strongly encouraged me to move this book project forward.

During my PhD research, the European Network for Political Ecology (ENTITLE) generated an exceptional group of colleagues and friends. The feedback I received on my book's core arguments and framing through our Barcelona reading group—from Diego Andreucci, Rita Calvário, Irmak Ertör, Gustavo García López, Marien González Hidalgo, Santi Gorostiza, Panagiota Kotsila, and Julie de los Reyes—stimulated and challenged me, and definitely improved my work. Extra thanks to my dear Irmak swimming by my side as I wrote the book proposal, and Santi, who always encourages me and lends a hand, be it for navigating archives, unearthing rich historical facts, or providing detailed insights into how to best translate various Catalan- or Spanish-language concepts into English. I value their friendships immensely. I am also grateful to my ENTITLE mentor Guy Baeten for organizing a five-week stay in Uppsala and Lund. Many seminars and discussions I had there and in Gothenburg were extremely helpful as I started formulating chapters. Thanks in particular to Brett Christophers, Irene Molina, Carina Listerborn, Jennifer Mack, Chiara Valli, Catherina Thorn, Håkan Thorn, Cathrin Wasshede, Juan Velazquez, Anders Lund Hansen, Henrik Gutzon Larsen, Emil Pull, Eric Clark, and Nura Alkhalili. Double thanks to Brett, who read my full draft manuscript and gave me encouragement during the long publishing process.

Over the last five years in Barcelona, Isabelle Anguelovski has been a phenomenal mentor, animating me from day one to make this book a reality and helping me create the time and space to do so. Despite having a million demands on her time, she always provided thoughtful feedback on proposals and revised chapters. Words fail to communicate how grateful I am for her continuous support and guidance; if academia had more people like Isabelle, it would be an enriching, caring, and flourishing place. I am also so thankful for the encouragement and support from fellow members of the Barcelona Lab for Urban Environmental Justice and Sustainability, housing struggle scholar-activists in Barcelona Mara Ferreri, Lorenzo Vidal, and Carlos Delclós, and the editorial collective of the *Radical Housing Journal*: dear Mara (again), Michele, Meli, Erin, and Ana. Thanks to Sid for making his home ours during a very fruitful writing retreat where I rejigged many elements of the book.

At the University of Georgia Press, I thank Mick Gusinde-Duffy for his continuous editorial support throughout the process. I am also very grateful to the two anonymous reviewers who pushed me to think beyond and dig more deeply into several critical framings in the first draft of my manuscript, which helped make the final version even stronger and more relevant. I also want to thank Brenda Parker for taking the time to share her experience publishing with the Press and giving me advice on moving forward in the process.

This book would not exist without the Platform for Mortgage Affected People (PAH). Countless compañerxs (companions/comrades) and friends in PAH Barcelona and PAHC Sabadell not only made this research possible, but also gave me support and *ánimos*, especially as I churned out my doctoral thesis. I am still humbled and inspired by their/our struggle, which marked a milestone in my life, despite political and ideological divergences that eventually led to the expulsion of the Obra Social commission from PAH Barcelona, shifting our energies to other projects.

Last but not least, I thank my parents, brothers, and sister-in-law, for their constant love and encouragement. My partner Diego has always, always believed in me, and has never ceased to give his unconditional support and love. Little Júlia was with us as I shaped this book. I hope the stories and learnings can inspire her, and others who didn't live these times in their flesh, about the possibilities of collective struggle for more egalitarian and just futures.

Non-Performing Loans, Non-Performing People

INTRODUCTION

Life and Struggle with Mortgage Debt

Two Stories from Performing to Non-Performing Loans and People

BUILDING A SECURE FUTURE?
MORTGAGE INDEBTEDNESS FROM HOUSING BOOM TO CRISIS

In the early 2000s María was a tenant in Sabadell, an industrial city fifteen kilometers away from Barcelona, with her partner, Carlos. Originally from Ecuador, they were just two people out of nearly five million, attracted by the
promise of a better life, who were part of Spain's largest ever wave of immigration from the late 1990s to mid-2000s. Spain was a European success story,
with record levels of economic growth and employment due to booming construction and tourism sectors. As a caregiver and a shop attendant, respectively, María and Carlos also had what they thought were stable jobs.

They decided to buy as rents began to rise in 2005, with the hope of saving
rather than throwing money away. The idea of saving through buying housing was on everyone's minds at the time in Spain. Housing prices were rising
quickly, doubling between 2000 and 2005, making María and Carlos feel that
they should buy before they missed their chance. As in other places at that
time, such as the United States, homeownership rates were reaching their historic peak as more and more people bought homes.

María and Carlos approached a real estate agency to help them find an
apartment. The agency arranged everything: visits to different homes, closing the sale, and mortgage financing from the bank. The agent told María
and Carlos that he found a great mortgage—one that he would even give to
his own father—with excellent conditions. No down payment was required,
and interest rates were variable, as typical at the time. Trusting the agent, they
moved forward with the financing arrangements.

María and Carlos never received the mortgage documents previous to signing but did talk over the details of their mortgage directly with the bank, which offered the couple a five-year waiting period, meaning that a reduced monthly mortgage installment covering only the interest on the mortgage capital would be paid during this period. María in particular was adamant in her refusal of the five-year waiting period, and the bank ultimately told them they would eliminate it from the documents. Based on the couple's combined income of €1,600 per month, the bank calculated their monthly mortgage installments at around €600 or €700—slightly less than they would have paid in rent. When María and Carlos asked about possible interest rate increases and what this would mean for their monthly mortgage installments, the bank said they might rise twenty euros a year in an exaggerated scenario. Interest rates do go up but always only a little, the bank emphasized.

When the bank saw that Carlos was a guarantor on the mortgage of two other couples' mortgage loans, they insisted that these couples, also from Ecuador, reciprocate and act as guarantors for María and Carlos's mortgage. This was standard practice, the bank explained, intended for María and Carlos's safety: if one or both of the couples did not pay their mortgage, nothing would happen to María and Carlos's apartment. Known as crossed guarantors, this arrangement was common especially among immigrants during the housing boom. This operation made it appear as if applicants' income levels were higher than they really were, ensuring that the Bank of Spain would approve the mortgage application.

When they signed the loan at the notary, María and Carlos officially owned their own apartment and a thirty-five-year, no-down-payment mortgage loan of €215,000, the average price of an apartment on the outskirts of Sabadell at the time. The next day the couple went to the office of the bank director, Monica, to discuss some final details. Unexpectedly, Monica shared that the bank had to include a one-year waiting period in the mortgage contract because María and Carlos couldn't start paying the €700 a month mortgage installment immediately. To ensure the mortgage deed was notarized as planned, the bank had included it in the final contract. Monica also explained that the bank had its original calculations wrong and that the couple had to buy mortgage nonpayment insurance, at a cost of €4,000. This insurance, according to Monica, would pay the monthly mortgage installment if either María or Carlos lost their job during the first five years of the mortgage. When María stated that she wouldn't pay for it, Monica threatened to begin the process of home repossession. María and Carlos grudgingly accepted the insurance, able to pay only half of the cost with their savings, the remainder to be paid in the coming years.

When the one-year waiting period on the mortgage was over, María and Carlos paid €700 a month for six months. But as interest rates crept up, affecting millions of mortgage holders across Spain, the monthly installments increased €150. One year later, they were up €300 a month. In other words, the couple's total monthly payment was €1,000, far above the promised €700 a month. And as interest rates hit their maximum in 2008, María and Carlos's monthly mortgage installments reached €1,270.

During this period, when they had two children, the couple started to have problems, largely driven by the tension that radiated daily as they were barely able to pay their mortgage. Furthermore, as the 2008 economic crisis hit, María was one of millions across Spain who lost her job. Non-European immigrants like her were the hardest hit, as their unemployment rates rose in Catalonia from a low of 9.3 percent in 2006 to a peak of 45 percent in 2012, according to the National Institute of Statistics. María received €600 in unemployment payments, three-quarters of which went to pay the mortgage. When the couple separated, however, Carlos refused to pay his share. At that point, the monthly installments were €800 a month due to a dramatic fall in interest rates in 2009–10, but María was unable to keep up. In addition, she learned that the mortgage nonpayment insurance the bank obliged them to purchase didn't cover the payments.

In 2010 María went to the new bank director in tears to find a solution. She was terrified of losing her home. She asked for a waiting period, but the bank said it would agree only if Carlos and their four guarantors signed. Despite María's pleas, Carlos and the guarantors said no. The bank also refused to forgive the mortgage debt in exchange for the home. Under Spanish law, it is not possible to declare personal bankruptcy, and debtors must meet their obligations through present and future payments. The bank told María that despite the fact that she was insolvent, the debt was permanent and there were five other people who could potentially pay: Carlos and the four guarantors.

The foreclosure documents arrived after four months of nonpayment. María consulted various lawyers, who all told her it was her fault and that nothing could be done, scolding her for not having read the mortgage contract before signing. Colloquially known as "the tome" (*el tocho*), these financial documents are hundreds of pages long, filled with cryptic text and fine print. The bank proposed that María and Carlos give them power of attorney so that they could maximize the sale price of the apartment; then the couple would owe just the remaining debt. No way, said María. How could she authorize the bank to sell her home without knowing the sale price?

Feeling guilty and hopeless, suffering insomnia, and fearing eviction, María thought she would never achieve resolution. While she was walking down the street one day in early 2011, someone handed her a flyer announcing the first meeting in Sabadell of a social movement called the Platform for Mortgage-Affected People (PAH). Skeptical, but with nowhere else to turn, she went to see what PAH had to say.

FROM HOPELESSNESS TO EMPOWERMENT IN CRISIS:
FIGHTING AGAINST INDEBTED LIFE

Pepe started to have problems paying his mortgage in 2010. He worked in the construction sector, which employed 14 percent of the population and generated 16 percent of Spain's wealth at the peak of the housing boom. Before buying an apartment, he lived with his girlfriend as a tenant in his hometown of Barcelona. In the mid-2000s, in Spain's booming and attractive second largest city and tourist mecca, the price of housing was continuously rising, and like many Spaniards since the time of the Franco dictatorship, Pepe had internalized the idea of buying a home. Although prices were more accessible in Reus, a city 120 kilometers south of Barcelona where Pepe worked and decided to buy an apartment, they were also rising daily.

When he signed his forty-year, €132,000, no-money-down, variable-rate mortgage in 2007, Pepe was paying €740 in monthly installments. He was earning around €1,800 a month with a permanent job contract. It was a manageable amount. Furthermore, he had shopped around for his mortgage, presenting proposals to different banks with the conditions he wanted—no guarantors, no down payment—and finally found a taker.

But with interest rate increases, an issue affecting 85 percent of mortgages in Spain at the time as variable interest rates were common, in the coming years Pepe found himself paying €1,200 a month. He couldn't make ends meet. To compound his problems, when interest rates fell in 2009–10, Pepe lost his job as the construction sector crashed: this was the main cause of mass unemployment, peaking in Spain at over 26 percent in 2013. His unemployment payments were only slightly more than his monthly mortgage installments.

Pepe did everything he could to pay as the bank demanded, even going hungry as he ate fewer meals, but after several months he couldn't keep going. The bank auctioned off his apartment, and the "solutions" they offered him in order to pay the €100,000 he still owed were impossible. After a lawyer told Pepe that he would be "screwed for life" if he didn't pay—if he had a property, a car, or any other asset in his name or if he earned over €1,000 a month, the bank could seize it—he was desperate and depressed.

Pepe's girlfriend had heard about the PAH, founded in 2009 in Barcelona, and encouraged him to attend a meeting. He started to go regularly in 2012, when the movement achieved its zenith. He explained his case to over 120 people in a packed meeting and was advised on what steps he could take. Pepe began to learn more about organizing against financial abuse, absorbing new legal and financial information about his case and about the political and economic situation that had created the housing boom and crisis.

Having never been part of a social movement, like the vast majority of people who come to the PAH, Pepe slowly became politicized. He began to ask all sorts of questions: Why do you have to continue to pay once you lose your home, when it was the bank and the state that speculated with housing, a basic need for all? Why was the financial system rescued with millions in public funds but was making millions in profits, at the same time that banks evicted people daily and the state actively enabled this process? Pepe learned about at least a dozen cases in every assembly he attended and saw countless numbers of people in need, especially compañerxs who immigrated from the Global South to Spain in search of a better life. He thought his situation was bad, but he heard and saw many people in the PAH suffering far greater abuses.

Through the PAH, with over 220 local assemblies across Spain, Pepe realized that thousands of people had been affected by housing scams. Article 47 of the 1978 Spanish constitution, adopted after the end of the almost forty-year Franco dictatorship and stating that everyone has the right to dignified housing, is simply not true. Pepe started to see how the government and financial sector benefited from the law. The banks facilitated indebtedness, granting loans to people in precarious conditions. Bancaja, the bank where Pepe got his loan, went bankrupt and after being bailed out by the state was merged in 2010 into a nationalized bank named Bankia, which now raked in tremendous profits. How was this possible?

With guidance from the PAH, Pepe fought for a solution from the bank. He used the knowledge he gained to advise his court-appointed lawyer on what steps to take. It was unfortunately normal that most lawyers didn't know how to defend these cases nor even start the proceedings because it was their first time representing a person undergoing foreclosure and/or eviction. Spain's housing crisis of the 2010s was unprecedented. Previously homeownership had been seen (and mostly experienced) as a safe bet, a path toward the "middle class."

As Pepe fought for debt forgiveness from 2012 to 2014, he attended as many of the PAH's direct actions as he could to help achieve solutions for his compañerxs when the state and banks refused to act. The first of dozens of evictions he blocked was Raquel's, a woman who had dejectedly come to a PAH assembly with an eviction order effective the following week. PAH members noted her details and asked everyone in the assembly to come and stop the eviction. The morning of the eviction Pepe arrived a bit before nine o'clock and saw a mass of people outside the apartment and five police vans. He felt a bit intimidated, but to chants of *no pasarán* (they will not pass), he piled in alongside others blocking the door. When the judicial retinue arrived a few PAH members spoke with them and prevented them from entering the building. Raquel came down and gave her ID to the court representatives, as they told her she had fifteen to thirty days to appeal the ruling, delay the eviction further, or archive her case. Shouts of *sí se puede!* (yes we can!) plus smiles, joy, and applause resounded from the dozens of compañerxs surrounding Raquel.

Pepe also participated in a collective action against a bank to collapse the daily operations of multiple offices simultaneously, forcing them to close their doors to the public for half a day. The action started at ten o'clock one morning with over a hundred people; by one o'clock the PAH had succeeded in signing with the bank a negotiation protocol, which outlined a standard communication procedure between the PAH and the bank for PAH members facing foreclosure or eviction.

Blocking evictions and forcing the closure of banks create unity, according to Pepe. People support each other and reclaim something that is right. He has lived in his own flesh and blood and seen from others' experiences that alone—isolated and helpless—they can't achieve anything. But those who support others will be supported. To force a dignified and just solution is possible only by working together. "Between us all, we can make them negotiate and we can be heard. That is the truth."

Pepe obtained debt forgiveness from Bankia in the spring of 2014. When he signed the paperwork, the bank's lawyer congratulated him, saying that Pepe should consider himself a lucky man. "It is extremely difficult to negotiate with the bank," the attorney confided. Pepe knew that he would never have liberated himself from indebtedness without the collective struggle of the PAH.

Life, Housing, and Debt Today

María and Pepe are just two of hundreds of thousands of stories from Spain about life and struggle with mortgage debt. But their tales are by no means unique to Spain. Becoming indebted to access basic needs like housing and education is increasing across the world and was manifest in the early 2000s in many parts of Europe and North America. For households and individuals, mortgages are one of debt's most pervasive day-to-day forms, constituting nearly 75 percent of household debt in the Global North and 43 percent in the Global South (McKinsey Global Institute 2015). That makes residential property, and the debt it entails, one of the largest assets in most people's lives, particularly in the Global North, and one of the largest financial assets in most economies. For example, in 2018 outstanding mortgage debt was €9.5 trillion in the United States alone and €7.2 trillion in Europe (European Mortgage Federation 2020). Household debt sat at over 100 percent of net disposable income in 2017 in Canada, the United States, and much of Europe, reaching over 200 percent in Norway, the Netherlands, and Denmark, according to the Organisation for Economic Co-operation and Development (OECD). Both outstanding mortgage debt and overall household debt are on the increase in many countries across the Global South, with South Africa, Chile, and South Korea standing out as leaders in their regions.

Housing is a universal basic need, but it simultaneously operates as an object of investment and an item of speculation. On the one hand, a home fulfills a fundamental psychological and emotional need, as a place of stability and security in people's day-to-day lives. On the other hand, housing is a commodity with an almost unique ability to incite economic growth and returns on investment at multiple levels. Significant capital is required to build housing, and in the private sector, which drives the construction of the vast majority of housing today, capital is attracted by the speculative possibilities of profit. Housing also needs a broad set of infrastructures to support it—roads, energy and water supplies, and sidewalks, to name a few—which further feeds private and public construction. At the household level there is the purchase of the home itself and all the objects that fill it, whose acquisition stimulates consumption, investment, and credit. Financial products like home and life insurance are often also required upon signing a mortgage loan. And from mortgage credit, there is investor demand for securitized financial vehicles like residential-backed mortgage securities. Taking all these material and financial processes together, it is clear that when housing booms, the economy booms.

The multiple planes on which housing functions have generated a paradox in many parts of the world, particularly in recent decades. Despite the universal need for housing and countless international declarations and national constitutions supposedly enshrining the right to decent and affordable housing, increasing numbers of people lack it. According to the Eviction Lab at Princeton University, an estimated 890,000 evictions took place in the United

States in 2016.[1] The International Tribunal on Evictions reported over 230,000 people evicted in Brazil through thirty-nine specific megaprojects across eighteen cities in 2018, while in São Paulo alone the Evictions Observatory recorded over 35,000 evictions and more than 204,000 households threatened by eviction from 2017 to September 2020.[2] Housing insecurity more broadly, referring to the inability to access affordable, stable, or decent quality housing, is a problem estimated by McKinsey Global Institute to affect 330 million urban households around the world. The lived dimensions that such realities generate are highlighted by Raquel Rolnik, the former United Nations Special Rapporteur on the right to adequate housing, as she relates scenes she witnessed upon her visits in the United States, Spain, Mexico, and Kazakhstan, respectively: "Millions of indebted or foreclosed homeowners, the 'subprime' victims of a decade-long credit boom; empty neighborhoods, depopulated towns, and bankrupted new developments; protesters occupying the streets and public spaces for months; a hunger strike by owners deprived of their promised apartments" (Rolnik 2013, 1058).

Yet just ten years earlier, as Rolnik continues here and further underscores in *Urban Warfare* (2019), housing was one of the most vibrant frontiers of late neoliberalism during the economic boom, as the state steadily withdrew from housing provision and liberalized market mechanisms to spur housing production and supposedly access. This was certainly the case in countries like the United States, Ireland, and Spain. In the latter, an unprecedented housing boom took place from 1997 to 2007. In a country with a population of forty-five million and an exceptional wave of immigration, almost six million units of housing were built—more than in France, Germany, and Italy combined—and housing prices increased over 200 percent in ten years. During that time, the acquisition of both primary and secondary homes accelerated. The built environment expanded exponentially thanks to the deregulation of housing, mortgage, and land markets, both mediated and compounded by various phases of Spain's integration into the European Union, which appeared to promise modernity, including a stable market and investment environment. What Ramón Fernández Durán (2006) dubbed the "urbanization tsunami" paved one-quarter of Spain's land area as the country, instilled with a construction obsession since the Franco dictatorship, became the European leader in housing production and cement consumption (Naredo, Carpintero, and Marcos 2008). Spain ranked fifth in the world's consumption of cement during this period—coming in after China, India, the United States, and Japan—and the construction sector represented a whopping 17 percent of Spanish gross domestic product (GDP) at its peak (Chislett 2008). Despite declining real average wages, Spanish financial entities granted over 9.4 million mortgages as the financial sector, public administration, and media actively promoted housing as a safe investment whose value would never decrease. From the Franco dictatorship's drive to create "a nation of homeowners, not proletariats" in the late 1950s, then through market-based strategies in the post-1978 democratic and modern European context, by 2007 homeownership was realized by almost 85 percent of the Spanish population—one of the highest homeownership rates in Europe.

In Spain, like in the United Kingdom, United States, Denmark, and Norway, real estate lending increased dramatically over the second half of the twentieth century, constituting around two-thirds of all bank lending in 2007 (Jordá, Schularick, and Taylor 2014). In many of these countries, credit was plentiful and interest rates hovered around 2 percent, marking historic lows, in the mid-2000s. Securitization, a process involving banks or financial intermediaries packaging mortgage loans and selling them on secondary financial markets to generate liquidity, became commonplace. As a seemingly magical tool to fuel mortgage lending and construction, securitization was hailed by the Bank of Spain (Banco de España 2007, 19) as "one of the main revitalizing elements of international financial markets." Securitization was a key element enabling extended mortgage lending and one of the main mechanisms driving the speculation with and financialization of housing, where the importance of the mortgage finance market came to rival or surpass the actual production of housing itself (Aalbers 2008). It often occurred at the same time that the state deregulated housing finance systems to facilitate the growth of banks and credit intermediaries, stripped tenants' legal protections, and reduced the provision of social housing. In other words, as the state stepped back from social provision and facilitated private market rule, securitization went hand in glove with broader processes of neoliberalization.

Of course, a growing quantity of homeowners was essential to increase mortgage lending and indispensable to ensure the success of securitization. This is what two of the cofounders of the PAH (la Plataforma de Afectados por la Hipoteca) term "mortgaged lives" (Colau and Alemany 2012). Yet in the 2000s mortgages were granted extensively across many countries under increasingly precarious conditions of life. Bellamy Foster (2006) highlighted the "growing squeeze" on wage-based incomes in the United States, as real wages were sluggish for decades and a typical household's real income fell for five years in a row through 2004. A similar story of income precarity manifested in Spain. During the years of the housing boom, around 30 percent of new work contracts were for short-term or temporary employment, while average salaries fell by 10 percent in real terms, as 40 percent of wage earners earned barely €1,000 a month (López and Rodríguez 2010). Furthermore, according to the Spanish National Institute for Statistics (INE), in 2008 workers' average annual earnings varied enormously by gender and especially nationality. Women earned over €5,000 less per year than men, and foreign workers made €7,500 less annually than Spaniards, with gender differences among non-Spanish immigrants also being pronounced. Yet despite this, due to an insignificant amount of social housing and poor legal protection for tenants, working-class and racialized people increasingly contracted mortgages to access housing. Many immigrants who came to Spain from 1998 to 2007—over 4.8 million in total according to the INE, largely from the rest of Europe (1.7 million), Latin America (1.8 million, especially Ecuador and Colombia), and Africa (650,000, over three-quarters from Morocco), to work in the construction and services industry—also found that mortgages were the best option to obtain stable housing or enable family reunification.

The neoliberal state's steady withdraw as a provider of social support through, for example, social housing or affordable rents has occurred as individuals have been pushed to secure their own future through mortgaged homeownership or other forms of indebtedness. Some authors have framed this as a shift toward a system of debtfare, as opposed to welfare (Hardt and Negri 2012; Soederberg 2014). In other words, individual or household loans, rather than state support, have become critical to meet basic needs for housing, education, and retirement. Reproducing society increasingly through private debt furthermore both re-creates existing racial, gender, and class inequalities and results in the intensification of social *in*security (Roberts 2013). At its extreme this has been expressed in recent decades through the rise of debtors' prisons in the United States, where punitive and coercive means are used to manage (and criminalize) poverty and the broader crisis in social reproduction (LeBaron and Roberts 2012).

As long as jobs are plentiful and people can pay their debts, this individualized financial responsibility amid reduced state support in the context of employment precarity does not appear to be problematic. But the U.S. subprime mortgage debacle and ensuing 2008 financial crisis brought a harsh reality to light for millions across the Global North, particularly in the United States, Ireland, and Spain, the countries hardest hit by the crisis. With the bust of Spain's real estate boom, according to the INE unemployment climbed steadily from its historic low of 8 percent in 2007 to 26 percent by 2013, with non–European Union foreigner unemployment—as the category is named by the Spanish National Institute of Statistics—reaching a whopping 40 percent, up to 45 percent in Catalonia. Unbeknownst to most households upon signing their mortgage loan, Spain's Civil Code (1911) and Mortgage Act (1946) do not cancel the full mortgage debt if the auction price of the home does not cover the household's outstanding mortgage debt and legal costs upon foreclosure and eviction. This element has not been amended despite the devastation these laws have wrought for hundreds of thousands of former homeowners. And unlike in the United States and other countries, individuals in Spain are unable to declare personal bankruptcy. This means that as housing prices plummeted and foreclosed homes were auctioned for a pittance or kept by the bank, hundreds of thousands of people were left with a lifetime of debt, what myself and coauthor Maria Kaika (2016) have called *mortgaged lives*, not infrequently totaling up to hundreds of thousands of euros. According to the Consejo General del Poder Judicial (General Council of the Judiciary), nearly 600,000 foreclosures occurred and 378,693 eviction orders were issued between 2008 and 2014, the peak years of the crisis.

This barbarity of foreclosures and evictions occurred as Spain had the largest empty housing stock in Europe—3.5 million housing units in 2011, according to the INE—and the financial system received a state bailout of at least €63 billion. Meanwhile, Spanish foreign direct investment capital rapidly shifted from Spain to Morocco's real estate and construction sector, spurring cries of an "Iberian invasion" driven by property speculators and illustrating how speculative housing booms in the Global North can have a domino effect in the Global South (Kutz 2016; Kutz and Lenhardt 2016).[3] The reality of evictions, private-sector bailouts, and shifting speculative investment has generated a political battle that cuts to the heart of the neoliberal and financialized system. In Spain and elsewhere the heart of the question has boiled down to what democracy really means and whose priorities rule. Is the priority of "democratic" states to buffer citizens and society from the crisis through people-centered solutions or to save, secure, and rejig the financial system to restart processes of economic growth that, ultimately, bring the vast majority of benefits to the economic and political elite?

These were some of the concerns of the Indignados (indignant) who burst onto the scene after the Arab Spring and before the U.S. Occupy movement in the early 2010s. The Indignados included hundreds of thousands of people who occupied plazas throughout Spain on 15 May 2011 to contest the way the Spanish state, arm in arm with the European Union, prioritized the rescue of the financial system rather than the people. This heated period of plaza occupations fueled the growth of local branches of the PAH across Spain, founded in 2009 in Barcelona as a grassroots process to unite and collectively find solutions to homeowners facing foreclosure, eviction, and a life of debt. The PAH provided concrete processes and actions to achieve personal and collective change.

The political battle is also unfolding at the subjective level, a core focus of this book. On the one hand, debt is shaping up to be a frontline battle of the future because for increasing numbers of people debts are the wages of the future that creditors claim long in advance (Ross 2017). And the increasingly interiorized discipline of the indebted self is what marks this period as different from past historic and colonial forms of debt (Mahmud 2012). On the other hand, the emancipatory potential of this social battle is huge as the regulatory and disciplinary nature of (mortgage) debt can be broken, as people no longer can be—and then no longer want to be—a financial subject who pays their debt no matter what. This is occurring as countless numbers first feel ashamed, guilty, and afraid because of their inability to pay and entrance into default, but then unite with others in the same situation and begin to understand the system as a scam. People started to see that they were mere objects used to further capital accumulation. Organized through movements like the PAH, they began to fight banks to liberate themselves and others from their nonpayable mortgage debt and press the state to change unjust housing laws. These struggles can be considered as a fight against capitalism at large (Suarez 2017) and generate a powerful politics of dissent (Gonick 2021). Debt, (urban) life, and housing thus emerge as key terrains of collective struggle.

As housing thus increasingly became—and remains—an object of speculation, the paradox between the universal need for housing and increasing housing speculation and precarity has deepened. Speculation with housing, and with life, generated a massive financial crisis, but the dynamics underlying the crisis have laid bare the true nature of supposedly securing a home through market mechanisms. Neoliberal and financialized housing models not only fueled what appeared to be stable routes for capital accumulation but also completely destabilized millions of lives and the entire global financial system. Better understanding the lived dimension of what it means when housing becomes a financial asset and the regulatory and disciplinary function of debt, as well as the resistance that has grown from those directly impacted by this process, can provide clues to theoretically and politically deepen critiques and alternatives to the financialized housing model, toward more equal and equitable access to dignified housing for all.

Mortgage Indebtedness:
Lived and Emancipatory Possibilities

In this book I tell the little-known story of how people obtain and live with mortgage debt in times of precarity, and how individualized indebtedness can be collectivized and fought against to stop foreclosures and eviction and free people from a lifetime of indebtedness. I tell this story, on the one hand, through a heterodox, Marxist-inspired political-economic perspective. On the other hand, the experiences of dozens of indebted compañerxs engaged in the PAH), as well as those of (ex-)bankers and government officials, compel me to move beyond a solely class-based Marxist perspective. Inspired by feminist scholars who have brought the everyday into their explorations of contemporary political economy (Hall 2020; Joseph 2014; LeBaron 2010; Montgomerie and Tepe-Belfrage 2017; Roberts 2013), what I learned from this lived experience highlighted the need to integrate a racialized, gendered, and decolonial analysis of mortgaged lives in order to get to the deeper roots of the financial and social processes I seek to uncover.

The need for a racialized analysis became clear as I understood in greater detail the experiences of obtaining a mortgage from formerly upper-middle-class Spanish, low-income Spanish, and non-European immigrant compañerxs. While class-based differences were relatively visible and present, clear racialized dimensions emerged in terms of the process of obtaining a mortgage and their terms and conditions. This reality begged deeper analysis, especially since racialized inquiries are largely absent in the Spanish context and can contribute to understanding how racialization configures housing insecurity more broadly. The need to consider gender emerged both from compañeras' productive and reproductive demands and struggles in the context of default, foreclosure, and eviction, as well as in the social composition of and feminist principles inspiring the PAH itself. Many almost passing comments that compañeras made about family and caring duties in the context of mortgage indebtedness pointed to deeper, gendered social impacts of indebtedness, while Spain's dominant patriarchal and machoistic culture meant that it was oftentimes women who sought out the PAH as a social support process, as other researchers have highlighted (Gonick 2021). Finally, in terms of a decolonial analysis, I attempt to destabilize a definitively Global North, "developed" reading of the everyday political-economic processes I explore. Spain has long been on the European periphery—economically, socially, and politically—and began to emerge into "modernity" only in the mid-1980s through full ascension to the European project. At the same time, the country is part of the famed PIGS (Portugal, Ireland, Greece, Spain), which have caused what are seen as excessive costs to, and thus problems for, European leaders of northern Europe, and it is sidelined from the Anglo-American axis of financial power. By integrating a racialized and gendered analysis and destabilizing Spain's "developed" position, I thus aim to deepen and make relational the lived impacts of mortgage indebtedness. In this light, I more deeply explore other elements of domicide (Porteous and Smith 2001) or root shock (Fullilove 2001), concepts that relate to the human consequences of the destruction of the home.

From this position, I seek to make visible and theoretically elaborate two critical phenomena related to housing, debt, and lived experience that have received limited consideration to date. First, I aim to understand how financial speculation with life is both lived in individuals' day-to-day experiences and *differentially* embedded in the dynamics of (urban) capital accumulation. Through the word "differential," I refer to entrenched racialized, gendered, and classed dimensions. I do this by digging deeper into the idea of mortgages operating as a "secondary form of exploitation" (Harvey 1982, 285) in the sphere of circulation and advancing a novel Foucauldian-inspired understanding of mortgage debt to illustrate how mortgages act as a technology of power to regulate and discipline life. Just as non-European, nonwhite (racialized) bodies are not valued the same as European white bodies in the sphere of production (Kish and Leroy 2015; Pulido 2017; Robinson 1983)—nor is women's (re)productive work versus men's market labor, or working-class versus wealthy bodies—the same reality becomes visible in the sphere of mortgage debt circulation. Differential technologies of power are used to regulate and discipline European upper-middle-class bodies, European working-class bodies, and non-European immigrant (Brown) working-class bodies through, for example, crossed guarantors or conditioning mortgage loans on contracting insurance or other bank products (cross-selling). Theoretically, I deepen understandings of the racialized, gendered, and classed lived dimensions of housing becoming a financial asset, a topic that has been underresearched in the housing financialization literature (Fields and Raymond 2021). In exploring this process more broadly I uncover the mechanisms and processes that create "the unequal differentiation of human value" (Melamed 2015, 77). I also contribute to critically understand the biopolitics of mortgage debt. This term refers to the role that household indebtedness can play in securing and ensuring capital accumulation in the context of neoliberal and financialized housing dynamics present and growing across the world. By understanding empirically and theorizing the dynamics of how bodies are differentially enrolled in complex financial relationships to obtain a home, a basic need for everyone, this book makes a previously missing yet urgently needed contribution.

In understanding this first phenomenon of how financial speculation with life is both lived in day-to-day experiences and differentially embedded in the dynamics of (urban) capital accumulation, I make two key arguments. First, I argue that the process of turning homes into financial assets to be bought and sold on secondary financial markets—what is known as the financialization of housing—is intimately tied to human life becoming an objectified financial asset. This is done as the government and financial sector attempt to instill investor or financial subjectivities into mortgaged homeowners who, in reality, become indebted people who serve as (differentially valued) objects, ensuring the circulation of capital. I maintain that this speculation with life itself is part and parcel of the dynamics of urban capital accumulation, suggesting that life is proletarianized not only through the capital-labor relation in the sphere of production, as has long been argued by Marxist scholars, but also in the mortgage debt relation in the sphere of circulation. Furthermore, I go beyond most Marxist scholars and build from feminist political economists by thinking through how processes of racialization are a lived and inherent part of the social and material nature of capitalism and the institutions that perpetuate it (Bhattacharyya 2018; Gilmore 2007; Goldstein 2015; Kish and Leroy 2015; Melamed 2015; Mitchell 2010; Robinson 1983). I show how this proletarianization occurs differentially between European upper-middle-class bodies, European working-class bodies, and non-European immigrant working-class bodies. When a person is able to pay their debt, being proletarianized in the sphere of circulation presents no apparent problem. But upon default, the mortgage becomes a non-performing loan, and debtors are in turn socially and economically branded a failure, a non-performing person, in both body and mind, in what is an intimate and deeply affective process with clearly gendered impacts (Dawney, Kirwan, and Walker 2020; Han 2012; Harker, Sayyad, and Shebeitah 2019).

My second argument is that mortgage debt serves to optimize a state of life and (re)production based in economic growth—maintaining the status quo—and to ensure circulation and security in view of the uncertain nature of life. I uncover the differential processes and strategies through which mortgages act as a technology of power in the Barcelona metropolitan region, underlining their impacts on everyday life and the body. Mortgages not only create a population that has to produce in order to meet their debt obligations but also operate through a subjective process. This happens through creating a perceived "security" of the home, reinforced by public policies and material conditions generating homeownership as the most secure tenure option. As eloquently shown by anthropologist Clara Han (2012), debt also slithers through and becomes enmeshed in intimate relations, as indebted people—often alongside family and friends—are locked into ongoing financial obligations that cannot be separated from everyday emotional and physical ties, damaging health and lives. When (mortgage) debt is securitized and sold on secondary financial markets, mortgages ensure further circulation in global financial flows through another upward redistribution of value. These speculative investments have no productive basis but appear to spur the security of the system through ensuring, at least in the short term, economic growth and capital gains for the few. The openly disciplinary dimension of mortgages came into play when people in Spain were unable to pay. Banks pressured and/or threatened households to pay their debts to ensure the circulation of capital no matter the cost. Yet when default hit and loans became non-performing— and in the eyes of the financial system, debtors, and their co-borrowers and/ or (crossed) guarantors, were non-performing, and the costs for the bank outweighed the benefits—the debt was sold for a fraction of its value to corporate investors. This further entrenched indebted lives in the operation of financial markets and transactions as these companies sought to extract rent from defaulters or the property itself.

The second underexplored phenomenon related to housing, debt, and lived experience that I unpack in this book is how individualized indebtedness is problematized, collectivized, and fought against: the emancipatory possibility of indebtedness. In other words, I consider how the financialization of housing life and the biopolitics of mortgaged homeownership can be disrupted. I look at the collectivization of individual problems of indebtedness through the experiences of compañerxs facing foreclosure and eviction through the PAH in the Barcelona metropolitan region. In the absence of the state, which prioritized rescuing the financial system over people, I analyze how the PAH's collective advising assemblies and direct actions—blocking evictions, occupying banks, and squatting empty bank-owned housing—disrupt the disciplinary and regulatory power of mortgage debt. I furthermore show how they rupture broader processes of urban capital accumulation and its urban forms and relations, reclaiming people's lives, bodies, and minds from complex financial entanglements. The PAH's forms of operation draw on feminist-inspired practices of care (Santos 2020), serving as a sharp counterpoint to the individualizing and mathematical logic of mortgage relations. While a feminist logic and practice is recognized by many in the movement—and visible in the processes through which compañerxs' lives are collectively reseized from abstracted financial relationships—an explicitly racialized analysis is absent. In exploring and reflecting upon these realities, I move beyond a common focus in social movement studies on demands or claims making to understand how processes of political subjectivation can challenge and even rupture, in a sustained and nonlinear albeit impermanent fashion, the way that housing becomes a financial asset and its underlying social relations. I seek to better understand how collective struggle can rupture, both subjectively and materially, a debt-driven housing model that dominates in Spain and many other parts of the world, underlining the possibilities—and, of course, the challenges—of collective organizing to fight mortgage indebtedness and housing and urban injustice more broadly.

In terms of the emancipatory possibilities of indebtedness, I argue for a new reading of the concept of political subjectivation. This concept refers to a process whereby society-abiding subjects reject the status quo and reconfigure material and subjective conditions through their actions, speech, and ways of being, toward becoming political subjects. Contrary to one of the most prominent readings of political subjectivation, advanced by Jacques Rancière (1989, 1992, 1999, 2001), a reading that proposes the political as a momentary act, I argue that it is a process emerging from an accumulation of collectively learned practices "from below." In other words, the political moment exists beyond a sole event or act and takes place over the course of repeated engagement and actions. Struggles to demortgage life turn the accepted financial, economic, and social status quo on its head and create new norms through collective organizing and material sociospatial disruptions to enact equality for so-called non-performing people, those people who have failed in the eyes of the system. This exploration finds an echo in Ananya Roy's (2017) insightful conceptual exploration of dis/possessive collectivism, a complex and often contradictory politics of emplacement enacted by people and supported through broader poor people's movements upon experiencing (foundational forms of) dispossession. Through this process, people facing mortgage foreclosure and/or eviction shift from being obedient society-abiding subjects—the indebted persons—to political subjects. Furthermore, I show how political subjectivation has both a disruptive and propositional nature: it materially and subjectively disrupts financialized housing life and the biopolitics of debt, and proposes new ways of inhabiting. In other words, it is dynamic and dialectic. The stories of mortgage-affected people and experiences of/in the PAH, however, show that political subjectivation is an uneven and unstable process with particular context-specific challenges. Its long-term outcomes are furthermore uncertain.

Unpacking and Upsetting Core Theories: Three Proposed Lenses

In this book, I propose a novel theoretical reading of mortgage indebtedness relevant for times of (racialized and gendered) precarity and cyclical financial and housing crises, one that ties a macro-level political-economic analysis to simultaneously apprehend everyday life. Specifically, I develop a heterodox framework to explore (1) the financialization of housing-life, (2) the biopolitics of mortgage debt, and (3) processes of political subjectivation. These three concepts are brought together to understand what it means for everyday life when housing becomes a financial asset, how external and internal processes related to indebtedness discipline and regulate different types of life, and the processes and actions through which both dynamics can be ruptured. Bringing these three concepts together addresses gaps that each concept alone is unable to explain, helping move beyond them.

In this theoretical reading, I unsettle what Barnor Hesse (2007, 644) terms "the constitutive racial tropes"—figures like whiteness, Europeanness, the West, or Christianity—of canonical (male) thinkers such as Michel Foucault, Karl Marx, and David Harvey. I question, as Ananya Roy (2016, 201) proposes, the adequacy of "dominant theory cultures" to explain not only places on the map that appear as marginal and different but also places or experiences that don't "fit" into dominant theorizations. In other words, inspired by the work of Katharyne Mitchell (2010, 256), I adopt a theoretical analytic that both works with Euro-American (white male) theorists like Foucault, Marx, and Harvey but avoids "purist, functionalist, and reductionist arguments and positions" through being "informed by concrete bodies and practices, in real times and places"—in this case the Barcelona metropolitan region. Toward thinking through and beyond the canonical traditions I draw from, which all contain a class analysis, in particular I expose racialized and gendered processes to help conceptualize what I learned from mortgage-affected compañerxs and from my engagement with the PAH movement more broadly. Following Howard Winant, I understand race as "a concept that signifies and symbolizes socio-political conflicts and interests in reference to different types of human bodies" (Hesse 2007, 645). Since these conflicts and interests are dynamic, I find racialization to be a more appropriate term, especially considering the Spanish context from dictatorship to democracy. I approach gender as a social process that helps unpack the structural and lived dimensions of women's marginalization and oppression, at the same time recognizing decades-old arguments from U.S. Black feminists that women are by no means a uniform or coherent population (Charusheela 2013; Crenshaw 1989; Predmore 2020). I now make these racialized and gendered processes more concrete through briefly outlining the lineage of the three conceptual approaches drawn together in this book.

FINANCIALIZING HOUSING, FINANCIALIZING LIFE

The notion of financialization has exploded in recent decades across an increasingly diverse number of fields. Yet approaches to the concept are heterogeneous, and its precise definition is often taken for granted. I draw together two approaches to financialization that at present tend to operate in silos. The first approach is regulatory and heterodox and understands financialization as involving structural and systemic shifts in capitalism. In this reading, production-based regimes of capital accumulation—where the capital-labor relation produces surplus value through processes of expanded reproduction—are being surpassed by finance-driven regimes of accumulation (Arrighi 1994; Krippner 2012). In other words, it is about profiting without producing, as Costas Lapavitsas (2013) neatly summarizes, meaning that already-produced value is siphoned off through relations of rent rather than relations of production. This approach theorizes the role of financialization in contemporary capitalism (Bryan, Martin, and Rafferty 2009; Lapavitsas 2013; Fine 2010). The second approach, from cultural economy, looks at the financialization of everyday life. Theorists here unravel how the financial world becomes embedded in subjectivities and identities, as money and finance shape increasing aspects of people's day-to-day experiences (Aitken 2007; French and Kneale 2009; Hall 2012; Martin 2002; Langley 2007). It considers how people are drawn into a range of financial products in everyday life—such as pensions, healthcare, and housing—to meet their basic needs and to secure their own financial futures in the context of the broader neoliberalization of society.

In this book I combine these heterodox macroeconomic and everyday life approaches to build an understanding of financialization related to mortgage debt, life, and the body. I furthermore underline an unfolding of financialization that articulates with "the devaluation of racialized life" (Kish and Leroy 2015, 646) or, as Laura Pulido (2017) frames it, the incorporation of devalued nonwhite bodies into economic processes. While such an analysis has emerged in the U.S. context in particular through considerations of housing financialization—thanks to the insightful work of Elvin Wyly and colleagues (2006, 2009), Gary Dymski (2009; Dymski, Hernandez, and Mohanty 2013), John N. Robinson (2020), and Desiree Fields and Elora Lee Raymond (2021), to name a few—in Spain it is generally absent. A "race-blind" consideration of Spanish society persists in mainstream media and thought amid an either purposefully forgotten or eerily glorified history of colonization (de Castro Rodríguez 2013; Martín Corrales 2017). As immigration trends increasingly shape the growth and life of cities, antifascist and allied activist collectives across Spain have certainly become more vocal about such issues in recent years, but critical racialized analysis is still quite marginal albeit deeply important to understand fundamental socioeconomic inequalities.

With this in mind, I approach the financialization of housing as the global expansion of speculative real estate investment through financial markets as a means to (temporarily) overcome the fundamental contradiction between the fixed nature of real estate and the need for capital to be in motion to create value (Aalbers 2008; Gotham 2006; Harvey 1978). Racialization operates both in the fixed place of real estate and in the mechanisms through which capital creates value. The contradiction between fixity and mobility is addressed through financial tools that create new avenues for surplus value and rent appropriation, with classed and racialized dimensions. When I say "classed," I refer to how these financial tools create an upward redistribution of value, while with "racialized" I mean the mechanisms through which these tools reinforce the unequal differentiation of human value (Melamed 2015). Finally, while the gendered dimensions of financialization and housing financialization more specifically have been articulated theoretically (Allon 2014; Predmore 2020; Wöhl 2017), my work further uncovers the gendered impacts of the "failure" of financialized housing (that is, of default, eviction, and/or indebtedness) in (re)productive spheres and everyday life.

Financial tools related to housing—increasing in their diversity and complexity, and implemented with more obvious or discrete "high-risk" racialized rationale in different countries—have been on the rise in recent decades. One prominent example is a residential mortgage-backed security (RMBS), an investment vehicle created by grouping hundreds of mortgage loans into a financial product through a process known as securitization. RMBSs are then sold to investors, who aim to profit on a bet that households will repay their loans. Created in the United States in the late 1960s, RMBSs became ubiquitous during the housing boom in the 2000s across North America and Europe. Between 2001–6, €13 trillion in RMBSs were issued in the United States, the

United Kingdom, Spain, and the Netherlands, the vast majority of these being in the United States (European Mortgage Federation 2011). Rather than facilitating access to homeownership, the ballooning of the finance market through these types of tools can lead to greater risk and uncertainty for households because the tools themselves become more important than granting mortgages and/or producing housing (Aalbers 2011). Indeed, the huge investor demand for securitized financial products like RMBSs was one of the key triggers behind the 2008 financial crisis. Research has furthermore made crystal clear the connection between investor appetites for high-risk, high-yield RMBSs and racist and classist subprime mortgage lending practices in the United States (Dymski 2009; Wyly et al. 2006; Wyly and Ponder 2011).

In this book I argue that embedded in this process of housing financialization is the differential financialization of life, calling to light the notion of biofinancialization (French and Kneale 2009, 2012), which refers to how financialization intermeshes and intertwines with the politics of life itself (Rose 2007) and produces distinctive capital/life/subject relations. The fostering of investor or financial subjectivities (Aitken 2007; Allon and Redden 2012; Langley 2006, 2007, 2008) "hides" the debt relation, but the lived realities of mortgages and other forms of indebtedness are rooted in a context of increasing precarity and processes of proletarianization that are raced and gendered in the sphere of circulation. Rather than understanding the proletariat as a static social class, proletarianization is understood here as a historically evolving process, moving from primitive accumulation to the factory and beyond. Following political theorist Jodi Dean (2012, 75), proletarianization is "the process through which capitalism produces, uses up, and discards the workers it needs," although, as I explain below, "workers" are valued unequally despite the mirage of upward social mobility through homeownership. In relation to housing and life, it is the fraction of the capitalist class that controls finance capital (e.g., rentiers) that acts, and in the sphere of circulation "workers" are mortgaged people.

Understanding proletarianization in this way means that the subjection of human life to capital accumulation occurs not only in production through processes of expanded reproduction, but also through mortgage and other debt forms in the sphere of circulation. The latter does not produce value but is the equivalent of extracting rent. This connects to David Harvey's (1982, 285) claim that mortgages are a "secondary form of exploitation." It also echoes Ugo Rossi's (2013) argument that contemporary capitalism has proved itself able to turn human life into a direct source of profit. Yet going beyond Harvey and Rossi, I show how the inherently racialized and gendered nature of capitalism means that not all human lives are valued the same, since capital needs to be in motion to create value and it accumulates by moving through relations of severe inequality (Goldstein 2015; Kish and Leroy 2015; Mitchell 2010; Robinson 1983). Racism, as Jodi Melamed (2015, 77) underlines, "enshrines the inequalities that capitalism requires." This is a reality that echoes through the experiences of non-European immigrant mortgage-affected compañerxs shared with me during the most recent housing boom-crisis, underscored even further by those who are women, as I outline in chapters 2 and 3.

THE BIOPOLITICS OF MORTGAGED HOMEOWNERSHIP

Financialized housing-life aims to maintain and expand a specific political-economic system and "state of life" (Foucault 2003, 246), where capital accumulation, economic growth, and the market prevail as the normalized, permanent state of affairs. This harkens back to the term "biopolitics," which Michel Foucault (2003, 245) defined as dealing "with the population as a political problem, as a problem that is at once scientific and political, as a biological problem and as power's problem." With the notion of the population at its core, biopolitics signals how knowledge and power began to be used as a way to control and mold human life. Biopolitics is, in this light, intimately connected with how a state attempts to regulate its people and territories or the "conduct of conduct," what Foucault dubbed governmentality (Gordon 1991). These concepts were first explored in a handful of books Foucault wrote in the early to mid-1970s, then expanded through a series of lectures in the late 1970s at the Collège de France that remained unpublished in French and English until the 2000s.

Inspired by Foucault's proposal that capitalism requires not only "the controlled insertion of bodies into the machinery of production" but also "the adjustment of the phenomena of population to economic processes" (Foucault 1978, 140), I move from the article I coauthored with Maria Kaika (2016) to more fully develop a novel biopolitical reading of mortgaged homeownership. Here, going beyond Foucault, I show not only the classed but also the racialized dimensions of this biopolitical process. I conceptualize mortgage loans as a technology of power at multiple levels: the state, the financial system, the individual. In chapters 2 and 3 I show how mortgages ultimately optimize a state of life and (re)production based in economic growth through a combination of differential political techniques and "technologies of the self" (*Homo economicus*) that the state actively enabled through deregulation and market-friendly legislation. Political techniques occur through, for example, the variety of overt and covert ways the state encourages homeownership and how financial entities differentially enroll people in mortgages and securitized debt, creating a variety of what Christopher Harker (2020) terms debt ecologies, which by their nature are classed, gendered, and racialized. Technologies of the self operate as individuals internalize the need to pay no matter what may occur upon signing their mortgage loan.

Mortgages can be conceived as a technology of power in terms of regulation and discipline. On the one hand, mortgages operate as a regulatory mechanism at the level of the human species through creating a system where a population of subjects has to produce in order to meet their mortgage debt obligations. In this regulatory capacity, mortgages enroll the population of mortgage signatories and their guarantors—where, in the Spanish context, the nature and number of guarantors is a key signal of the differential valuation of life—into the financial sector's rent extraction mechanisms in the sphere of circulation. If these mortgages are securitized, the population becomes subsumed directly into global financial flows. A secondary regulatory dimension thus takes place. Securitization is a tool that ensures extended processes of capital circulation into global flows, while it simultaneously regulates a shifting and differentiated population of (securitized) mortgaged homeowners. While mortgage holders can "fail" in the eyes of the system, securitization cannot.

On the other hand, mortgages contain a disciplinary mechanism centering on the body and producing individualizing effects. The body is a fundamental, interconnected part of life and subjectivity and is critical in the production, exchange, and circulation of capital (Haraway 1995; Harvey 1982, 1998). A mortgage builds a social relation between creditor and debtor, deepened through processes of subjectivation that—by no means consistently or evenly—produce a subject (un)consciously bound to pay their monthly mortgage payment. As Foucault notes (1991), discipline creates subjected, practiced, and docile bodies, increasing the forces of the body in terms of its economic utility while diminishing the same forces in terms of political obedience, ultimately disassociating power from the body. In other words, paying mortgage debt is a form of discipline and is, as Maurizio Lazzarato (2012) observes, a relation of both self-inflicted and externally imposed subjection. Life itself and the body thus move through, and are moved through by, mortgage debt servicing practices. Furthermore, the possible utility of individuals increases when mortgage loans are securitized, due to an added element of surplus value extraction. That is, individuals circulate not only in the creditor-debtor relationship with the financial entity that provides the mortgage loan, but also through global financial flows as their individual mortgage debt is packaged, secured, and sold on secondary markets. This is the ultimate level of housing-life finan-cialization, a reality whose problematic nature becomes visible when people default on their mortgage payments, triggering massive health impacts, as de-tailed in chapter 3. In these cases, the state actively enables the eviction of non-performing people in order to avoid the failure of speculation processes. The unquestionable, disciplinary notion that individuals must pay their mortgage, as an individual enterprise, both demobilizes any notion of collectivity and re-inforces the rational figure of *Homo economicus*.

A critical element in the biopolitics of mortgaged homeownership is the norm. That is, in order for mortgages to be able to operate as a technology of power, homeownership, as well as mortgage debt, must be normalized. This involves generating sociocultural desire/need and its political articulation through discourses, laws, and mechanisms of governance. The normalization of homeownership is a process that has occurred across most of the Western world in recent decades (Gurney 1999; Ronald 2008; Smith 2008), with dis-courses often equating homeownership to being a better citizen, providing safety and security, offering a place for caring and social reproduction, and ul-timately being "natural." Also normalized is the unequal differentiation of hu-man value (Melamed 2015), with race relations historically and relationally, particularly in the Spanish context, "constituted through the colonial desig-nations of *Europeanness* and *non-Europeanness*" (Hesse 2007, 646). Chapter 1 unearths the historic-material roots of Spanish homeownership, showing how it was a gendered racial hygiene project under the banner of creating upright, Catholic, patriotic Spaniards during the Franco dictatorship, while market mechanisms increasingly encouraged homeownership in democratic Spain. Chapter 2 shows how mortgage indebtedness became normalized during the 1997–2007 housing boom.

In this light, the regulatory and disciplinary technologies of mortgages, and the norms that circulate through them, operate to ensure the security of "the random element inherent in a population of living beings so as to opti-mize a state of life" (Foucault 2003, 246). Mortgages establish a homeosta-sis in part through furthering docility and compliance of the body and mind, where mortgage holders are concerned about meeting monthly mortgage pay-ments as well as maintaining or enhancing the value of their home. In this way, mortgages help achieve "an overall equilibrium that protects the secu-rity of the whole from internal dangers" (246). This security is ensured and/ or protected through creating a population that must produce and provide a flow of monthly payments to the bank over a given time period, meaning that bodies must produce in order to generate the income to maintain these flows. When mortgage securitization gains in importance, as housing becomes financialized, granting mortgages becomes more and more about adjusting "the phenomena of population to economic processes" (Foucault 1978, 140). Since credit/debt is the promise of payment and a financial asset like a share or bond is the promise of future value (Lazzarato 2012), biopolitical processes secure the realization of the circulations needed to bridge the gap between present and future.

POLITICAL SUBJECTIVATION:
COLLECTIVE MOVEMENTS OF RUPTURE AND PROPOSITION

Broadly speaking, "subjectivation" is a term that signifies the process of becoming a subject. As a process, not a state of being, it is ultimately an indeterminate, unanticipated becoming (Tassin 2012). Foucault's explorations of subjectivation—how people become ethical, active, moral subjects—have been particularly influential, as countless theorists have sought to both deepen and extend it (e.g., Gilles Deleuze, Maurizio Lazzarato, Michael Hardt, and Antonio Negri) as well as to contest it (e.g., Jacques Rancière, Alain Badiou). In this book I draw upon and extend the work of Rancière because his understanding of rupture is a particularly useful framing device. It is also a conceptualization that plays little or no role in other readings of subjectivation. Furthermore, Rancière's ideas on politics and political subjectivation provide critical insights into key theoretical and empirical processes at the core of this book: those that challenge dynamics of financialized housing-life and the biopolitics of mortgaged homeownership.

Political subjectivation, as stated by Rancière (1999), refers to new ways of acting, speaking, and being that break with the existing status quo and thus reconfigure it. In other words, it is a process involving emancipatory acts that make the invisible visible. This occurs as "the part of those who have no-part," people who are outcasts in the existing system, disrupt the police order, and voice a "wrong" for the sake of equality (Rancière 1992; Rancière and Panagia 2000). Take the African American activist Rosa Parks who refused to cede her seat on a bus in Montgomery, Alabama, to white people who in the 1950s were the only ones with the "right" to sit there. Similar to Judith Butler, Alain Badiou, and Slavoj Žižek, Rancière proposes that equality demands operate as universal demands (Davidson and Iveson 2014). Universal means that they benefit all regardless of race, gender, or class—although it is key to recognize that, as Ananya Roy (2016, 2017, A10) notes, "seemingly universal categories have been forged through historical difference." We will see this in the Spanish context in chapter 1 through how the Franco dictatorship sought to enforce a universal category of homeowner as an attempt to transform the mass of "second-class" Spaniards to upright, Christian, modern Spaniards.

Rancière's (2004a) distribution of the sensible, or what he also calls the police order, is an idea at the core of his understanding of political subjectivation. It also parallels Foucault's notion of biopolitics. Both assign or regulate certain social positions to ensure their circulation and proper distribution, with these accepted social positions operating as an implicit, often invisible, social law (Davidson and Iveson 2014). Clearly race, gender, and class are deeply imbricated in these social positions. As homeownership, mortgage debt, and financial tools become more and more ubiquitous and "normal," they can be understood not only as integral to biopolitical processes but also as elements of the distribution of the sensible. Homeownership through mortgage debt becomes implicitly inscribed as a self-evident and normal modality to access housing, supported by legal and regulatory mechanisms, discourses, and material reality. It is critical to underline here that distribution means both inclusion and exclusion, and that inclusion is differential. For example, Deborah James (2014) illustrates the both structural and intimate interplay between inclusion and exclusion through unpacking Black "inclusion" in the financial system in the aftermath of credit apartheid in South Africa.

Rancière sees the police order and biopolitics as directly opposed to a truly democratic politics, the latter as disruptive and exceptional, rooted in a presupposition of equality that when enacted sends liberal democracy into disarray (Hewlett 2007; May 2008). While democratic society was founded upon values like equality, freedom, and justice, these values do not preexist but rather have to be constantly verified. A political act is precisely this verification, according to Rancière. Politics and political subjectivation thus occur through enacting equality by disrupting the police order, whereby subjectivation is defined through a process of disidentification (Rancière 1992). Political acts, then, generate a collectively announced "we" through unveiling inegalitarian logics, through a dissensus (Rancière 2004a) that refutes a situation's taken-for-granted hierarchies and relations. They reconfigure the status quo in the name of equality. The people, Michel Foucault (2007, 66) states, "refusing to be the population, disrupt the system." In other words, they disrupt the systemic inequality that assumes that some life is not equal to others or worth the cost of its own reproduction.

In terms of mortgaged homeownership, disrupting the police order could make visible and reject the neoliberal premise that the principal role of the state is only to prevent extreme exclusion in accessing housing, denouncing the taken-for-granted social assumption of inequality at the core of market relations. Public political action could demonstrate that private home space has been ideologically constructed as autonomous and disconnected by making visible its material and social connections and contesting processes of individualization and fragmentation that are at the root of what is considered "home" (Kaika 2004). Resisting (housing) financialization ultimately means "allow[ing] ourselves to be disobedient to the test of an accountant's profit" (Christophers 2015, 193, citing Keynes 1933, 765). It means making visible a naturalized financial, social, and economic order by not following the rules or not doing what is "supposed" to be done.

Whatever they may be, these political acts are carried out by the very people who are being excluded and presuppose equality in enacting housing for all. In the context of South Africa's shantytown movement Abahlali, Anna Selmeczi (2012) details how speaking about and listening to each other's sufferings is fundamental to the movement's "living politics" and broader process of political subjectivation. Home liberations carried out by the Chicago Anti-Eviction Campaign, following the slogan "homeless people in people-less homes," are one way that housing as a human right is enacted (Roy 2017). Through collectively speaking and acting, people make visible a wrong and mobilize to question and disrupt the status quo order that allocates them unequal roles and spaces. Here, the depth to which race and intersectional identities are questioned requires further unpacking, which I address in chapter 4.

At the same time, in the very different context of mortgaged homeownership, it is fundamental to ask how, exactly, a process of political subjectivation can mobilize the indebted person and what kind of political potentiality it holds. As Balibar (2013) notes, collective political resistance faces deep-seated challenges because debt is individualizing and negative, and it is difficult to find common professional or cultural spheres to build a shared political front. This makes the building of solidarity, sharing, and trust difficult. Furthermore, following Roy's (2017) reflections on what she terms "dis/possessive collectivism" in the Chicago Anti-Eviction Campaign, the PAH's practices of emplacement like blocking evictions or occupying empty bank-owned housing have complex relationships with the political potentiality of new visions of property and personhood. It is thus critical to understand more deeply the modes of individual and collective subjection related to debt in order to uncover the emancipatory possibilities of indebtedness. In chapter 2, I show how lives, bodies, and minds became differentially wrapped up in mortgage debt and its complex financial relationships. I illustrate the enormous individualizing challenges people, upon defaulting, live with in chapter 3, and how many of these are overturned through a movement that builds a shared and collective struggle in chapter 4.

Questioning Research:
An Engaged Ethnographic-Activist Approach

In order to ground the theoretical framework to understand the lived dimension of everyday life and struggle with mortgage debt, I used an engaged ethnographic qualitative research approach in the Barcelona metropolitan region, specifically in the cities of Barcelona and Sabadell (Figure I.1). Box I.1 outlines the characteristics of this region and why it was chosen. During an eleven-month period, I employed multiple qualitative data collection strategies, including participant observation in over eighty assemblies and thirty actions (mostly blocking evictions and occupying banks), producing forty weeks of detailed field notes; thirty-eight semistructured interviews with mortgage-affected compañerxs, financial sector employees, former or current government officials/technicians, and academics; a focus group with mortgage-affected people; official statistics; and extensive press and financial document analysis. I conducted the research in Spanish and translated interviews and documents, in some cases facing challenging questions of translation. The biggest difficulty was the use of *compañeras* or *compañeros*, a term that sometimes gets translated to comrades, but as fellow housing activists Tom Youngman and Laura Barrio (2021) note, this term has militaristic or communist connotations that do not fit. Hence, I used *compañerxs*, with an "x" to refer to male and female, or *compañera* for female and *compañero* for male fellow PAH movement members. When citing a compañerx in text, I sometimes decided to include the phrase in Spanish with a translation following in parentheses since there are some literal meanings and sayings whose power can be lost in translation.

Through these methods I sought to unpack three dynamics. First, I wanted to embed the processes of mortgaging and liberating life within their broader political, economic, social, and historic context in order to understand both more fully. Second, I sought to grasp the relationships, processes, and conditions that unfolded between mortgaged households and financial entities in the context of financialized housing, from the contraction of the mortgage to its regular payment and its nonpayment. And third, I strove to comprehend how financial (indebted) subjectivities are ruptured through collective processes and practices, understanding this from and through the voices, actions,

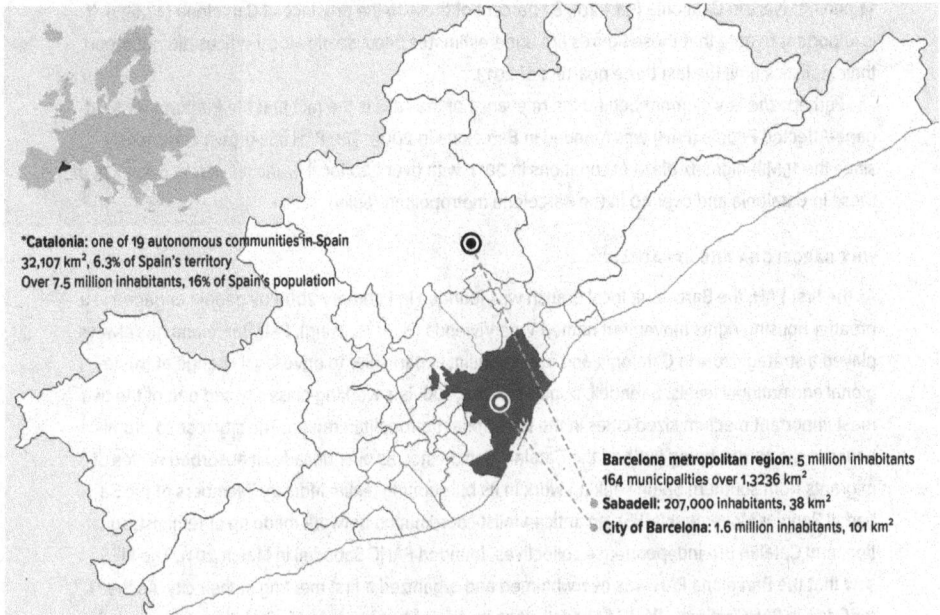

*Catalonia: one of 19 autonomous communities in Spain
32,107 km², 6.3% of Spain's territory
Over 7.5 million inhabitants, 16% of Spain's population

Barcelona metropolitan region: 5 million inhabitants
164 municipalities over 1,3236 km²
Sabadell: 207,000 inhabitants, 38 km²
City of Barcelona: 1.6 million inhabitants, 101 km²

FIGURE I.1. Location of Barcelona and Sabadell within the Barcelona metropolitan region.
SOURCES: IDESCAT, Shutterstock, and Carpintero, Sastre, and Lomas (2015).

BOX I.1. Why the Barcelona Metropolitan Region?

The Barcelona metropolitan region (Figure I.1), containing almost half the population of the autonomous community of Catalonia, has specific characteristics that make it a meaningful location to dig deeply into understanding life and the struggle with mortgage debt in times of precarity. Catalonia is one of the wealthiest autonomous communities in Spain, and the Barcelona metropolitan area produces half of the Catalan gross domestic product (GDP). It has historically been an attractive region first to industry and construction, and most recently to services, IT, and tourism. Between 1996 and 2006, the construction sector's production grew at a rate above Catalonia's total GDP, reflected in 1 million of the 6.5 million housing units initiated in Spain during this period being located in Catalonia (Carpintero, Sastre, and Lomas 2015). Average housing prices in Barcelona in particular were the highest of all cities in Spain from 2005 to 2008. According to the Spanish Department of Public Works, even the price of the lowest tenth percentile of housing during this period surpassed the national average housing price per square meter.

The 2008 bust of the housing boom reverberated deeply across Spain, and Catalonia in particular. On top of plummeting housing prices, a crash in construction and skyrocketing unemployment, foreclosures, and evictions were particularly acute in Catalonia. According to the General Council of the Judiciary, 578,546 foreclosures took place across Spain from 2008 to 2014 inclusive, with Andalusia and Catalonia each experiencing 20 percent of the total. Of the 115,000 foreclosures in Catalonia, just over 60 percent (70,426) occurred in the province of Barcelona. During the same period 378,693 eviction orders were issued and 244,267 executed across Spain. Of the latter, at least

14 percent were in Catalonia (54,520), 87 percent of these in the province of Barcelona (47,637). It is important to note that these figures are underestimates because nine local offices did not report their statistics until the last three quarters of 2013.

Perhaps *the* key element behind the relevance of the case is the fact that the Platform for Mortgage-Affected People (PAH) was founded in Barcelona in 2009. The PAH has grown enormously since the 15M Indignadx plaza occupations in 2011, with over 220 local branches across Spain, 75 of these in Catalonia and over 40 in the Barcelona metropolitan region.

WHY BARCELONA AND SABADELL?

As the first PAH, the Barcelona local branch was founded in February 2009 by people engaged in a broader housing rights movement named V de Vivienda (H for Housing). PAH Barcelona has always played a strategic role in Catalonia and across Spain, in particular to drive legal change at the regional and national levels. Sabadell, population 210,000, is a working-class city and one of the two most important medium-sized cities in the Barcelona metropolitan region. The city rose to prominence in the 1960s, being dubbed the Catalan Manchester, as over decades it absorbed waves of migrants from southern Spain seeking work in its burgeoning textile industry. Members of the Sabadell Popular Movement (MPS), an anticapitalist coordination network made up of feminist, squatting, and Catalan pro-independence collectives, founded PAHC Sabadell in March 2011. The MPS saw that the Barcelona PAH was overwhelmed and organized a first meeting in their city. As the "C" for Crisis in PAHC reflects, PAHC Sabadell since its origins has struggled for solutions for people facing all types of housing problems. It is also one of the most important sites of the PAH's Obra Social (building occupation) campaign.

Thus, while both (and all) PAHs work with a similar process and toward the same broad goals, the Barcelona and Sabadell PAHs reflect different strategies within the metropolitan region. This book does not *compare* these two sources but rather approaches them as exemplifying different dynamics within the metropolitan region that have emerged due to particular histories, social relations, and material realities. In this book I therefore consider how different forms of political organizing in the context of housing rights struggles support the subjectivation of people affected by mortgage debt.

---

and experiences of people who are living it. My aim was to piece together a form of narrative inquiry (Flyvbjerg 2006), developing descriptions and interpretations of phenomena from the perspective of different compañerxs, a variety of data sources, plus my experience and analysis.

The very nature of these three dynamics, however, raised many personal and political questions in terms of how I would engage with the movement and its members. Before starting, I was aware of the roots of "research" as a European imperialist and colonialist project (Tuhiwai Smith 1999), a trajectory that goes beyond the colonial context. Countless authors have written about how research is embedded in unequal power dynamics (lisahunter, Emerald, and Martin 2013; Pain and Francis 2003; Pulido 2008). Furthermore, research in the West or Global North has been heavily influenced by positivist epistemology connected to objectifying practices, deterministic thinking, and rigid categorization, conducted from a supposedly "neutral" and "scientific" position. I was also aware of both the postmodern turns in social theory in the 1980s that have disturbed this position (McDowell 1992) and the significant amount of (participatory) action or militant research that contests this approach in different ways (Bookchin et al. 2013; lisahunter, Emerald, and Martin 2013; Malo 2004). Action research strives to have an agenda for positive social change, where those who are part of the research benefit from it. From the various strands of action research, critical and/or participatory action research strategies are two that attempt to explicitly address the objectifying tendencies of research and the researcher-"researched" power dynamic.

My research was *informed* by these action research approaches, at the same time that—similar to the Autonomous Geographies Collective (2010) and the Durham Community Research Team (2011), among many others—I recognized their challenges. For a variety of reasons, not having been previously engaged in the movement and time constraints, to name just two, I felt that a participatory action research approach would not be feasible or realistic. I thus came into the field with broad research questions and a theoretically shaped perspective, both of which evolved significantly through an engaged ethnographic approach (Casas-Cortés, Osterweil, and Powell 2013; Scheper-Hughes 1995), a type of activist research (Hale 2006) that is characterized by a researcher's commitment to contribute to a movement through theory and practice. It also meant, following a postcolonial spirit, opening up what I was learning to self-reflexive critique and to multiple alternative knowledges inside and outside the academy (Sharp 2009).

This research approach was unquestionably shaped by the nature of the PAH and my experiences becoming engaged in the movement. Upon attending assemblies and getting involved, it quickly became clear that the PAH *produces* and diffuses knowledge based on the experience of compañerxs, knowledge that moves against expert or established knowledge. In other words, PAH assemblies generate what Donna Haraway (1991) calls situated knowledges. In terms of methodology, this reinforced the need for an engaged approach that blurs formal researcher-researched boundaries and promotes a more relational approach (Casas-Cortés, Osterweil, and Powell 2008). I therefore considered the PAH not as a research object or a case study but as a social process that generates its own analysis, concepts, and practices, unfolding in a specific time, place, and context. Building from Haraway, Casas-Cortés, Oster-weil, and Powell (2013, 215) call this "situated sources" of knowledge. On top of knowledge generated in assemblies and experiences shared in interviews, I have both learned and built from the base of current and former PAH members' militant analysis and reflections (e.g., Adell, Lara, and Mármol 2014; Co-lau and Alemany 2012, 2013; Jiménez 2013a, 2013b; Llonch 2013; Macías 2013; Sorinas 2015; Sorinas and Giné 2017). Alongside my empirical investigation, these sources served as building blocks from which I sought to develop the-oretical and political reflections related to housing debt-life relations, specifi-cally urban capital accumulation, indebted subjectivities, and political subjec-tivation. In summary, I immersed myself in spaces where housing precarity was lived and felt in order to enrich and make political-economic housing analysis more relevant to lived realities (Lancione 2020).

I also feel it is important to underline how several social interactions also shaped my research approach. The first was upon navigating entrance into the PAH. A Catalan academic asked a PAHC Sabadell acquaintance if I could get in touch. The response was affirmative, although "that being said," remarked the academic, "he told me they are a little bit annoyed with people who come with the mentality that they are going to study a tribe from the Amazon." Another was at an assembly in Sabadell in early 2014, when I was greeting a mortgage-affected woman I had come to know well in the previous months. As we were chatting, her distress over a foreign television crew that interviewed her for hours in her home in a collectively occupied PAH building suddenly came pouring out. The TV crew asked her to take them to her former home, which she had been evicted from three years before: "It was really painful and diffi-cult," she told me. "These are the kind of experiences you just don't want to re-live. Why are there so many researchers here? It seems like we are an endan-gered species from the Amazon, that we're going extinct. In any case I am not taking part in any more studies or interviews, I just can't do it anymore." Fi-nally, I was in a handful of assemblies where students came to request inter-views with people being foreclosed or evicted for an assignment due in a few weeks. On several occasions, especially in assemblies in Sabadell, a compañerx would underline the importance of students sharing their research findings, and above all that mortgage-affected people are subjects, not objects.

These "epistemological encounters" (Juris and Khasnabish 2013) reinforced the need for openness and flexibility in my research, transforming myself and my ideas in the process. They also illustrate the intersubjective and dialogic nature of my research (England 1994). For me these experiences, among many others, reemphasized the importance of spending an extended amount of time in the movement to build trust and rapport, to be sensitive to the reality people are living and reflexive about my own privileged positionality. My experiences also made clear the need to relate to the lived experience of life and struggle with mortgage debt delicately and with deep empathy. People face severe mental and health impacts upon losing, or the threat of losing, their home, and I actively decided not to ask many people for an interview due to the heartbreaking and deeply trying realities they were living. I found that an engaged ethnographic approach, despite its challenges, was an invaluable way to provide in-depth, qualitative accounts of the processes, meanings, and nuances of sociospatial life (Hall 2016; Herbert 2000).

While I generally felt like a tightrope-walking insider-outsider during my research, a position constituted in what feminist geographer Cindy Katz (1994, 72) calls "spaces of betweenness," I walked as conscientiously as I could manage, juggling a balance between gaining insights into my research and being another member of the movement. I strived to move from a place grounded in my own politics of solidarity, mutual aid, and respect, a position critical of the relations of exploitation and domination inherent in capitalism and that is ultimately driven by and concerned with critical ways to understand the world toward making it a more emancipatory, egalitarian place. I also made contributions to the movement—for example, researching financial actors for bank actions, translating materials from Spanish or Catalan into English, creating organizational and information tools, developing campaign material, taking minutes or updating wall calendars, and being another body participating in dozens of bank occupations, home occupations, and eviction blocks—a process that has continued after finishing my fieldwork and becoming an activist, and sometimes activist-researcher, in the housing rights movement in Barcelona more broadly.

Chapter Outline

The book weaves together a critical political economy of housing and mortgage debt in Spain, and how this was lived in the day-to-day experiences of compañerxs in the Barcelona metropolitan region, focusing on the 1997–2007 housing boom and the post-2008 crisis. In order to more acutely understand this more recent process, chapter 1 provides a historic backdrop to the main political-economic dimensions of housing in the second half of twentieth-century Spain during both the Franco dictatorship and post-1979 democracy. It provides context to more deeply understand how the material and discursive processes driving the financialization of housing and of life and the biopolitics of mortgage debt unfolded in Spain during the boom and the post-2008 crisis. I outline the principal ideological and material processes around the promotion of homeownership and housing policy during the Franco dictatorship and illustrate how the groundwork was laid for Spain's housing boom and the subsequent mortgaging of life. In this chapter I show how the production of housing and homeowners was continuously stimulated through different means but toward the same end: to create and maintain a specific social and economic order based in fostering growth through the production of ever-increasing numbers of housing units and controlling/regulating the population through homeownership. We see how the latter was first focused on regenerating the Spanish race under the dictatorship and became part of the struggle for European modernity in the democratic period.

Chapter 2 narrates the process of mortgaging lives during Spain's 1997–2007 urbanization tsunami and how this was normalized, where the increase in household "wealth" masked a reality of indebtedness and job precarity, highlighting the existence of Spanish subprime mortgages. Unlike in the United States or the United Kingdom, subprime mortgages do not exist as a specific financial product in Spain, but millions were granted in practice during the boom. I approach the lived dimension of mortgage debt by unpacking the specific conditions, mechanisms, and relationships through which mortgaged homeownership adjusted the population to economic processes during the housing boom in the Barcelona metropolitan region. Through the stories of mortgage-affected compañerxs, I highlight their racialized and classed operation. I uncover the ways in which mortgages acted as a tool to regulate and discipline the population, illustrating that human life and subjectivities were crucial components of the process to financialize housing, pointing to an interconnected process of financializing life. Through racial and class differences, we see how mortgage holders are proletarianized as their labor and life are packaged into financial products and vehicles of financial speculation through debt repayments.

The continuities and consequences of the financialization of housing-life and the biopolitics of mortgage debt during Spain's housing bust and the post-2008 crisis are the focus of chapter 3. I weave together the deep-seated restructuring of the Spanish financial system with the evolving relationships of compañerxs introduced in the previous chapter with financial entities as they struggle to pay their mortgage debt and ultimately default amid extensive unemployment, increasing monthly mortgage payments, and plummeting housing prices. We see how households are forced to choose between the mortgage or life—deciding whether or not to sign mortgage refinancing or credit offers from the bank in order to keep paying—and how complex debt ecologies (Harker 2020) can become as mortgaged lives are caught up in financial sector restructuring processes, having been securitized and/or sold to foreign investment funds. The set of regulatory and disciplinary techniques underlying mortgages are reconfigured as financial entities attempt to maintain rent extraction from mortgaged (under-/unemployed) households at any cost. Finally, this chapter underlines the lived experience of the treatment of life, and the body, as an accumulation strategy (Harvey 1998).

Chapter 4 turns to look at the emancipatory possibilities of indebtedness, showing how the status quo that maintained a state of life rooted in the financialization of housing and of life itself is ruptured when people accept to not do what is "expected" of them, as they stop paying their mortgage, fight for debt forgiveness, and undertake actions to enact housing equality. Upon explaining the origins, emergence, and demands of the PAH in Barcelona and Sabadell, I unpack the movement's main activities at the peak of its influence, specifically weekly assemblies and regular actions—blocking evictions, occupying empty bank-owned buildings to rehouse households, and disrupting/occupying banks to demand solutions—and unravel how they can be understood as processes of political subjectivation. I illustrate how engaging in collective advising assemblies and direct actions to enact equality for those ejected from the status quo are co-constitutive dynamics that turn mortgaged financialized subjects into political subjects. Specifically, these dynamics disrupt the regulatory and disciplinary power of mortgages and fundamentally challenge their underlying dynamics of financial rent appropriation. At the same time, I discuss some of the main challenges and tensions in this uneven, nonlinear process.

The concluding chapter reviews the theoretical, methodological, and empirical findings of the book, reflecting on the main insights and what they mean for broader debt-life struggles. I summarize how the financialization of housing is intimately tied to human life becoming a financial asset, how mortgage debt serves to optimize a state of life and (re)production based in economic growth and to ensure circulation and security in view of the uncertain nature of life, and how political subjectivation is a process with both a disruptive and a propositional nature. Having both engaged with and moved beyond Anglo-European (white male) theorists, I reflect on what a racialized and postcolonial analysis has brought to understand and broaden the learnings from the Spanish case. I return to consider how this book helps us rethink the role of mortgage debt and housing access more broadly, outlining the possibilities and challenges of collective organizing to fight mortgage indebtedness and housing and urban injustice more broadly. Briefly considering the political and housing situation today in Spain, and particularly into four years of an attempt at radical municipal politics in Barcelona from the citizen platform generated in part by cofounders of the PAH, I reflect on what the future brings for housing debt-life struggles here and beyond.

CHAPTER 1

Grounding Spanish Housing Financialization and Mortgage Biopolitics

Spain's housing stock underwent a major transformation in terms of its quantity and dominant tenure in the second half of the twentieth century. The country went from having poor-quality and insufficient housing in the 1940s to an amount that almost tripled the increase in population, leaving Spain with the largest quantity of second and empty homes in Europe by 2011. Similarly, over half of the country's population were renters in the 1950s—characterizing up to 95 percent of households in Madrid and Barcelona—while by the turn of the twenty-first century over 85 percent of Spain's residents were homeowners.

While these changes may appear to be simple facts, reflecting development and modernity, or perhaps an illustration of the famed 1960s tourism slogan that "Spain is different," this chapter tells a more profound story. Through unpacking the political economy of housing and its deeply embedded culture from the Franco dictatorship to democratic Spain, I reveal how the production of housing and homeowners was continuously stimulated through different means but toward the same end: to create and maintain a specific social and economic order. This order was based on two interconnected elements. The first element involved fostering economic growth through the production of the built environment. Developing the construction and infrastructure sector was fundamental for Spain to overcome its long-standing economic "backwardness." Spain's early modern colonialist empire was dependent on external markets for commercial goods and on the profitability of metals and mining in the Americas, a reality that proved detrimental to the development of Spanish industry centuries later (Charnock, Purcell, and Ribera-Fumaz 2014). Spanish capitalism, in other words, has long been peripheral in the European context because its production of goods and services has not been competitive. This is in part why Spanish capital was encouraged by the dictatorial Francoist state

Key political events		Key housing policies
Spanish Civil War	1936–39	
Franco dictatorship established	1939	
	1939	National institute of Housing established
	1939	National Housing Act adopted
	1944	National Housing Plan 1944–54 released
	1944	Discounted Housing Act adopted (viviendas bonificables)
	1946	National Housing Act extended
	1946	Urban Letting Act adopted (Ley de Arrendamientos Urbanos: LAU)
	1954	Subsidized Housing Act adopted (Ley de Viviendas de Renta Limitada)
	1955	Urban Letting Act (LAU) amended
	1956	Land Act first adopted (Ley de Suelo)
	1957	Ministry of Housing created
	1957	Madrid Social Urgency Plan enacted
	1958	Barcelona Social Urgency Plan enacted
	1959	Vizcaya Social Urgency Plan enacted
	1959	Stabilization Plan adopted (beginning of desarrollismo period)
	1960	Horizontal Property Act adopted
	1961	National Housing Plan 1961–76 released
	1962	Parent Act adopted
	1963	State subsidized Housing Decree adopted (Vivienda de Protección Oficial: VPO)
	1964	Urban Letting Act (LAU) amended
	1975	Land Act amended
End of Franco dictatorship (death of Franco)	1975	
Democratic transition	1975–77	

FIGURE 1.1. Timeline of key political events and housing-related policies, 1936–1977.

to seek sanctuary in the construction and real estate sectors (Llordén Miñambres 2003). Professionalizing and making the real estate sector profitable, a growth sector in its own right with close ties to tourism development, was thus an important order to establish.[1]

The second element needed to create and maintain a specific social and economic order was homeownership. This served as a way to improve the "Spanish race" by forming Catholic, tradition-abiding Spaniards during the dictatorship, putting women in their "proper" place at the home, then fitting into a larger project of Europeanization under democracy. Creating homeowners was a key discursive and material strategy of the dictatorship, which faced "a mass of second-class Spaniards" (Maestrojuán 1997, 173) living in poor-quality rental housing and tainted by communist and leftist thought in general after the end of the Spanish Civil War in 1939. Homeownership also played a key role in adjusting the population to economic processes (Foucault 1978) under democracy: as construction became increasingly core to the country's economic growth, the creation of homeowners—and the purchase of second residences—was a necessary component to ensure its expansion, especially within the project of Europeanization.

This chapter uncovers the deep roots permeating Spain's 1997–2007 "urbanization tsunami" (Fernández Durán 2006), illustrating how homeownership and house building became both possible and normalized through a variety of ideological, institutional, and legal changes that took place over a period that lasted well over half a century. I illuminate how state intervention dominated during the Franco dictatorship (1939–75), shifting completely to market mechanisms under democracy (1975–onward), the latter reflecting broader shifts toward neoliberalization in Europe and across the world. This historical context provides a necessary basis to more deeply understand how the financialization of housing and everyday life occurred during Spain's 1997–2007 real estate boom and its consequences in the subsequent crisis, as detailed in the following two chapters.

I now turn to explain how under the nearly forty-year dictatorship of Franco—the longest dictatorship in European history—homeownership was inscribed at the political, economic, social, and cultural levels. Figure 1.1 outlines the key housing-related policies during this period. I then unpack the housing, land, and financial policies that more recently undergird the financialized housing boom in the post-1979 democratic Europeanization period. The chapter finishes by outlining how these elements came together in the 1997–2007 Spanish housing boom, with the penultimate section and conclusions critically tying this historical period together in order to set the stage to understand the lived experience of mortgaged compañerxs in subsequent chapters.

Housing Shortages, *Barracas*, and Second-Class Spaniards in the Early Franco Dictatorship

The insufficient quantity and poor quality of housing in Spain at the turn of the twentieth century were compounded by the destruction unleashed during the Spanish Civil War (1936–39). Yet even before this time, as historian Chris Ealham vividly describes in his classic book *Class, Culture and Conflict in Barcelona, 1898–1937* (2004), living conditions for working-class people in cities like Barcelona were awful. Housing construction across Spain was limited in the 1920s and 1930s due in part to the rising cost of construction materials in the wake of the First World War (Llordén Miñambres 2003). Some of the first public interventions that attempted to provide affordable housing were the 1911 and 1924 Low-Cost Housing Acts (Ley de Casas Baratas). Some of these *casas baratas* in Barcelona are eloquently described by Stefano Portelli (2015) in his ethnography *The Horizontal City*; these spaces became deeply appropriated by the working-class "others" of the city over decades. But in their totality these Housing Acts were unable to address the massive housing shortages for working-class households (Tatjer 2005). The latter was increasingly composed of people fleeing the countryside in southern Spain to industrializing cities in Catalonia and the Basque Country, driven by poverty, hunger, the promise of a better life, and, after the Civil War, political exile or repression (Díaz Molinaro 2010).

Facing extreme overcrowding of the existing housing stock, many urban migrants had no other option but to build their own shacks or *barracas*, echoing processes we see in cities termed as "developing" across the world today. Despite efforts to suppress and counteract barracas in cities such as Barcelona (De Andres Creus 2011), they continued to expand into the 1970s. In Barcelona these areas included El Somorrostro and El Camp de la Bota on the beach (Figure 1.2) and the multiple barracas of *Montjuïc* or *El Carmel* on the hills (Figure 1.3). Across the city around 6,500 barracas existed in 1927, growing to almost 20,000 by the 1960s (MUHBA 2010). In Sabadell, fifteen kilometers from Barcelona, the Saint Olaguer caves (Figure 1.4), housing the first settlers in the region thousands of years ago, provided a home for an estimated 1,500 people by 1952 (Masjuan 2010). Overcrowded sublet rooms, barracas, and caves were often the only housing options for many of the tens of thousands of immigrants pouring in from Murcia and Andalusia from the mid-1940s onward to work in various industries flourishing in Barcelona, Sabadell, and other nodes in what is now the metropolitan region. Most of these poor urban migrants were seen as the "other" by their middle-class and especially bourgeois Catalan counterparts, memorialized in the 1964 censored book *The Other Catalans* (*Els altres catalans*) by Francesc Candel and reflected in derogatory terms like *xarnego* used by "natives" to signal working-class immigrants to Catalonia (Vilarós 2003).

According to the dictatorship, the housing situation was generating a "mass of second-class Spaniards" (Maestrojuán 1997, 173) and therefore grow-

FIGURE 1.2. Demolition of barracas in El Somorrostro, Barcelona, 1966.
SOURCE: TAF Helicòpters SA, Arxiu Nacional de Catalunya.

FIGURE 1.3. Barracas on Montjuïc, Barcelona, 1968.
SOURCE: TAF Helicòpters SA, Arxiu Nacional de Catalunya.

FIGURE 1.4. Sant Olaguer caves in Sabadell, 1950.
SOURCE: Unknown, Arxiu Històric de Sabadell.

ing social dangers that had to be avoided at all costs. Improving housing thus emerged as one of the key fronts of action for the Franco regime when it came to rule in 1939. In terms of the broader Spanish political economy, Francoist housing policies sought to create "adequate conditions of profitability to open up a new field of capital accumulation" and to help birth "large, professional real estate developers and their corporate configuration" (Llordén Miñambres 2003, 145). The use of political prisoners after the Spanish Civil War—defeated fighters for the Spanish Republic—as slave laborers was fundamental in building the productive capacity of the construction sector, with the dictatorship implementing and regulating forced labor in the public and private sectors for infrastructure development (Mendiola Gonzalo 2011). Several construction companies established with slave labor during this period still exist today (Crawford 2003). Three of these in particular rank amid the top ten construction companies globally, actively building infrastructure across Latin America in what can be interpreted as a process of neocolonization or the *reconquista* (Baklanoff 1996; Chislett 2008).[2]

Yet the housing policies taken up in the early part of the dictatorship struggled to achieve their material and social goals. The National Institute of Housing was established in April 1939 with a legal mandate to coordinate the production of low-income housing (*viviendas protegidas*), but production was limited due to an unprepared and poorly coordinated public sector and unattractive economic returns for private developers. An extension to this 1939 act in 1946 stipulated that all businesses with more than fifty workers had to ensure the construction of worker housing—facilitated through tax relief, interest-free state loans, and forced expropriation of land, among other incentives—but due to the lack of building materials and capital it failed to reduce the growing housing deficit in industrial cities across Spain (Masjuan 2015). The 1944 Discounted Housing Act (*viviendas bonificables*), in turn, largely benefited middle- and upper-income groups who could pay for it; the state provided important benefits to private capital to stimulate investment, and developers were able to sell housing "with truly scandalous profit margins" (Tamames, cited by Capel 1975, 121). This act was, however, noteworthy because it introduced housing for sale rather than for rent and also began to professionalize developer-construction activity within a corporate structure that thus far did not exist in Spain (Llordén Miñambres 2003).

The shortage of building materials, limited capital investment, and an unprepared private sector meant that housing production was limited in the 1940s. The first two in particular are unsurprising conditions considering the post–Civil War period in Spain and the Second World War ravaging Europe as well as the dictatorship's policy of autarky until the early to mid-1950s (López Díaz 2003). Rent freezes were initiated in the first 1946 Urban Letting Act (Ley de Arrendamientos Urbanos), which continues to be an important regulation of the rights and duties of renters and landlords. Freezes were renewed in 1955 due to continued housing scarcity and the dictatorship's desire to please a broader social base including shopkeepers, industrialists, and renters (Artola Blanco 2012; Leal 2005).

As the 1944–54 National Housing Plan produced far less than half of the projected 1.4 million homes, in cities like Barcelona the decade following the Civil War "brought hunger, misery and a new explosion, this time more intense, of slum development (*barraquisme*) and other forms of sub-standard housing" (Oyón and Iglesias 2010, 35). Construction activity in the 1940s and even into the 1950s was thus largely reduced to solvent demand, benefiting the bourgeoisie faithful to the regime (Masjuan 2010). While the first steps to professionalize the developer construction sector were secured, housing production was minimal. The poorly housed "mass of second-class Spaniards" remained.

Bettering the Environment through Homeownership:
Spanishness and Racial Regeneration

Especially in the early period of the dictatorship, there was great concern over how to civilize and domesticate these hordes of second-class Spaniards, many of whom had been "tainted" by anarchism, republicanism (anti-monarchic pro-republic), or liberal or democratic thought. One member of Franco's close ring of collaborators over various decades, a psychiatrist and lieutenant colonel named Antonio Vallejo-Náguera, played a key role in defining a "scientific" way for the dictatorship to take action to transform this unacceptable proportion of the population that was dangerous to the regime. Vallejo-Náguera envisioned eugenics as a way to reverse the "degeneration" of the Spanish race in recent decades and ultimately create a *supercasta hispana* or Hispanic super caste (Álvarez Peláez 1998, 87). Women, in turn, were seen as inferior beings with an atrophied intelligence, whose singular role was to be at the service of motherhood (Mestre 2014).

Eugenics at the time was a burgeoning, white-supremacist pseudoscience that sought to defend, promote, and/or develop a (superior) race. According to historian Raquel Álvarez Peláez (1998), Antonio Vallejo-Náguera and Manuel Buñuelos were two prominent medical professionals who were avid proponents of eugenics in 1930s Spain. They adhered to the teachings of Francis Galton, who saw it as a logical, Darwinist path to improve the (white) race and as a way for difference to rightly determine social status. Keenly in line with their fascist counterparts in Germany, both Buñuelos and Vallejo-Náguera saw racial hygiene as a process to recover the essence of the Spanish people (*el pueblo español*) and the (Nordic) Castilian race. Yet the two differed in that Vallejo-Náguera believed that the genetic notion of the Aryan race wasn't valid for the Spanish because in fact there were very few Spaniards of a "pure race"; they were, as Vallejo-Náguera said, "a hybrid of a thousand milks" ("*el cruce de mil leches*"). Rather, the racial policy of new Spain required a behavioral focus, eliminating the "red gene" (communist and leftist thought more generally) through the betterment of the environment, including not only putting women in their "correct" place as child bearers and homemakers but also submitting them to the will of their husbands in all aspects of life (Díez 2017). Vallejo-Náguera advocated, in other words, for "environmental eugenics" (Campos 2016).

In his understanding of racial hygiene and improvement, Vallejo-Náguera became a fervent proponent of Spanishness (Hispanidad), inspired by Ramiro de Maetzu's 1934 essay "In Defense of Spanishness" ("Defensa de la Hispanidad"). Maetzu's notion of Spanishness built upon a nostalgia for Spain's glorious colonial past and sought to reclaim a social model based on hierarchy, honor, and loyalty from the values and traditions of sixteenth- and seventeenth-century Spain (Marcilhacy 2014). The Catholic order of hierarchy and inequality was fully embraced—with the equality of races possible through salvation beyond earth—and Maetzu unabashedly saw the European white race as the only truly civilized race and thus superior (Álvarez Chillida 2014). Ideas foreign to "being Spanish" like the Enlightenment, liberalism, and Marxism were rejected, seen to have degenerated the Spanish race upon taking root under decades of democracy (Campos 2016). Vallejo-Náguera, in this light, called for a return to the Hispanic race that forged the empire in the sixteenth century, focusing on the moral and spiritual—rather than biological—dimensions of Spanishness. His interpretation of racial hygiene thus focused on instilling a Catholic culture, respect for tradition and the "correct" place of women at the home, and hierarchical elitism as a "natural" outcome of the differential talent of superior (vs. inferior) classes (Álvarez Peláez 1998).

Spanishness thus became a key symbol in the fascist, totalitarian, and Catholic "new Spain" under Franco. An important facet of bettering the environment, toward improving the race and building a new social order, was homeownership. Falangists—Spanish fascists who believed in national syndicalism and were republican and Catholic in their outlook—viewed homeownership as a symbol of social peace and as an anticommunist strategy, since "a man who has a warm and agreeable home does not think the same as a man who sleeps in the terrible filth of a shack (*chabola*)" (Ochotorena 2019, citing José Luis Arrese, first minister of housing). The following quote from journalist José Cañas describing commonplace housing conditions for Barcelona's working classes in 1952 illustrates what the dictatorship saw as immoral and unspiritual living conditions, an environment that must be changed: "The spectacle before our eyes cannot be described. Families heaped on top of each other, children without the warmth of a home nor education, belongings in piles, stoves and many rags. The rags were not in the sun; rather some serve to separate one house from another. Modesty does not exist. It is a scene of the absolute promiscuity and complete demoralization of people that no longer have faith in anything and do not believe they will ever have a house of their own" (Venteo 2012, 83, 88).

The poor living conditions that remained prevalent especially across rapidly growing cities in the 1940s and 1950s spurred the creation of the Ministry of Housing in 1957, with Falangist José Luis Arrese appointed as its first minister. A deeply patriarchal figure, he declared war on slums and subleasing, seeing these areas as particularly rampant hotbeds for immoral, proletarian thought and action. Aresse framed the ministry's action as a social revolution to create a new way of thinking, which involved "abolishing man's temporariness and melancholy, walking through life with no right to accomplish with his hand the possession of what surrounds him and implant, like a hymn of glory, the support for his family in the warm and friendly environment of the home" (ABC 1959, 42).

Building a Country of Homeowners, Not Proletariats

Material efforts were redoubled in the mid- to late 1950s to address the continued proliferation of housing problems. In 1954 the Subsidized Housing Act (Ley de Viviendas de Renta Limitada) was adopted, with the dictatorship guaranteeing the profitability of private capital invested in the promotion and construction of social housing through tax breaks, land expropriation, subsidized materials, and long-term credit (Betrán Abadía 2002). José Luis Arrese, the minister of housing, perceived the problem of housing as one of public order, and to achieve social peace he proposed the "destiny" of the ministry as "making a spring of homes grow in Spain" (Naredo 2010). As historian Francisco Javier Maestrojuán maintains, Arrese conceived the task of building the Ministry of Housing as "a true mission, inspired by the ideals of the social revolution of the Christian and Falangist type: the family is the first fabric of coexistence that man forms and the principal guarantee of stability; the home, the sublimation of the house, is the only—indispensable—medium through which the family can grow, and, lastly, at a higher level, the homeland (la patria) is the home of all Spaniards. Family, Home, and Homeland are, consequently, the foundations of the regime and to this its protection and development responds" (1997, 173).

Through state-subsidized housing policy, the ministry intended to transform the mass of second-class Spaniards into first-class homeowners—a regeneration of the Spanish race—to guarantee social stability. Urban development was geared toward building a hierarchical and traditional society. The deep-seated belief in homeownership driving Arrese's vision is crystal clear in the oft-cited statement from his first official speech upon taking the reins of the ministry: "We want a country of homeowners, not proletarians" (queremos un país de propietarios, no de proletarios). Arrese repeated this phrase upon receiving an award during an official Real Estate Agents Association event, where, to great applause, he underlined the role of real estate agents in leading the conquest toward the Christian and revolutionary idea of private property and thus a homeownership society (ABC 1959). The latter statement generates eerie echoes with the classed and racialized practices of real estate agents during the 1997–2007 real estate boom, as I explain in chapter 2.

Residential construction started to become an economic motor and building a country of homeowners became possible during Spain's developmentalism period (*desarrollismo*) in the 1960s, marked by the incipient emergence of a market economy. The objective of the 1961–76 National Housing Plan was "to support housing construction as one of the alternatives for the country's economic take-off" (Rodríguez Alonso 2009, 135). Mitigating the housing question was also pressing due to increasing waves of internal migration seeking work in rapidly industrializing areas: in the 1950s, 400,000 people moved to Catalonia, half of these settling in Barcelona, while between 1961 and 1965 there were 800,000 new arrivals, 128,000 of these in Barcelona and over 160,000 in the metropolitan area (Ferrer 2010). The Social Urgency Plans published in 1957, 1958, and 1959 for Madrid, Barcelona, and Vizcaya, respectively, outlined new terms for private capital to collaborate in solving the housing problem (Betrán Abadía 2002). The 1959 Stabilization Plan—the central axis in the shift from the dictatorship's autarkic phase to desarrollismo (Fernández Navarrete 2005)—established the legal bases for external capital to enter Spain (Tascón 2003). New regulations on foreign investment enabled up to 50 percent ownership in all Spanish firms, and a decade-long boom took place in Spain's most important growth industries including steel, textiles, shoes, and construction, a period when mass tourism attracted vast inflows of external capital (Charnock, Purcell, and Ribera-Fumaz 2014). Finally, the 1962 Parent Act made key changes to adapt the financial system to new economic growth strategies through an interventionist regulatory framework, ultimately reinforcing the role of banks as suppliers of capital (Altuzarra et al. 2013).

Coordinated and regulated through the National Housing Plan, 180 working-class housing estates (*polígonos de vivienda*) across 15,000 hectares were financed by the state by 1970, with the number of housing units per estate ranging from 500 to 10,000 (Capel 1975). Private initiatives to construct state-subsidized housing (*vivienda de protección oficial* [VPO]), legislated in 1963 and regulated in 1968, also grew as the state enabled access to mortgage credit, facilitated legal processes for developers to expropriate land, and provided financial help for construction. This made working-class demand more profitable for private developers. Most housing estates, however, were low cost and of poor quality, peripherally located and lacking infrastructure, leading some to dub them as vertical barracas (De Andres Creus 2011). Tatjer (2005) furthermore notes that VPO in general was unable to provide housing alterna-

TABLE 1.1. Housing Stock in Spain, 1950–2011

	1950	1960	1970	1980	1991	2001	2011
Total housing stock	6,687,200	7,726,400	10,657,000	14,726,000	17,160,677	20,823,369	25,208,623
Main residence	6,327,800	7,028,700	8,504,300	10,430,900	11,736,400	14,270,656	18,099,406
Second home	177,900	331,000	795,700	1,899,800	2,923,600	3,323,127	3,681,565
Empty housing	181,500	366,700	1,355,700	2,396,200	2,546,400	3,091,596	3,443,365

SOURCE: Rodríguez Alonso (2004). 2011 data from INE (2013).

TABLE 1.2. Housing Tenure in Spain, 1950–2019 (percentage of households)

Year	Homeownership	Rental	Cession of use	Other (social housing)
1950	45.9	—	—	—
1960	51.9	43.0	—	—
1970	63.4	30.1	4.6	1.9
1981	73.1	20.8	3.1	3.0
1991	78.3	15.2	4.5	2.0
2001	80.7	11.0	6.0	2.0
2006	87.0	10.4	4.0	1.5
2011	79.9	13.5	5.5	1.5
2019	76.0	18.0	4.0	2.0

SOURCE: Rodríguez Alonso (2004). 2006 data from Palomera (2014). 2011 data from INE (2013). 2019 data from INE Household Survey.

tives for the poorest of the working class, who were left in precarious housing until the final decades of the twentieth century. Indeed, the 1961–76 National Housing Plan produced far more housing than projected—3.7 million housing units were planned but 4 million were built—but largely at market rates. The proportion of actually built VPO units was 20 percent below planned levels, with virtually all offered for purchase, not for rent (Rodríguez Alonso 2009). The 1973 petroleum crisis cut this first housing boom short, but the end of the desarrollismo period set a new legacy of second and empty homes (Table 1.1).

A final key piece in the dictatorship's push for homeownership was the 1960 Horizontal Property Act, critical legislation that enabled the sale of individual apartments within a building. Its prime objective was to encourage large swaths of the population that lived as renters to invest capital by purchasing property (Betrán Abadía 2002). The various strategies in this desarrollismo period thus successfully ignited housing production (Table 1.1) and increased the number of homeowners (Table 1.2), establishing a social and economic order that would set the bases for the subsequent decades.

Market Rules: Housing, Land, and Finance in Democratic Spain under Europeanization

The increasing social and political turbulence of the 1970s culminated with Franco's death in 1975 and the subsequent end of the nearly forty-year dictatorship, inaugurating what was for many a long-awaited return to democracy in Spain. Figure 1.5 provides a timeline of the key political events and housing-related policies in this period. The three axes that reconfigured the real estate

Key political events		Key housing policies
Democratic transition	1975–77	
First Spanish president elected Adolfo Suárez (UCD—center right), 1977–81	1977	
	1977	Ministry of Housing suspended, subsumed under Ministry of Public Works
Spanish Constitution ratified	1978	
First president of Catalonia elected Jordi Pujol, center-right (CiU), 1980–2003	1980	
	1981	Mortgage Market Regulation Act adopted
	1981	National Housing Plan 1981–83 released
Spanish president Felipe González elected (PSOE—socialists), 1982–96	1982	
	1984	National Housing Plan 1984–87 released
	1985	Boyer Decree adopted
	1985	National legislation on savings banks adopted (new governance structure)
Spain joins European Economic Community (EEC)	1986	
	1988	Savings banks' territorial barriers completely removed
Maastricht Treaty (EU)	1992	
	1992	Securitization Vehicles Act adopted
	1992	National Housing Plan 1992–95 released
	1994	Urban Letting Act (LAU) amended
Spanish president José María Aznar elected (PP—conservatives), 1996–2004	1996	
	1998	Land Act amended
	1998	Royal Decree 926/1998 to secure assets other than mortgages
	1998	National Housing Plan 1998–2001 released
Spain joins European Monetary Union	1998	
Spain adopts euro	1999	
	2002	44/2002 Act creating Asset Securitization Funds adopted
	2002	2/2002 Land Act (Catalonia) adopted
Catalan president Pasqual Margall elected, left-wing tripartite coalition, 2003–6	2003	
President José Luis Rodríguez Zapatero elected (PSOE—socialists), 2004–11	2004	
	2004	Ministry of Housing reinstated
Catalan president José Montilla elected, left-wing tripartite coalition, 2006–11	2006	
	2007	Housing Rights Act adopted (Catalonia)
	2010	Ministry of Housing suspended, subsumed under Ministry of Public Works
Center right (CiU) majority in Catalan Parliament, Artur Mas president, 2010–15	2010	
President Mariano Rajoy elected (PP—conservatives), 2011–15	2011	

FIGURE 1.5. Timeline of key political events and housing-related policies, 1978–2015.

market under democracy were policies and legislation addressing residential housing, land use, and mortgage finance (López and Rodríguez 2010).

Although the Spanish economy was opened up and somewhat liberalized during the dictatorship's desarrollismo period in the 1960s, the posterior democratic period was characterized by profound deregulation to stimulate industrial growth and the production and purchase of housing. The rise of neoliberalism in Spain occurred symbiotically with European integration, led by the Socialist Party from 1982 to 1994; the party successfully depicted the old regime as in need of reform and modernization as the country subsequently underwent intense labor market and industrial restructuring (McVeigh 2005). While there was a contradiction in the Socialist Party's desire for a nationally negotiated social partnership between capital and labor and a continent-level economic liberalism, it was eventually resolved to the benefit of neoliberals in government (Holman 1996). Europeanization—full membership in the European Community—became Spain's principal foreign policy objective, and the unquestioned path to reach it was through neoliberal reforms (Baklanoff 1996; McVeigh 2005). Indeed, the "challenge of modernity," as Barcelona's long-standing bourgeois newspaper *La Vanguardia* stated, began on 1 January 1986, when Spain officially became part of the European Economic Community. The paper's cover, as seen in Figure 1.6, depicts a "modern-day" rendition of *The Surrender of Breda*, a famous painting by quintessential Spanish artist Diego Velázquez. The Dutch surrender to the Spanish in 1635, which Velázquez symbolized through a key handed from the former to the latter, is depicted 350 years later by the Catalan illustrator Peret, with Europe bestowing its key to Spain. Spain of 1986 is thus portrayed as reclaiming its historic glory and power within the European context. The idea that "Africa begins at the Pyrenees"—first proposed by Napoleon and repeated for centuries by modern European neighbors—would finally be dispelled once and for all.

Becoming fully European was thus a process broadly seen as ushering in economic prosperity and democratic consolidation, critical for Spain to become a truly developed or "emerged" country—with Spanish industries even able to embark on a *reconquista* of Latin America in the 1990s (Toral 2001). Arguably, following Barnor Hesse (2007), this achievement of modernity also has a clear racial dimension, being a synonym of Europeanness and the West, and in turn Christianity and whiteness. Modernity was also reflected in shifting gender relations. Women's employment in the formal labor market rose dramatically—albeit in more precarious and poorly paid positions while continuing to perform most unpaid care work and social reproduction tasks—and the European Commission pressed Spain to institutionalize gender equality in

LA VANGUARDIA

FIGURE 1.6. Spain's ascension to the European Economic Community. (Translation: Modernity will be Spain's biggest challenge upon its integration into the European Economic Community, after having broken its centuries-old isolation. This transcendental historic fact has been interpreted with a vanguardist air by our collaborator Peret, in an allegory of *The Surrender of Breda*.)
SOURCE: *La Vanguardia*, 1–2 January 1986.

Europa, el reto de la modernidad

the 1980s (Lombardo 2017). Here began a complex and nonlinear movement from the dictatorship's embrace of Spanishness as tradition, conservatism, and patriotism to enfolding democratic Spain within Europeanness, modernity, and progress, activating different imaginaries of the country's historic relationship with its past and with its formulation of the "other."

Some of the first steps in Spain's transition to democracy and move toward European modernity involved decentralizing many competencies that were formally the sole authority of the central state to autonomous communities and municipalities.[3] Control over urban planning and housing development was one of these. Much of Spain's and Catalonia's current mortgage and housing system, outlined in Box 1.1, was established at this point.

The restructuring of housing policies, land use, and mortgage finance during the 1980s and 1990s came together in a particularly important configuration in Spain's 1997–2007 real estate boom, the third and deepest cycle of its kind. Coinciding with Spain becoming fully modern through joining the European Monetary Union in 1998 and subsequent adoption of the euro in 1999,

BOX 1.1. Overview of the Spanish and Catalan Housing and Mortgage System

While some core elements maintain their roots dating to the early twentieth century and the Franco dictatorship, most of Spain's current housing configuration was laid in the transition to democracy in the 1970s. Government competencies around housing are highly decentralized: while the state retains a number of powers (property rights, eminent domain), its seventeen regional governments hold the powers of land use, urban planning, and housing (González Pérez 2010). The Spanish government is in charge of overarching housing policy, through the development of housing plans and their fiscal control. At the same time, fiscal transfers to regional governments have steadily decreased in quantity since the early 1980s, with some autonomous communities able to make up the shortfall and others not (Trilla 2014). Housing plans seek to aid access to housing for low- and medium-income households through the production of state-subsidized housing (*vivienda de protección oficial* [VPO]), virtually all of which is for purchase.

Catalonia has exclusive competency in "territorial and coastal planning, urbanism and housing," as dictated by Article 9.9 of the 1978 Statute, although successive Catalan governments limited themselves to distribute funds from the central government for housing plans and to maintain, repair, and when needed substitute the state-subsidized housing park inherited from the Francoist period (Fernández 2004). Upon the transfer of powers to regions in 1985, in Catalonia Incasòl and the Department of Architecture and Housing were created to produce and oversee public and officially protected housing, and ADIGSA (now the Catalan Housing Agency) managed the public housing park.

In terms of private, market-based housing production, the predominant model in Spain, the developer (*promotor*) is an essential figure. Developers ensure the management of circulating real estate capital in the commodity-housing transformation phase (Llordén Miñambres 2003), acquiring land and building buildings, in some cases also carrying out construction and the final sale of buildings. Thus the developer/construction role is often conflated (TAIFA 2008). Furthermore, some savings banks work hand-in-hand with property developers and commercialize the resulting housing through their own in-house real estate agencies. Housing is sold to the consumer by an entity that can combine all or some of the sector's activities, being a developer, constructor, real estate agency, bank, and/or savings bank (TAIFA 2008). Mortgage brokers can also be present "at the bottom of the chain," taking a mortgage application to a bank or savings bank to be analyzed and approved/rejected by the entity's loan officer in exchange for a commission (García Montalvo 2014, 501).

The foundations of Spain's mortgage configuration were laid in the 1946 Mortgage Law, and the Spanish mortgage market was created by Law 2/1981 of 25 March 1981, when mortgages became more readily available. The Spanish legal system consecrates the principle of universal patrimonial responsibility through Article 1911 in the Civil Code, which states that "the debtor responds to the fulfilment of obligations with all their goods, present and future" (Ayuso 2011). In other words, a person is unable to declare personal bankruptcy and always owes the full amount of the mortgage debt contracted with the financial entity, no matter the final sale price of their mortgaged home. This debt can be inherited only if inheritance is accepted. The law stipulates that mortgage loans can be granted for 80 percent of the total value of the home, with a household having to pay the remaining 20 percent plus indirect taxes, the Stamp Tax, notary costs, and land registration fees. As a whole these total 10 percent of the cost of the property, although as of 2019 most of these costs are borne by banks due to changes in the 2017 Mortgage Law. Appraisal companies play an important role in the process: if the appraised value of the home is higher, loans can be granted for 80 percent of the appraised value rather than the listed market price. Contracting home insurance is obligatory when signing a mortgage loan.

State-subsidized housing began to be substantively produced in the 1960s but has never constituted more than 2 percent of Spain's total housing stock. Both private and public developers produce VPO housing, coordinated and incentivized by each regional government according to their housing plans and central government budget allocations. The vast majority of VPO housing is built for purchase at 20 percent below market prices, with social rental housing making up a very small proportion of state-subsidized housing production (e.g., in Catalonia, there are 14,321 units, owned by Incasòl and managed by the Catalan Housing Agency). To access this housing, families must register themselves and be in a specific social category, not surpassing a maximum income level or not owning a main residence, among others. Mortgage finance is obtained from private financial institutions, although under particular conditions regulated by the regional government, and a family is unable to sell VPO housing for a certain period of time, in order to prevent speculation (van Gent 2010). The state provides up to 80 percent of the project financing to developers at very low interest rates. Since market-rate housing production provides much better returns for developers, they are not very motivated to build VPO housing (TAIFA 2008).

---

housing prices skyrocketed from €720 per square meter in 1997 to a peak of €2,100 in 2008, and the country's total housing stock increased by almost six million units. This peak represented more than the housing production in Italy, France, and Germany combined (López and Rodríguez 2011). I now turn to briefly unpack the housing-land-mortgage nexus from the end of the dictatorship onward, then illustrate how this nexus made possible Spain's unprecedented 1997–2007 financialized housing boom.

HOUSING POLICY AND PRODUCTION: REINFORCING HOMEOWNERSHIP

Culminating the dictatorship's desire to build a nation of homeowners and instigate the construction sector as an economic growth motor, the first housing boom peaked in the early 1970s with between 400,000 and 500,000 housing units constructed per year (Naredo 2004). Spain's first housing boom (1969–74) was spurred by public subsidies attempting to deal with rapid urbanization, provide state-subsidized housing, and meet internal demand fueled by a booming tourism industry (Charnock, Purcell, and Ribera-Fumaz 2014). It was during this period that the Spanish economy's competitive advantage in capturing flows of capital in the construction sector, through its tourism–real estate specialization, was established (Observatorio Metropolitano de Madrid 2013). The project to expand homeownership and spur the construc-

tion industry continued in the decades that followed the end of the dictatorship in 1975, albeit through a different institutional framework and ideological rationale.

Renting was dealt a double blow as a form of tenancy in Spain in the 1980s,
as the country emerged from the 1973 oil crisis and the democratic transition.
This occurred first through the 1985 Boyer Decree, which eliminated rent control and tenant protection clauses in all new rental lease contracts. The theory
behind liberalizing the rental market—that rental prices would fall and the
housing supply would rise, following market logic—did not manifest in practice (Pareja Eastaway and San Martin Varo 2002). The decree also outlined a
series of economic measures that sought to "stimulate private consumption
and investment, encourage employment, and propel the construction sector"
(Rodríguez Alonso 2009). Although the 1994 Urban Letting Act (LAU) later
tied rent increases to the growth of the consumer price index, similar to laws
regulating rent in other European countries, the slowness of legal rulings in
cases of unpaid rent discouraged an increase in market rental properties (Leal
2005).

At the same time, income taxes strongly encouraged housing purchases
through making mortgage principal and interest tax-deductible. From 1985 to
1989 this included both main *and* second residences, explaining the increase
in second home purchases between the 1981 and 1991 censuses, which contrib-
uted to Spain's second short but intense housing boom (1985–92) upon joining the European Economic Community in 1986 and before Barcelona's 1992
Olympics (García Montalvo 2003). The wealthy benefited most from this tax
policy, as the more expensive the home, the larger the mortgage and the greater
the deduction (Cabré and Módenes 2004). Thus despite the public sector recognizing the need to increase the proportion of rental housing, their policies
relying on the invisible hand of the market to balance demand and supply did
not operate as planned. Instead, it was largely the socially excluded and lowest income classes of the population who lived as tenants, mainly because they
were unable to purchase property (Cabré and Módenes 2004; García Montalvo 2008; Trilla 2014). Thus, the deregulation and liberalization of the rental
market and tax incentives for housing purchase, alongside the increasing price
of rental properties, encouraged property purchases, initiating the path of increased indebtedness.

The two housing plans executed during the 1980s continued to leave out the
poorest segments of the population, with market production far surpassing
state-subsidized housing production, benefitting middle- and upper-income

groups (Rodríguez Alonso 2004). A former Catalan secretary of housing explained to me how state-subsidized housing (explained in Box 1.1) functions only in times of recession because developers completely swear off building it during housing booms as the benefit margin is "ridiculous" compared to what they earn building private-market housing. Both this secretary of housing and another, alongside numerous authors, underline the anticyclical nature of state-subsidized housing production, as it ultimately serves as a strategy to maintain construction activity during times of recession.

Into the 1990s, following broader processes of neoliberalization, the state largely withdrew its intervention into housing. The two social housing programs in the 1990s continued to encourage low-income households to become owner-occupiers through reducing market prices and providing subsidies, also serving to reactivate the building sector during the 1992–95 recession (Pareja Eastaway and San Martin 1999). During the 1997–2007 housing boom, one government informant told me that Catalan housing policy was "modernized" to European levels by the Socialist coalition government then in power, but the dedicated resources and public spending were absolutely insufficient to achieve these new policy goals.

The Catalan population expressed deep concerns about housing access through opinion polls in 2004–6, but efforts to mitigate the increasing unaffordability of housing through the 2007 Housing Rights Act and related policies and plans failed. Two Catalan secretaries of housing in office during this period underlined the difficulties they faced and their ultimately unsuccessful attempts to counteract the status quo rooted in over-indebtedness and over-production. Despite their institutional and political struggles to address this, in the end, as one noted, "we are in a free market, of course. So prices can't be controlled by decree, that's the big dilemma." They also noted that from the 1990s onward those responsible for housing policy could say nothing to the financial sector, as the latter has "total autonomy" and in essence laid the rules of the game.

In conclusion, housing policy acted as a carrot and rental legislation as a stick to encourage the Spanish population to become owner-occupiers. This resulted in mortgaged homeownership becoming the most attractive option for low-income households to access housing post-1990 (Palomera 2014; Pareja Eastaway and San Martin Varo 2002). Indeed, tax relief for homeowners has "powerfully influenced" both the development of homeownership and the indiscriminate production of housing, reducing taxes for medium- and high-income households and driving construction activity (Leal 2005, 76).

This reality has led Hoekstra, Heras Saizarbitoria, and Etxezarreta Etxarri (2010, 129) to conclude that "Spanish policies for the provision of housing—both private market housing and social or subsidized housing—have been shaped more by a desire to stimulate economic activity than by social policy per se."[4] Thus housing policies have by and large failed in providing accessible and affordable housing for all, as rental legislation, tax incentives, and housing plans have encouraged homeownership. State-subsidized housing, meanwhile, has largely served to sustain the construction sector during times of economic recession.

LAND POLICY: FROM THE SOCIAL FUNCTION OF OWNERSHIP TO THE BUILD ANYWHERE ACT

The original 1956 Land Act was the first attempt to regulate the expansion of Spanish cities. It classified land uses and planning processes, but legal loopholes allowed the free play of private agents and enabled land speculation (Capel 1975). While the act sought to provide an integrated order to urban growth, the reality of rapid rural to urban migration placed significant pressure on building housing immediately and infrastructure later (Leal 2005). The subsequent 1975 act maintained the same principles and categories as the original act but extended the distribution of benefits obtained from urban development to the public sector and municipalities (Narváez Baena 2013).

After Spain joined the European Economic Community in 1986, new ideas around economic liberalization began to penetrate urban planning and land use institutions, coinciding with the neoliberal reengineering demanded by the 1992 Maastricht Treaty, which set the constitutional base of the EU (López and Rodríguez 2011; Rullan 1999). Fierce debates around state intervention by the Spanish liberal right and sectors of the left in this period resulted in the adoption of the 1998 Land Act under the Conservative (Popular Party) Aznar government. With an overall objective of reducing land prices, the 1998 act sought to increase the supply of land, whereby, as stated in the act itself, "all land as yet unincorporated into the urban process is considered eligible for development, when no objective reasons for its preservation arises."

The fundamental change in the 1998 act involved a new model for the classification of land. The concepts of "developable" and "nondevelopable" land were redefined, where the latter became regulated to extend the potential of urban development to all land across the country (Puig Gómez 2011). This led to its popular nickname as the "build anywhere act" (*la ley del "todo urbanizable"*). As the social function of ownership was significantly removed from planning obligations, private land ownership came to operate at the core of the urban development process. In other words, the profit (rent) that previously went to public bodies for the development of their planning policies was channeled into private hands (Roca Cladera and Burns 2000). As explained to me by an employee of Incasòl, the Catalan agency that regulates public land, the 1998 act in essence "transformed the business expectations around land in a radical way because any landowner is potentially a land developer (*urbanizador*)." Enormously lucrative possibilities for money making thus began to appear.

Since the central Spanish government defines broad categories such as property rights and land values, and the autonomous communities oversee and implement land use, urban planning, and housing policy, the application of the 1998 act was uneven across the Spanish territory. That being said, many regional laws changed to reflect it, and close to 30 percent of municipalities across the country revised their master plans accordingly (González Pérez 2010). Catalonia, for example, adopted the 2/2002 Act in lieu of the 1998 Land Act to control urban planning and regulate housing development by clearly defining land owners' obligations to cede a proportion of land for public use. But rather than build social or affordable housing, municipalities often sold this land to developers or leased it for private use. Attempts by the Catalan leftist coalition government in power at the time to reduce land speculation, foster the rental market, and curb skyrocketing housing prices during the boom were ultimately unsuccessful.

The failure of these attempts also had to do with legislative reforms occurring in parallel to the 1998 Land Act that reduced local government tax intake. A lucrative new avenue to finance municipal activities involved taxes tied to land and housing, which stimulated the approval and execution of aggressive urban plans and generated extensive corruption in local governments across the country (Naredo 2010). For example, a report published by the bank BBVA (Pou 2007) states that in 2004 alone local land and building tax revenues generated over €9 billion for municipalities across Spain, a figure not including urban development income such as fees for the private use of public land. It is estimated that the income related to housing and construction during the housing boom period constituted at least 25 to 35 percent of municipalities' total revenues (García Montalvo 2008).

While economic theory dictates that liberalizing the land market leads to a decrease in the price of land and housing, as the "invisible hand" of the market would guarantee its fully rational and efficient use, quite the opposite took place. The price of housing rose exponentially and the profit expectations produced immediate supply effects. The 200,000 housing starts in 1993 rose above 500,000 in 1999, over 600,000 in 2003, and up to the record numbers of 729,000 and 863,800 in 2005 and 2006, respectively. These figures represented by far the most housing produced by any one country in Europe at the time.

The changes to the Land Act from 1956 to 1998 thus resulted in its progressive liberalization, as continent-level dynamics intermixed with and pressed such changes. Catalonia's legislative attempts to control speculative practices were unsuccessful, as broader changes in local government financing made land- and building-related taxes an attractive source of income for municipalities across Spain. The 1998 act and the 2002 Catalan Act, despite the latter's attempts to prevent it, both acted as pieces in a larger web reorganizing nested structures to facilitate capital flow into land development, paving the way for land to become a form of fictitious capital—that is, "a flow of money capital not backed by any commodity transaction" (Harvey 1982, 265)—and for property to be freely traded as a financial asset. The way in which ever-increasing levels of both fictitious capital and interest-bearing capital flows were enabled through mortgage financing systems and processes is the final element I now turn to examine.

MORTGAGE FINANCE: DEREGULATION AND EXPANSION

The liberalization of Spanish housing finance systems in the 1980s was a critical step in enabling the credit explosion in the 2000s. This liberalization was related to the broader financial system deregulation that took place in the wake of the country's severe industrial and banking crisis. Until 1980, channels to finance housing production in Spain were publicly controlled, while consumer mortgages were provided either by the public mortgage bank or by local savings banks (*cajas de ahorro*). The 1981 Mortgage Market Regulation Act deregulated access to finance by enabling the entrance of private operators, privatizing financing avenues, and building a deeper integration of financial and mortgage markets (Alberdi 1997). Adopted under the simple-majority Central Democratic Union government, a party headed by ex-Francoist minister Adolfo Suárez, the act increased the proportion of the final house price that could be financed through a loan from 50 to 80 percent and introduced variable-interest-rate loans. This enabled lower-income households to more easily obtain mortgages—as well as become more deeply indebted.

The 1981 act also established the financial infrastructure to securitize mortgage and other debt—that is, to package debt into portfolios and sell it on financial markets to generate liquidity for financial entities. The latter were able to issue covered bonds (*cédulas hipotecarias*), a type of securitization left on banks' balance sheets considered to be relatively safe and low-risk because investors have privileged claims if issuers go bankrupt (Anguren Martín, Marqués Sevillano, and Romo González 2013; Avesani, Garcia Pascual, and Ribakova 2007). A decade later the 1992 Securitization Vehicles Act created the legal basis for Spanish residential mortgage-backed securities (RMBS), an instrument that moves debt off the balance sheet and thus diffuses risk globally (Nasarre-Aznar 2002). Spreading risk through RBMS was a common strategy used for U.S. subprime loans in the 2000s (Blackburn 2008).

The 1992 act sought to create the institutional conditions to generate a new real estate takeoff after the crash of Spain's second property boom, falling housing prices, devaluations of the peseta, and the signing of the 1992 Maastricht Treaty (López and Rodríguez 2010; Naredo 2004). While the financial framework to securitize assets other than mortgages was adopted through Royal Decree 926/1998, the 44/2002 Asset Securitization Funds (FTA) Act enabled the securitization of higher-risk mortgage loans like second mortgages and mortgages whose loan-to-value ratio exceeded 80 percent (Ezcurra Pérez 2012). The 1992 and 2002 acts in particular attracted vast amounts of fictitious capital into Spain's mortgage finance market, as I outline in the next section.

Spain's forty-five savings banks were the main actors mobilizing credit and securitization, granting over half of all mortgage credit during the boom. The fact that savings banks were the originators of over 85 percent of total covered bond securitizations by the end of 2006 exemplifies their importance within the financial system (Fuentes Egusquiza 2007). Historically connected to charitable institutions, savings banks were legally defined as nonprofit private foundations that provided banking services but had a statutory obligation to dedicate funds to social and charitable works, the latter called *obra social* (Maixé-Altés 2010). However, as a banker I interviewed underlined, "There is nothing nonprofit about savings banks." They did not have shareholders, nor were they listed on stock markets like banks, but they nonetheless were aggressive profit seekers, in particular during the 1997–2007 housing boom.

The drive for profit by savings banks started in part in 1985 through national legislation that integrated depositors, local governments, founders, and employees into three governance bodies. Yet autonomous community legislation on voting rights meant that local and regional governments came to exercise considerable control over how savings banks were run (Illueca, Norden, and Udell 2014). Regional and district councils, in turn, saw significant profits to be made by rezoning sites for urban development and selling the land to a developer—who would pay for it with a loan from a savings bank run by the same councilors or their friends (López and Rodríguez 2011). The rampant

TABLE 1.3. Number of Offices and Staff of Spanish Financial Entities, 1984–2008

	Savings banks		Banks	
Year	Offices	Staff	Offices	Staff
1984	10,477	69,438	16,399	164,330
2000	19,297	101,718	16,027	122,374
2008	25,035	134,867	15,612	115,114

SOURCE: Serra Ramoneda (2011); data from Bank of Spain.

corruption that emerged led Naredo (2010, 24), among others, to characterize savings banks as "the financial hand of local and regional neo-despotism (*neo-caciquismo*)" used to execute large real estate operations and megaprojects of dubious profitability. Indeed, many savings banks were attracted by the profits reaped by real estate developers and decided to get directly involved in the business (Serra Ramoneda 2011).

Savings banks were originally able to operate only locally, but after lobbying for branching deregulation to improve their competitiveness in 1998, they were able to operate across Spain (Illueca, Norden, and Udell 2014). This geographical deregulation led to a spectacular growth in offices and personnel, as illustrated in Table 1.3. This expansion required new offices to turn profit as quickly as possible, an activity most easily achieved through providing development loans and residential mortgages. Banks faced a dilemma vis-à-vis savings banks' aggressive business strategy and decided to change their policy, lowering the requirements for credit provision to developers and families rather than losing market share (Bernardos Domínguez 2009).

Furthermore, a study by economists José García Montalvo and Josep Maria Raya Vilchez (2012) illustrated how appraisers systematically overvalued housing in order to facilitate mortgage lending during the boom. While the average loan granted in relation to the *appraised* value of a home was 82 percent, the maximum level recommended by the Bank of Spain, the average ratio of loan to *market price* was close to 110 percent. So, say the market price of an apartment was €100,000, but its appraised value sat at €130,000. A financial entity often granted a €105,000 mortgage loan, which was 105 percent of the market price of the apartment, but only 81 percent of the appraised value. The fact that over half of the appraisal companies carrying out appraisals during any given year had banks or savings banks as majority shareholders (García Montalvo 2014) illustrates how speculation in part unfolded on future profit and ever-increasing housing prices. In any case, real-estate-related lending as a proportion of total bank lending more than quadrupled, from 12 percent in 1970 to 58 percent in 2007 (Jordá, Schularick, and Taylor 2014).

Spain's "Urbanization Tsunami" Unleashed:
The 1997–2007 Housing Boom

The implementation of the European Monetary Union in 1999 suddenly brought interest rates in Spain to historic lows, from 16 percent in the early 1990s to 3 percent in 2004 (European Mortgage Federation 2012). This descent removed the past braking effects of Spain's internal financial limits, while the adoption of the euro in 1999 created a mirage of stability and safety for investors. After all, if anything went wrong, Spain's supporting European infrastructure was now "backing up" the country, which had now truly achieved its main foreign policy objective since the late 1970s: Spain was now officially and fully Europeanized (Baklanoff 1996).

These factors intertwined with neoliberalized housing, land, and finance-related legislation to unleash the country's "urbanization tsunami" (Fernández Durán 2006). In just over a decade, one-quarter of Spain's land area was paved over and built upon, with the country proudly becoming the European leader in cement consumption and fifth in the world after China, India, the United States, and Japan (Chislett 2008; Naredo, Carpintero, and Marcos 2008;). According to a report by the bank BBVA (2007), construction represented 16 percent of Spain's GDP, 10 percent of the gross value added of the economy, and 14 percent of employment in Spain in 2006. The most populated and economically central regions like Catalonia, Madrid, Valencia, and Andalusia accounted for more than half of the country's housing construction at the peak of the boom. One million of the 6.5 million housing units initiated between 1996 and 2006 were located in Catalonia (Carpintero, Sastre, and Lomas 2015).

Getting in on construction—be it through developing, building, financing, or selling housing and its related infrastructure—was the most profitable activity in Spain. Total housing-related credit rose tenfold during the boom, from €97 billion in 1994 to €1 trillion by 2007, with well over half of this credit used for housing purchase or renovation and the remainder for construction activities (Murray Mas 2015). As illustrated in Figure 1.7, the number of mortgages issued per year climbed steadily from over 600,000 in the early 2000s to over 1 million annually between 2003 and 2007, peaking in 2006 when over 1.3 million mortgages were granted. During this peak period, 15 to 20 percent of Spain's total mortgages were granted in Catalonia.

Securitization played a fundamental role in the expansion of mortgage lending, as the financial sector was able to move beyond the previous limits of bank deposits and internal savings thanks to new legislation and inves-

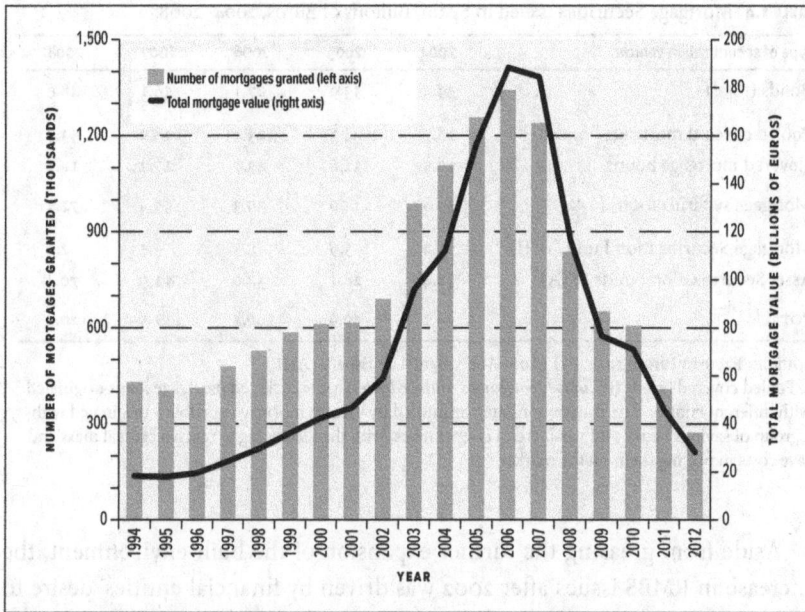

FIGURE 1.7. Number and value of homeownership mortgages granted, 1994–2012.
SOURCE: INE (2014b).

tor demand for securitized mortgage bonds. Over one-third of total Spanish mortgage debt was securitized by 2007, and Spain's securitization bond market came to occupy third place globally, after the United States and the United Kingdom (Naredo, Carpintero, and Marcos 2007; Rodríguez-Castellanos et al. 2013).

Extended mortgage lending was thus enabled as spatial fixity (e.g., a house) was turned into liquidity (e.g., a covered bond or RMBS); financial entities could then use this liquidity to grant more mortgage loans. Fictitious capital escaping the bust of the so-called new economy dot-com bubble in 2000 in part fed the dramatic investor demand for securitized bonds (Fernández Durán 2006; Puig Gómez 2011). German capital also purchased significant quantities of Spanish covered bonds, the latter becoming one of the largest asset classes in the European bond market (Charnock, Purcell, and Ribera-Fumaz 2014). During the boom, foreign investors purchased around 62 percent of the securitization bonds issued (Avesani, Garcia Pascual, and Ribakova 2007). By 2008 Spain stood next to the United States in receiving the largest net import of capital, most being private foreign investment fueling the real estate sector (García 2010).

TABLE 1.4. Mortgage Securities Issued in Spain, Billions of Euros, 2004–2008

Type of securitization vehicle	2004	2005	2006	2007	2008
Bonds (total)	39.2	55.9	67.1	56.1	48.0
Pooled covered mortgage bonds[a]	18.7	24.3	23.4	28.9	33.9
Covered mortgage bonds	20.5	31.6	43.7	27.2	14.2
Mortgage securitizations (total)	19.8	34.0	39.3	55.4	72.4
Mortgage Securitization Fund (FTH)	6.4	5.9	5.3	3.5	2.0
Asset Securitization Funds (FTA)	13.4	28.1	34.0	51.9	70.4
TOTAL	59.0	89.9	106.4	111.5	120.4

SOURCE: Ezcurra Pérez (2012, 97) (from AIAF, Banco de España, AHE).
a. Pooled covered bonds (*cédulas hipotecarias multicedentes*) are securitized mortgage loans originated with different entities. The transactions are constituted by various mortgage portfolios originated with a group of savings banks and small credit cooperatives, with the idea being to reach a critical mass and save costs in placing them on the market.

Aside from greasing the further expansion of the built environment, the increase in RMBS issues after 2002 was driven by financial entities' desire to spread their exposure to real estate risk. This was responding to the reality that by 2007 nearly 70 percent of total bank credit was made up by construction loans and mortgages, and Spain ranked first in the world in its overall exposure to real estate risk (Naredo, Carpintero, and Marcos 2007). Upon analyzing a database of securitization transactions issued in the Spanish market from 1998 to 2009 and selecting operations that could be considered subprime due their later ("failed") performance, Ezcurra Pérez (2012) argues that creating RBMS through Asset Securitization Funds (FTA) permitted Spanish financial entities to grant riskier loans, especially in 2006–7. This is because FTAs were guaranteed by lower credit quality loans and ultimately resulted in higher default rates. Table 1.4 details the progression of mortgage securities by type of securitization vehicle issued from 2004 to 2008.

Ezcurra Pérez (2012) thus estimates that a total of thirty-eight "subprime" securitization transactions valued at €49.9 billion were carried out in Spain during the housing boom, making up 21 percent of the total volume of RMBS issued from 2003 to 2008. These findings align with Jiménez et al. (2010), who maintain that banks that securitized loans had a much stronger growth in credit lending to new clients from 2004 to 2007, with new credit granted as riskier and a third more likely to default. Although subprime mortgages have no formal legal or financial definition in Spain, such realities absolutely highlight the existence of what has been called subprime *a la española*, discussed in depth in the next chapter.

As long as housing prices increased, interest rates were low, and housing construction boomed, the housing finance market appeared to be a magical tool to fuel the credit and liquidity needed to sustain the expansion of the built environment. Economic growth levels flew above even the wealthiest European neighbors: Spain had made it. Especially toward the end of the boom, the housing finance market also worked beautifully to spread banks' exposure to real estate risk. From the inherently speculative nature of mortgages themselves—as a form of rent to financial institutions where land and housing titles are given to "homeowners" as claims on future labor—the expanding housing finance market created an even greater scale of speculation. Yet as banks became more and more exposed to real estate debt, chinks in the supposedly never-ending growth, or at least stabilization, of housing prices began to appear and soon after shattered.

From a Renter to a Homeowner Society: Housing Shortages to Millions of Empty Houses

The shift from one end of extreme housing conditions in the 1940s to another in the 2000s—a majority-renter society to a solidly homeowner society, massive housing shortages to boundless empty homes—was accompanied by other extremes: from Spanishness to Europeanness, from dictatorship to democracy. The historical explorations in this chapter show, following Ananya Roy's (2017) proposal, the essence of how seemingly "universal" categories (e.g., homeownership) are truly forged through historical difference. Among the many developments in the move from the state-instilled growth of housing and homeownership under the Franco dictatorship to the market-driven growth of both as facilitated by the democratic Spanish state, this section provides some deeper reflection on several key points.

The dictatorial regime was unable to fully realize its Falangist (national syndicalist) ideal of depoliticizing society and fomenting Spanishness through housing, but it proved successful on two other fronts. First, the regime created the legal basis and corporate structure to professionalize developer and construction activity, a necessary action to effectively manage circulating real estate capital and thereby turn housing into a commodity. This step was fundamental to later attract private capital and launch residential construction as an economic motor for Spain in the 1960s, establishing its construction sector and triggering an unprecedented housing production and, for the first time in history, a stock of second and empty homes. It also enabled several of the most powerful Spanish construction companies in the world today to build their base from the slave labor of defeated fighters for the republic in the post–Spanish Civil War era, a dirty secret behind the Spanish "reconquest" of Latin America in the 1990s that has been much lauded, especially by the private sector (Chislett 2008).

The second success of the dictatorship was to instigate a deep-seated shift from a majority-renter to an ever-increasing homeowner society through a variety of legal mechanisms and discourses rooted in eliminating all leftist thought, instilling family values and thus improving the Spanish race. In Catalonia alone, homeownership doubled in two decades, from 25.7 percent in 1950 to 53.3 percent in 1970 (Trilla, cited in Tatjer 2008). A clear project of sociopolitical control underlying the push to homeownership became clear in this chapter, reminiscent of projects encouraging homeownership in other countries decades later (e.g., Allon and Redden 2012; Langley 2008; Ronald 2008; Smith 2008), albeit with a blatant nationalist-fascist twist of Spanishness. Homeownership offered a "stable" and "harmonious" form of property for the Franco dictatorship and a means to pacify the population, which can be understood in Foucauldian terms as increasing the docility and utility of the population. The Francoist period laid the foundations for radical changes in the practice and perception of the status of homeownership in Spain to such an extent that, as Colau and Alemany note (2012, 33), by the 1980s the Spanish homeownership "culture" was considered completely natural, "like a lucky genetic code inscribed in our DNA that differentiates us from other mortals and determines our behavior. Just another expression of the *Spanish way of life*." Homeownership thus served as a "security mechanism" to control a "random element inherent in a population of living beings so as to optimize a state of life" (Foucault 2003, 246), one that sought to maintain and expand a specific social and economic order grounded in homeownership and housing production.

Thanks to the evolution of housing policy, land legislation, and mortgage finance under democracy, the Francoist drive to create a specific economic and social order continued, but through a neoliberal strategy of governing for the market. The market—enabled by the state under modernizing pressures of broader European neoliberalization and Spain's keenness to become Europeanized—became "the indispensable regulating function of the economy" (Foucault 2008, 240). For example, economic growth underwrote any purportedly social goals of housing policy, whereby rental market liberalization, tax policy encouraging housing purchase, and easing access to mortgage finance were used as tools to stimulate homeownership in the 1980s and beyond. The regulatory changes that took place illustrate how various housing-, land-, and mortgage-finance-related frameworks were carefully crafted to organize a society where market mechanisms could supposedly rule. At the same time the state promoted housing purchase through tax regimes and the (insufficient) production of state-subsidized housing in times of recession to keep the construction sector rolling. This new post-dictatorship configuration was successful in continuing to stimulate both the production of housing and more homeownership: the housing stock increased by over seven million units from 1970 to 1991, with the quantity of second homes quadrupling and empty housing almost doubling (Table 1.1). The number of owner-occupiers rose 15 percent during the same period in Spain (Table 1.2), while in Catalonia homeownership increased from 53 percent in 1970 to 80 percent in 1991.

Heterodox Spanish economist José Manuel Naredo (2010) avers that the advancement of homeownership established through Franco's housing policy from 1939 to 1975 culminated in the bust of the 1997–2007 housing boom, albeit, as historian Eduard Masjuan (2010) specifies, without the public promotion of affordable rents or "ultra-cheap" property from the paternalist Franco era. Indeed, the drive to become fully European under Spanish democracy necessitated a more complete shift to the market to ensure continued growth, increased investment, and a definitive exit from economic backwardness that (too) long characterized Spain as a backwater. The fact that housing production ultimately almost tripled population growth was secondary: the desire of Franco's first minister of housing to make a spring of homes grow in Spain was finally coming true.

Conclusions

This chapter illustrated the deep roots of the 1997–2007 housing boom and crisis by showing how housing served as a tool to create a specific social and economic order in Spain. Homeownership was instilled in and inscribed on the Spanish population under the dictatorship, where a clear pro-owner-occupier discourse was backed by legal and material changes that began to facilitate housing purchase. This provided stability for the regime and served to pacify the population, increasing their docility and utility (Foucault 1991). The latter occurred in particular as the population was connected to the incipient growth and development of the construction sector at the end of the dictatorship, after significant efforts to professionalize the development of the real estate sector. Then, from dictatorship to democracy, there was an increasing shift toward governance through the market, toward what Foucault (2008, 116) calls "a state under the supervision of the market rather than a market supervised by the state," a reflection of broader neoliberal shifts across continental Europe, the United Kingdom, and the United States. Housing policy reinforced homeownership and free-market housing production, while the steady deregulation of land and housing finance systems, intertwined with the dynamics of formally becoming European through full EU membership, created the conditions for an unprecedented growth of the construction and infrastructure sector.

The production of housing and homeowners through market mechanisms resulted in the establishment of "a sort of homeostasis, not by training individuals, but by achieving an overall equilibrium that protects the security of the whole from internal dangers" (Foucault 2003, 249). In other words, mortgaged homeownership became a key component to ensure homeostasis and continued economic growth through the construction and financial sectors, as the mortgaged population could ensure growth and guarantee the system's stability. The adjustment of the population to economic processes (Foucault 1978) was thus deepened beyond, although in relation to, the labor-capital relation. The financialization of housing thus shows itself to be a process where the mortgage finance market comes to be just as vital as or more important than building housing (Aalbers 2008) and where the economic and social reproduction of the workforce becomes more deeply integrated in the financial system (Fine 2010; López and Rodríguez 2010). The mechanisms and processes through which the latter unfolded are explored in detail in the next chapter.

This chapter also made clear how, from the dictatorship to the present, there was a political construction of nonalternatives, or the building of nonchoice, in homeownership and economic growth through housing production, fueled by an unprecedented influx of speculative capital. This configuration was by no means accidental but was carefully assembled by the Spanish state. The state deregulated and liberalized land, housing, and mortgage finance to facilitate the supposed rule of the market, including, for example, the institutional conditions and legal mechanisms to transform real estate into a liquid financial asset abstracted from local conditions (Gotham 2009). At the same time, tax relief encouraged housing purchase, the liberalization of the rental market increased rental prices while decreasing rent stability as a tenure option, and state-subsidized housing was underproduced. Through these direct and indirect mechanisms, what emerged was a mixture of no alternative than to continue producing market-based housing and extend homeownership. As I will underline in the next chapter, this was articulated as the sensible choice, celebrated as a boon for the economy and a path to a wealthier society. Transforming housing into a "highly leveraged debt vehicle" parceled and sold on secondary markets thus not only depoliticized the underlying indebtedness of households (Montgomerie and Büdenbender 2015, 389) but was the stable and logical path to access housing under the tenure status of "homeowner."

The figures depicting housing and homeownership growth over five decades in Spain appear to illustrate the success of creating homeostasis and stability through the twinned processes of stimulating the construction sector and building a population of owner-occupiers. Yet evidence suggests that toward the end of the boom the mortgage finance market was operating not to facilitate housing construction, but purely to make money (Aalbers 2008). The emergence of Spanish-style subprime mortgages illustrates this, as they in essence represent lending to households despite uncertain repayment capacities and conditions. While this point will be discussed in greater depth in the next chapter, it is important to highlight here because it illustrates how the population is both a necessary component of and a limit to the financialization of housing. In other words, they are needed as recipients of mortgage loans, which can then be securitized and sold on secondary markets, but precarious lives and labor that may lead to defaulted loan payments en masse can destabilize the system. As Aalbers (2008, 160) notes, "The financialization of home was never designed to enable homeownership; it was first and foremost designed to fuel the economy," and ultimately it increases risk and insecurity for families. While used as a strategy that attempts to overcome crisis and the limits of capital, the financialization of housing ultimately creates a deeper catastrophe when the inevitable crisis hits. But first, the next chapter will zero in on the role of the population in the financialization of housing during the 1997–2007 housing boom, taking an ethnographic look at how mortgages played a regulatory and disciplinary role in facilitating housing construction and the mortgage finance market.

CHAPTER 2

The Biopolitics of the
1997–2007 Housing Boom

The previous chapter illustrated how Spain's 1997–2007 financialized housing boom was the culmination of a particular social and economic order laid during the nearly forty-year Franco dictatorship and subsequent democracy and ascendance to modernity through formal Europeanization. The objective of this order was both to fuel the production of the built environment as a core economic growth machine and to create a nation of upright, properly Spanish—and then modern European—homeowners. In this chapter I turn to detail the processes and pathways through which lives became mortgaged and financialized during the country's 1997–2007 urbanization tsunami. In other words, how and why did lives become tangled up in domestic and international financialized housing flows? What were the racialized and classed ways in which mortgages regulated and disciplined the population? In this way, I make visible the biopolitics of mortgage debt during a housing boom.

To do this, I weave together two narratives: a macrolevel political-economic overview of the housing bubble and the lived experience of mortgage-affected compañerxs plus stories from a handful of (ex-)bankers working in the decades previous to and during the boom. My aim is to illustrate how the political and economic changes that led to the expansion of mortgage credit lending also served to integrate not only the social and economic reproduction of the workforce into global financial systems (Fine 2010; López and Rodríguez 2010) but also everyday life, showing the racialized, classed, and gendered ways this unfolded. I argue that mortgages operate differentially as a "secondary form of exploitation" (Harvey 1982, 285) in the sphere of circulation, as they *appeared* to modify the real income of workers through wealth generation but in reality were rooted in deepening debt relations. These relations furthermore differed according to race and class and, in turn, created differentiated debt ecologies (Harker 2020).

Beginning with a focus at the level of the population, I illustrate how the mortgaging of housing-life was normalized by the state and private sector during the 1997–2007 housing boom. Then, the narratives of Spanish and non-European immigrant compañerxs explain how they experienced this process in their day-to-day lives. We then see how the rapid and remarkable increase in household wealth, which supposedly reflected the success of Spaniards and immigrants alike, masked shared but different realities of indebtedness, job precarity, and subprimes *a la española*. I then uncover exactly how mortgaged homeownership differentially adjusted the population to economic processes (Foucault 1978) during the housing boom in the Barcelona metropolitan region and how life became financialized. At its base, this process unwittingly relied on precarious job contracts, and the social reproduction tasks underlying the maintenance of the family borne largely by women, to advance the performance of global financial markets and successfully respond to the rise and fall of interest rates. Under conditions of the creation of nonalternatives to homeownership in terms of accessing housing stability and security, rich ethnographic material illustrates the racialized, gendered, and classed process of finding and contracting a mortgage. Here it becomes clear exactly how mortgages operated as a "technology of power over life" (Foucault 2003, 236), that is, a form of biopolitical control, to differentially regulate and discipline the population.

The findings show how human lives and subjectivities, unequally valued (Melamed 2015), were crucial components of the process to financialize housing and maintain economic expansion, suggesting an interconnected process of financializing life. I argue that this occurs as mortgage holders are proletarianized—"produced, used up" (Dean 2012, 75)—as their labor and life is differentially packaged into financial products and vehicles of financial speculation through debt repayments. But these lives are not discarded, as Dean notes, since in the Spanish context a debt contracted is a debt for life due to the impossibility of declaring personal bankruptcy and Spanish law obliging debtors to pay their debt with all their "past and present goods." In the penultimate section I reflect on the theoretical insights from these findings and the subprime loan as a racial/postcolonial, moral, and economic referent (Chakravartty and Silva 2012) in the Spanish context. I now turn to detail the mainstream messaging around homeownership and mortgage indebtedness in the 2000s from the public and private sectors as well as mortgaged compañerxs' experiences.

Housing as a Safe Investment: "Mortgage Yourself!"

Starting in the late 1990s, the Spanish population heard the same motto from the public administration, real estate agents, developers, builders, financial institutions, and the mass media, among others: "The price of housing never falls, housing is a safe investment" (Colau and Alemany 2012; García Montalvo 2008). Such messaging was reinforced through media representations connecting the dominance of private property to an almost genetic predisposition of Spanish citizens to own their homes (Palomera 2014). This dehistoricized and manufactured interpretation of the "naturalness" of home-ownership was also echoed by the financial sector. For example, the Bank of Spain's 2007 annual report asserted that factors favoring real estate expansion in Spain were "amplified in some measure by the marked preference of Spanish families for real estate assets." The 2006 annual report of the savings bank La Caixa (now CaixaBank) declared that "despite the escalating price of housing and rising interest rates, the demand for mortgage credit is being maintained at a high level thanks to demographic factors and factors related to the social environment." These are but two illustrations of how "preferences" for mortgaged homeownership and its related "social environment" were understood as neutral, objective, preexisting realities that were somehow naturally engrained in Spaniards' bodies and the Spanish fabric of existence.

The reality impelling the growth of mortgaged homeownership from 1997 to 2007 has a decades-long, deep political-economic and cultural history, as explored in chapter 1. The new element was that "the entire financial system hurled itself on families so that they would ask for [mortgage] credit," as underlined to me by a former Catalan secretary of housing. Financial institutions competed for clients through aggressive marketing campaigns, selling mortgages based on their supposed distinction, singularity, and originality (Fernández Rincón 2013). Mortgages were offered through the internet, direct-mail advertising, television ads, and unsolicited emails. They appeared to be tailor-made to fit each social group and need: "the young mortgage; the easy mortgage; the free mortgage; the open mortgage; the serene mortgage; the global mortgage; the paid-off mortgage; the wild mortgage; the super mortgage; the revolution mortgage" (Colau and Alemany 2012, 66–67).

The message of housing as a safe and surefire investment, and the ease in accessing mortgaged homeownership, was a winner for millions of people. Part of the demand was fed by a massive wave of international immigration, the largest in Spain's history. The documented foreign population increased by 4.8 million people from 1998 to 2007, with Madrid experiencing rapid and

¿por qué?

FIGURE 2.1. Caja Madrid mortgage advertisement targeting Arab-speaking immigrants. (Translation: Caja Madrid has the biggest immigrant client base in the country, with about 35.5 percent of immigrants as our clients. This proves that Caja Madrid can adapt to the changes that the country has faced in recent years. We are fast at realizing and assessing job opportunities and that immigrants like Mohammad [man in the ad] and his family will be a part of the economic future of the country. That's why Caja Madrid has taken a chance on them and that's why we offer you all the special monetary services that will help you advance economically. That's why we have a training process to hire more people from different nationalities. Caja Madrid was the first to believe in Mohammad, Ingie ... etc. [Translation by Gida Homam].)
SOURCE: *El País*, 14 December 2003.

unprecedented growth (Gonick 2021) and over one million newcomers settling in Catalonia. According to the Spanish National Institute of Statistics, immigrants came to Spain largely from Latin America (1.8 million)—in particular from Ecuador (408,394) and Colombia (272,266)—the rest of Europe (1.7 million), and Africa (650,000), with over three-quarters of the latter from Morocco. About half of these new Spanish residents filled the growing number of jobs in the construction and service sector, and increasing numbers shifted from renting to homeownership in the face of apparently stable employment, the reunification of family members, and easy access to credit (Bernardos Domínguez 2009). Homeownership also gave the newcomers the impression of truly being part of the Spanish economic and cultural way of life. Advertising from financial entities dedicated expressly to immigrants was prevalent, as seen in Figure 2.1, which depicts these entities as generous (patriarchal) saviors. A former Catalan secretary of housing underlined how the entire façade of the Barcelona Cathedral, under rehabilitation at the time, was covered in ads promoting mortgages "with the very best conditions" for immigrants.

FIGURE 2.2. Banco Comercio mortgage advertisement. (Translation: It is said by those who know the most: our mortgages have no [olive] pits. And now AENOR quality certified. At Commerce Bank we are specialists in mortgage loans. In fact, we were the first to take the pits out of mortgages with the 100 percent Mortgage, giving you up to 100 percent of the housing price. But we are also guaranteed by over 25,000 mortgages we've granted in recent years. Innovative solutions, flexible, tailor-made, and of maximum quality. For this reason, the concession and administration of our mortgage loans has obtained one of the most rigorous quality certifications: AENOR. So that you can count on the maximum guarantees and security, in our mortgages you will find no pits. Confirm it in any Commerce Bank. Commerce Bank. We will understand each other.)
SOURCE: *La Vanguardia*, 21 July 1997.

FIGURE 2.3. BBVA mortgage advertisement. (Translation: Go ahead, now buying your house is easier. Pay up to 40 percent less on your mortgage payments during the first years. The BBVA easy mortgage. Buying a house is always a decision that requires special effort, especially at the start. At BBVA we know this, which is why we offer you a mortgage that adapts and allows you to pay up to 40 percent less on your fees, because during the first 3 years you pay only interest. In addition, you can leave the amortization of up to 30 percent of the capital until the end of the loan. All this with the possibility to protect your mortgage through a large range of insurance options. In short, we help you choose the fee you want to pay so that you can enjoy what is really important, your house. Come on, visit BBVA and we will make you a personalized offer.)
SOURCE: *La Vanguardia*, 10 January 2005.

Figures 2.2 and 2.3 are further illustrations of mortgage advertisements prevalent in popular media during the boom. The translated text below each figure illustrates how the complexity of mortgages was brushed away, making them appear as simple, straightforward, and ordinary products. As found by Martin (2002) in the United States and Pellandini-Simányi, Hammer, and Vargha (2015) in Hungary, mortgage finance appears to be an easy subject.

Due to the growth and profit objectives spurred by their territorial deregulation in the late 1980s, many of Spain's forty-five savings banks developed tight ties with the real estate sector. These expanding savings banks were particularly aggressive mortgage credit lenders, but banks also lowered credit provision requirements to get in on the game. Mortgages with a 100 percent to 120 percent loan-to-value ratio became commonplace. The following quote from Vicky, a banker at La Caixa, provides insight into the general climate:

> Of course, there was competition, total competition between entities to earn that piece of the pie. Granting a mortgage means a sudden increase not only in the office's volume but also of its business, because of commission, interest over thirty years, plus insurance. With entities, especially small savings banks, it was crazy. . . . All they wanted to do was grow and grow, but they did not assess that if a person had a €300,000 mortgage with a very unstable job, or if only one of two signatories worked, if interest rates rose they could no longer pay. Instead, the bank gave them the mortgage, and even said, "Do you want 10 percent more for expenses, to furnish the apartment?" Since the price of housing had never fallen recently, I suppose they didn't think about it too much.

Two of the four bankers or retired bankers remarked that many potential clients expressed a right, even an entitlement, to receive mortgage credit during the housing boom. If their loans were not approved, they would go to another savings bank "who wanted in, whatever the cost" and their request for a mortgage would be approved. In the face of benefits generated for multiple actors, Vicky emphasized how this attitude of entitlement was promoted by developers, by the state, and at all levels: "Mortgage yourselves!" In one transaction real estate agents could make up to a 10 percent commission and the state received 6 percent VAT (value-added tax), alongside a 0.5 percent stamp duty (*Impuesto sobre Actos Jurídicos Documentados*), and financial entities earned a 1 percent commission. Local land and building tax revenues generated billions each year. These monetary flows constituted important incentives to maintain and increase the volume of mortgage and housing sales, also stimulating predatory practices particularly targeted toward immigrants and low-income

Spaniards as detailed in this chapter. Thus, this specific context of easy access to credit spurred by savings bank expansion and unprecedented liquidity led to more and more households being induced, through advertising and "expert" guidance, to buy housing, something a broad range of social actors depicted—and even continue to depict today—as a natural, even genetic, component of the Spanish way of life.

Purchasing a Home: "It Was Like Going to Buy Bread"

As compañerxs explained to me why they bought a house and their experience finding their home and mortgage, over half highlighted the social and contextual pressure they faced to become a homeowner. Two compañeros, one Spanish and one Ecuadorian, underlined how "housing prices were increasing every day, every day" in the early to mid-2000s. Almost every time they walked past a real estate agency, housing prices had shot up. As a former Catalan secretary of housing explained, during the boom the upward speculative spiral in housing prices "generated a feeling of, well, we're missing the train." Many compañerxs expressed a feeling that they needed to buy immediately before prices were out of reach.

Spanish compañerxs predominantly spoke about being instilled and inculcated to purchase housing by family members, although over half spoke of buying as a societal norm, illustrating the deep-seated success of Franco's inculcation of homeownership. Compañerxs expressed this through the idea that homeownership is "stuck deep inside" (Elena) or that one is taught to "work to have a roof" (Daniel). The following three quotes express these sentiments: "Here in Spain the problem that we have, that we inherited from our parents and our grandparents and such, is having a house. I have lived it that way. You have to buy a house, I always have heard that housing, you have to buy it. Of course, that's how it is, you are born that way" (Pepe, 35 years old). "Yes, it is really true that it was hammered into you to buy an apartment, because you had to buy one . . . and of course, if you paid €700 per month in rent and it cost €800 to buy, well of course, it was clear. The option was to buy, buy, buy" (Joana, 50–55 years old). "The idea that has always been held here is that the future for common people was investing in housing. You have your house so that day after tomorrow when you have children or if you are elderly, you have the stability of a home" (Bea, 40–45 years old).

When a Spanish compañera explained how a friend warned her and others at a social gathering in 2006 to "be careful, don't go there, [the housing bubble] is going to burst," they all laughed, incredulous. Rather, virtually all compañerxs, both Spanish and immigrant, emphasized the general pressure to contract a mortgage and the ease in doing so, as there was a tightly wrought chain of agents making mortgages more easily "accessible." Carlos, an Ecuadorian compañero in his late thirties who worked in the offices of an infrastructure company, illustrates this:

> A: When I arrived [from Ecuador], it was not necessary for me to go to a bank and say, "Hey bank, I want a mortgage." Everything was made easy for me. There were people who came and offered mortgages with conditions that you never in your life thought you would find.
>
> Q: *They came to your house?*
>
> A: They came to my house, to my workplace. Representatives, real estate agents came because I tell you, this was not just at the level of the banks, here everyone benefited. The real estate agent, the bank, the seller, everyone. If you went to a real estate agency, they would send an agent to your house. He ate you up, he told you many things, he described it in a very lovely, wonderful way, this was your life's dream, many things. You get excited, and you end up falling in their web.

Real estate agents, brokers, bankers, friends, and even acquaintances encouraged virtually all immigrant compañerxs I interviewed to buy housing. Real estate agents and bankers said that buying a home was an investment, and all repeatedly expressed renting as "throwing away money." Mortgaged homeownership was conveyed as key to security and stability and an asset that would grow to realize future returns (Langley 2008). This was compelling for many immigrants, provoking perceptions that buying "was the opportunity of your life" (Carlos) or "like winning the lottery" (Julián). At the same time, José, a Colombian mechanic in his early forties, noted that "I saw it as something normal, most people were doing the same thing. . . . It was like going to buy bread." The sole exception I ever heard from this narrative—in interviews, in informal conversations, or at PAH assemblies—was expressed by Isa, a compañera from Ecuador who at the time was in her late twenties and worked in a supermarket. She explained her experience when she went to the savings bank La Caixa in 2005: "An elderly worker there told me, 'But my dear, you don't know what you are getting yourself into, you don't know what a mortgage is. How old are you?' I told him, 'But I want to save.' He said, 'If I were you, the first thing I would do is take a trip around the world. Don't get yourself into a mortgage.' We [my husband and I] left feeling so angry. Now I say: why didn't I listen to him?"

Of the ten immigrant compañerxs I interviewed, half discussed buying a home explicitly as a way to save money. This notion of saving through buying was often held in relation to returning to one's home country in the future, an idea often inculcated by real estate agents, brokers, or bankers. For example, Marta, a supermarket worker in her late forties from Ecuador, lived in a rented room for five years with her husband and teenage son. With €6,000 in savings, in 2005 they went to a real estate agent to rent an apartment. The agent told them that "the bank is giving 100 percent financing to be able to buy.... Listen, it is better for you to buy because renting is like throwing money into a broken bag.... Apart from saving money, when you leave [return to Ecuador], even though you don't make any money you have it there. When you leave you sell the apartment and your money is there, stored. You just have to sell the apartment and take your money."

Saving money aside, four immigrant compañerxs expressed further motivations to become a homeowner. Two explicitly stated the desire to provide security for their children, to leave them something in the future, thus reproducing and echoing similar thoughts as those heard around them. Sara, a Moroccan chef in her late thirties, exemplifies this position: "Since our roots are outside Spain, at least I'll leave something for my kids, like an inheritance, so they don't have to suffer like when we lived in rented rooms." In their minds, buying a home equaled social mobility, increased financial security, and social integration. For compañeras in particular, social reproduction concerns were at the forefront, especially finding a stable home to fulfil provisioning and caring demands. They clearly saw household indebtedness as the most secure path to achieve this (Allon 2014; Predmore 2020). Half of the immigrant compañerxs I interviewed lived in sublet rooms upon arriving in Spain, two of them as single men before bringing their families, and Sara and Marta as a family unit squeezed into one room in an overcrowded apartment. This was often the only accommodation option for undocumented immigrants, as they awaited their official documents, at an exorbitant price. Isa, also from Ecuador, lived in a shared room with her husband and two extended family members. They were charged €100 each per bed per month. Several other people lived in the apartment, and no one was allowed to receive visitors. Isa explained that since she was an undocumented immigrant upon arrival in Spain, they were unable to complain or demand anything else.

Family reunification—the right of immigrants to Spain to bring their close family to their place of residence—was also an important element behind the decision to buy. This process was usually in itself gendered, as the common pattern was for the male breadwinner to migrate to Spain, then bring his wife and children once he was established. Applying for family reunification required holding a Spanish residence permit for at least two years, a minimum level of income, and adequate living space, among other requirements. Sublet rooms did not count as adequate living space, while an apartment rented in its entirety had size requirements depending on the number of children in the family. Julián, a forty-year-old Ecuadorian compañero who used to work in a cleaning company stated: "I started looking for an apartment precisely for family reunification, because it was an essential requirement to be able to bring your children. Many of us indebted ourselves in order to reunite our families." Patricia, a Colombian in her early thirties, was the other compañera I interviewed whose husband, working as a truck driver in Spain, brought her to Barcelona through the family reunification process. Patricia explained that her husband searched a long time for a reasonably priced and adequately sized rental apartment but was unable to find one: "In the end he found mortgages, all mortgages, mortgages."

Paying (often high) rental deposits also compelled residents to seek a mortgage. Four compañerxs, almost all of them immigrants, discussed the difficulty in meeting increasing rental prices during the boom and their inability to gather the money for a rental deposit, as the latter ranged from €3,000 to €6,000. This played a large role in their decision to buy housing. Several of the Spaniards I interviewed lived as renters previous to the housing boom and once in long-term relationships decided to buy. Elena, for example, lived as a renter in Barcelona her whole life and was paying €320 per month. But in 2004 her eight-year rental contract ended and her monthly rent doubled under the new contract. Unable to pay this amount, she sought to rent an apartment together with her partner, but down payments were €3,000, with monthly rent around €600. Buying a home was the logical choice.

While a few Spanish compañerxs interviewed lived with their parents before purchasing a home, five other middle- to upper-income compañerxs were already homeowners before the housing boom. These compañerxs saw the price of their previous home skyrocket and were able to leverage it either by selling it and buying a new home or by obtaining a bridge mortgage to "make the leap" into a larger, single-family, detached dwelling. For example, in 2001 Ángela and her partner contracted a mortgage with a savings bank to purchase their first apartment in the center of Sabadell for €119,000. The bank appraised the property in 2007 at €338,000, and then approved €260,000 toward the purchase of a 350-square-meter second home whose total cost was €369,000 (officially appraised at €601,000). The rest of the loan was taken out with another savings bank. Ángela and her partner were in their early thirties and had a combined income of €4,500 per month working in business administration and information technology and were confident they could pay both mortgages until the first apartment was sold for its appraised amount. But their first apartment was never sold as the crisis hit, and the couple was left paying two mortgages and, shortly after that, unemployed. Another middle- to upper-income compañero is Joan, a fifty-five-year-old self-employed builder with thirty years' experience who sold his two-garage single-family home in 2006 for €240,400, over three and a half times what he bought it for in 1988. He purchased land in the northern outskirts of Barcelona for €138,000 in 2006 and contracted a mortgage for €200,000 to build his 380-square-meter home. With a monthly income between €3,500 and €4,100 and his wife who earned €1,050, paying the mortgage seemed manageable.

Debt Disguised as Wealth:
Socioeconomic Precarity and Subprimes a la Española

The housing boom was praised for increasing Spanish households' net wealth. The latter appeared to grow from 767 percent of gross disposable household income in 1995 to 1,185 percent in 2006, with virtually the entire surge corresponding to property wealth (Naredo, Carpintero, and Marcos 2008). But this increase in household "wealth" was in reality an increase in household debt, underpinned by inflated housing prices. By the end of 2009 Spanish household debt stood at 84 percent of annual GDP, up from 32 percent in 2002 (García 2010; García Montalvo 2003). According to the European Mortgage Federation total outstanding mortgage debt in Spain increased over fourfold, from €154.5 billion in 1999 to €674 billion in 2008. The Bank of Spain reported that debt contraction was four times higher in 2006 than it was in 1990, with 42 percent of people over the age of twenty holding debt, well over half of which was mortgage related.

Debt size and duration also grew as the price of the average mortgage loan granted tripled—from €47,284 in 1994 to €168,677 in 2007—and the average repayment period increased from twelve years in 1990 to twenty-seven years in 2007 (Murray Mas 2015). During the boom, thirty-five- or forty-year mortgages were not uncommon. Indeed, the consumer magazine from the Basque supermarket chain Eroski reported that some Spanish savings banks were even offering a fifty-two-year mortgage. Remarkably, journalist Pablo Ximénez de Sandoval reported in Spain's largest newspaper, El País, that the financial intermediary CreditServices offered a sixty-nine-year mortgage. These longer time periods served to simultaneously stretch a family's debt payment capacity, generate greater interest payments for financial entities, and create more deeply indebted households (TAIFA 2008). Furthermore, Article 1911 in Spain's Civil Code obliges (mortgage) debtors to pay their debt with all their "past and present goods," resulting in a debt for life. In other words, there is no personal bankruptcy law in Spain. The moral legitimization of debt was legally guaranteed.

The exponential increase in indebtedness took place at the same time that real average wages, and thus gross disposable household income, decreased, reflecting trends in other countries like the United States (Bellamy Foster 2006). From 1995 to 2005 the purchasing power of the average Spanish salary fell 4 percent (TAIFA 2007), one of the impacts of profound labor market re-structuring in the 1980s. With an eye to Spain's full ascension to the European Economic Community in the mid-1980s, the Socialist government sought to "clean up" and reconvert unprofitable industrial sectors. This resulted in a 35 percent reduction in industrial sector jobs and the partial or full privatization of forty-six firms (Charnock, Purcell, and Ribera-Fumaz 2014). Changes in la-bor laws during this period and beyond steadily enabled workforce flexibiliza-tion and thus more temporary and precarious contracts, whereby in the third trimester of 2004 nine out of ten new job contracts were temporary, and av-erage contracts lasted twenty-one days (TAIFA 2005). Labor rights were thus steadily eroded over decades.

The construction sector played a key role in the reorientation of Spain's economy and labor force flexibilization, a process also tied up in liberaliza-tions demanded by Spain's increasingly tight membership in the European Union. Out of 8.1 million new jobs created between 1996 and 2007, 20 percent were in the construction sector and over 50 percent were low-skilled jobs in the service sector (Romero, Jiménez, and Villoria 2012). Many of these jobs ex-plain Spain's almost top-ranking position in the global tourism industry and the country's ability to produce millions of main and second homes for Span-iards and expatriates. The wave of new immigrants—from Latin America and Africa in particular—were key in filling low-paid job positions in both sectors. Around 30 percent of new contracts were for short-term or temporary em-ployment, while average salaries fell by 10 percent in real terms. Of wage earn-ers, 40 percent barely made one thousand euros a month, a status popularly known as *mileuristas* (López and Rodríguez 2010). The accumulated increase in housing prices between 1997 and 2007 grew *seven times* more than con-sumer prices and salaries during the same period (Spanish Ministry of Hous-ing, cited by TAIFA 2007).

But no matter the fact that one-third of work contracts were temporary and 60 percent of wage earners were living on an average annual salary of €10,935

TABLE 2.1. Distribution of Wage Earners in Spain by Income Scale, 2007

Salary scale	€0–15,977	€15,977–39,942	€39,942–59,913	€59,913–79,884	>€79,884
Number of wage earners	10,863,957	7,017,173	958,288	275,817	193,796
—Foreigners (%)	16.7	4.6	1.9	2.4	4.2
—Women (%)	50.4	35.4	28.0	22.0	14.2
% of total wage earners	60.0	35.8	5.0	1.4	1.0
% of total salaries	25.2	49.2	13.0	5.4	7.2
Average annual salary	€10,935	€26,175	€47,599	€68,111	€129,852

SOURCES: Spanish Tax Agency (AEAT 2007) and López and Rodríguez (2010, 233).

per year in 2007, financial institutions were making mortgages available to an ever-broader spectrum of the population. Table 2.1 shows the distribution of wage earners by income scale in Spain in 2007. The lowest salary scale held the largest proportion of "foreign" (e.g., non-Spanish citizens) and female workers, reflecting the differential valuation of racialized life, long-existing structural gender inequalities, and intersectional forms of discrimination more broadly (Bhattacharyya 2018; Bustelo 2009; Ezquerra 2014). Despite continued growth in women's employment in the formal labor market since the 1980s, their positions have been more precarious and poorly paid, while they simultaneously continue to perform most unpaid domestic care work and social reproduction tasks (Lombardo 2017). Skyrocketing housing prices amid stagnant salaries translated to an escalation in household indebtedness from 65 percent of net disposable income in 1995 to 149 percent in 2007, according to OECD data. Spain became the country with the highest proportion of long-term household mortgage debt to disposable income in the world (Naredo, Carpintero, and Marcos 2007, 2008). Mortgaged homeownership was thus mushrooming despite precarious job contracts and stagnant salaries, much of it helping feed financial instruments in the (subprime) mortgage market.

As the U.S. subprime debacle unfolded, virtually all Spanish politicians and bankers said that subprime mortgages did not exist in Spain. The country, after all, had obtained its official European status of modernity. The Spanish minister of economy, Pedro Solbes, stated in October 2007 that "there are practices that the [Spanish financial] sector should correct, but it has nothing to do with subprimes in the United States" (Pérez 2007). Unlike in the United States or the United Kingdom, subprime mortgages do not have a formal legal or financial definition in Spain because the Spanish mortgage market is opaque and difficult to disaggregate. Specifically, the European Data Protection Act shields data on the credit quality of borrowers and origination of mortgage loans. Yet Spanish economist García Montalvo (2007) was among the first voices to state that a household holding a forty-year variable-interest-rate mortgage for 80–100 percent of the value of the home, paying interest only during the first two years of the contract and with monthly mortgage payments over 30 percent of a family's income, will end up in what could be considered the subprime market. These were regular conditions for many people asking for a mortgage in Spain during the boom.

As the U.S. subprime crisis hit with full force, the term "Spanish-style subprime" (*subprime a la española*) was used by a handful of economists to denote high-risk mortgages contracted at variable interest rates at a time of abnormally low interest rates, inflated housing prices, and close to full employment (Calleja 2008; Naredo 2009). Variable-interest-rate mortgages—making up 87 percent of mortgages issued in Spain during the boom, the highest in Europe according to the European Mortgage Federation—made indebted households more vulnerable to global financial risk through increased interest rates during periods of global financial turmoil. Mortgages issued in foreign currencies like the Japanese yen or Swiss francs are also in this high-risk category. Although they were not as prevalent as in countries like Poland (Halawa 2015), at least 30,000 foreign-currency mortgages were issued in Spain in attempts to take advantage of (what were at the time) favorable currency exchange rates—although with the onset of the crisis, foreign currency mortgage debt repayments rose up to 40 percent (Quelart 2013). Two of the cofounders of the PAH, Ada Colau and Adrià Alemany (2012), added to these Spanish subprime characteristics the extensive use of crossed guarantors (*avales cruzados*). Crossed guarantors, explained in depth later in this chapter, are a prime example of racialized practices by banks to ensure that mortgage requests would be approved for non-European immigrant households by having friends, or even mere acquaintances who perhaps shared only a country of origin, guarantee each other's loans, which helped "guarantee" the feasibility of the mortgage process.

Researchers have estimated that Spanish financial entities granted at least one million mortgages to vulnerable segments of society between 2003 and 2007, with a securitized volume reaching €49.9 billion, or 20.7 percent of the total volume of residential mortgage-backed securities (RMBS) issued from 2003 to 2008 (Ezcurra Pérez 2012; López and Rodríguez 2011; Otero-González et al. 2015). Such estimates are supported by stories in mainstream newspapers like *El País* about franchised financial intermediaries—in this case, CreditServices—that targeted "welcome mortgages" issued by American entities to immigrants with a minimum of a three-month work record in Spain, covering 120 percent of the value of the home (Ximénez de Sandoval 2010). According to the head of CreditServices, American banks were especially interested in this profile since they could surreptitiously charge higher interest rates. The extensive granting of mortgages to more vulnerable segments of society also became starkly visible as more and more people defaulted on their mortgages when the crisis hit and began pouring into the PAH.

Deeper political and conceptual reflection on subprime mortgages is sorely lacking in Spain. Before turning to unpack the terms and conditions of sub-primes a la española through the experiences of compañerxs, I want to lay out Paula Chakravartty and Denise Ferreira da Silva's (2012) insights about "the racial/postcolonial, moral and economic referent" of the subprime. They read it as a process that "resolves past and present modalities and moments of economic expropriation into *natural* attributes of the 'others of Europe'" (Chakravartty and Silva 2012, 365). What were the deeper practices and processes through which this occurred in the Spanish context? What were these naturalizations that sustained subprime logic?

Obtaining a Mortgage:
Uncovering Racialized and Classed Dynamics

The majority of the twenty-one mortgage-affected compañerxs I interviewed in depth purchased their home at the height of the boom. The median year of purchase was 2005, with seventeen people buying in 2005 (eight), 2006 (five), or 2007 (four), when the most mortgages were granted in Spain (see Figure 1.7) and the price of housing was at its peak. This coincides with data from the Spanish National Institute for Statistics, which reported in 2014 that 52 percent of foreclosure proceedings in the second semester of 2014 were for mortgages granted between 2005 and 2007. The median mortgage loan amount held by compañerxs was €221,500, and the median loan length was thirty years, although a handful of compañerxs had thirty-five-, forty-, or even forty-five-year mortgages. Virtually all compañerxs bought their home with their husband, wife, or partner, although the two people who were able to purchase on their own were men (Pepe, a Spaniard with no guarantors, and Carlos, an Ecuadorian the bank obliged to have multiple guarantors). This reflects larger trends I saw among compañerxs in the PAH. All mortgages granted to compañerxs had variable interest rates, like 87 percent of those granted during the housing boom across Spain.

Over two-thirds of the compañerxs I interviewed received 100 percent financing, with five receiving mortgage loans for 110 to 130 percent of the listed market price of the home. Monthly household income ranged from €1,400 to €3,000 per month for low- to middle-income compañerxs and from €4,500 to

€5,000 for what were previously upper-middle-income (four) compañerxs, demonstrating the wide range of incomes and classes that became affected by the financial and mortgage crisis. During the boom compañerxs worked in construction (six), in restaurants (two), as supermarket cashiers (two), as factory workers (two), as truck drivers (two), and as an elderly caregiver, a mechanic, a local government worker, a security guard, an entrepreneur, a business manager, and in a family-run business (one each).

Compañerxs who at the time were upper to middle income bought single-family detached houses in affluent suburbs or semirural areas. Low- or low-middle-income compañerxs, both Spanish and immigrant, bought apartments in peripheral parts of Sabadell and Barcelona, or in the case of Barcelona in working-class cities immediately adjacent, including l'Hospitalet de Llobregat to the southeast and Badalona to the northwest. Housing prices in these two often-stigmatized areas also increased dramatically, although not as much as in the more central parts of the city. As Sara, a Moroccan compañera, noted, "We decided to leave Barcelona to buy an apartment because we couldn't buy in Barcelona. An apartment in Barcelona used to be worth over €400,000. The cheapest option was Badalona or Santa Coloma." These housing prices, "untouchable" according to Sara, were confirmed by Sebas, a sixty-five-year-old Catalan entrepreneur: "An apartment in Barcelona used to cost €360,000 to €420,000. If it was a three-bedroom apartment, the price wasn't below €480,000 to €540,000." Indeed, according to the real estate intermediary Tecnocasa's 2007 annual report, based on twenty thousand listed apartments for sale, the average price in Barcelona peaked at €4,487 per square meter in the second half of 2006, among the highest in Spain. Even the lowest tenth percentile of housing cost €3,506 per square meter in Barcelona, far above Spain's (€2,101) and Catalonia's (€2,457) peak average housing prices per square meter in the first quarters of 2008 according to the Spanish Department of Public Works.

Some similarities emerged in mortgage-affected compañerxs' experiences of obtaining a mortgage. Over half expressed trust in "experts," specifically real estate agents, bankers, or notaries. These professionals performed a critical role in (mis)guiding people through the process of accessing and signing a mortgage loan. This is reflected by María, a compañera in her late thirties from Ecuador who worked as a caregiver: "When the real estate agent told us that he found a great mortgage with great conditions, as if it were for his father, we trusted him." Daniel, a Spanish former painter in his late thirties, said, "If you are in front of a notary, always trust him, that's what my parents taught me." Two of the bankers interviewed also underlined the importance of people's trust in the advice of savings bank employees in particular, arguably carried over from historical perceptions of these institutions, many existing since the late 1800s, as being charitable (Maixé-Altés 2010). Several mortgage-affected compañerxs also noted that they were not given much detail on the terms and conditions of mortgages and especially what would happen if they were unable to pay. The latter was an issue that—if mentioned at all—was brushed away by experts. After all, in theory everyone could sell their home in the future and recuperate the money invested.

Yet as compañerxs explained the various facets of the mortgage relationship, specific classed and racialized dimensions became clear. The two principal dimensions were the way that mortgage finance was accessed and the bank-imposed requirements for co-owners and guarantors. This highlights differential debt ecologies (Harker 2020), in the way that debt shapes the movement of racialized, gendered, and classed bodies through space and time, entangling financial, geopolitical, economic, and cultural processes. The four upper-middle-income Spanish compañerxs received mortgage financing from the same bank that granted their past mortgage. Due to their elevated incomes and previous properties, none were required to include guarantors or coborrowers in their mortgage loan contract. Joan, for example, told me that obtaining mortgage financing during the boom was "child's play. First, because I had my own business. Second, because things were going well. Third, because banks were looking for people to give mortgages to." In his early forties, he requested €200,000 to build his house, to be paid back in the next twenty years. The bank's response? "'Don't be silly! Make it thirty years.' I said: man, in thirty years I'll be seventy-two. . . . Fine, in the end, it was a thirty-year loan." Sebas similarly explained that "they made it very easy for me. . . . They would have given me €100,000 more, they would have given me credit to buy a car. They made it so easy for me that despite being fifty-eight years old they gave me a thirty-year mortgage, when I think that an eighty-eight-year-old person is no longer alive. . . . But of course, they knew that I had a paid property and that I could access money, didn't they?"

Low-income Spaniards and non-European immigrants, however, had quite a different experience both in accessing their mortgage and in the terms of their mortgage conditions, generating an entirely different debt ecology embedded in predatory and racist practices. The following two subsections provide further detail.

REELING IN IMMIGRANTS:
THE BUCCANEER-STYLE PRACTICES OF REAL ESTATE AGENTS AND BROKERS

The majority of immigrant compañerxs obtained their mortgage through an estate agent or a broker, never stepping foot in the bank until the day they signed their loan. Bea, a Spanish compañera in her early forties who worked in a factory, was one of only three (working-class) Spaniards who found her apartment through a real estate agent. She explained that direct transactions between homeowner and buyer were common before the housing boom, when the buyer would subsequently go to the bank to sort out their mortgage. But during the boom "more and more real estate agents came onto the scene and almost all apartments were sold through agencies. They resolved everything for you. They even looked for the bank and helped you if you had any problems getting a mortgage."

Many immigrant compañerxs spoke extensively of abusive or illegal practices by real estate agents and savings banks upon signing their mortgage loan. When Marta, her husband, and their two guarantors were waiting at the notary to seal the deal, the real estate agent told her, "You won't speak. We will. Everything has been discussed with the savings bank. . . . Don't say anything, otherwise they won't give you the mortgage." The notary arrived in a hurry and quickly read bits of the contract out loud. Everyone signed as required. Three months later Marta received the mortgage deed and was shocked to see that all four signatories were listed as co-borrowers: Marta, her husband, their nephew, and Marta's friend. "When we went to the real estate agent to complain they said, 'You two, you weren't enough. Besides, your husband doesn't even have a work permit.'" Furthermore, the €6,000 deposit she gave the real estate agent at the beginning of the process vanished. That is, Marta never received a receipt, nor was it discounted from the price of the property. Similar to Marta, a compañero from Pakistan named Ahmed found out only upon signing his mortgage that his guarantor would be a co-borrower. "But don't worry," he was told, "if you can't pay one year from now, the bank will keep the apartment and pay you back. No problem." Such experiences were regularly echoed by non-European immigrants at the PAH's collective advising assemblies.

David, a branch director for the bank Ibercaja who has worked in the sector for thirty-five years, underlined how common it was during the boom for real estate agents to build relationships with banks to obtain mortgages for their clients:

> There were all types of real estate agents (APIs, *agentes de la propiedad inmobiliaria*), qualified and less qualified ones. . . . I even remember one case where

a restaurant chain selling hot dogs was reconverted into an API. The only thing that changed was that there was a toilet on-premise, the owner poured on two liters of Varón Dandy [a cheap cologne] every day and put on a tie. That's it, that's all it was. Obviously prices were inflated, but at the time that was not a problem because everything was being financed with commissions of up to 10 percent, and with truly buccaneer-style practices. . . . I remember an API who told me, "Don't worry, if you can't give me mortgage financing, I'll go to Caja Laietana or Caixa Catalunya [savings banks bailed out by the state in 2012]. They swallow everything."

Reflecting on the term "buccaneer" in reference to the behavior of housing intermediaries like real estate agents and brokers provides an intriguing insight into what was happening during the Spanish housing boom. Anna Neill (2000, 165), in "Buccaneer Ethnography," characterizes buccaneers as "outlaws of the seas" in the seventeenth and eighteenth centuries, central to the English colonization of the New World. Neill's narration of the uneven shift of the buccaneer from being seen as a sea raider (savage) to a man of science (civilized) reflected in part the state's increasing need for their activities. There is an uncanny parallel here to the Spanish story, where real estate agents were indeed "needed" by the state and financial sector to increase housing sales and mortgage lending, respectively, especially among harder-to-reach groups like non-European immigrants and low-income Spaniards. They not only were advertisers and brokers of property but also facilitated and increased the provision of mortgages—and the millions of euros of debt accumulated and then repackaged throughout the process.

While having an office and official status as a business gave them legitimacy (e.g., they were "civilized"), real estate agents' and brokers' practices were often predatory and savage. Manel, a mortgage technician at Santander's central office in Catalonia from 1992 to 2007, saw real estate agents falsifying paychecks. Once he sat at the notary's office with a couple signing a mortgage where the real estate agents "took the money [down payment] and never appeared." Vicky, an employee of La Caixa, underlined that real estate agents could easily make €30,000 in one transaction. "At that time, you saw unbelievable things. Real estate agents made incredible amounts of undeclared money," she told me.

Real estate agents' and brokers' abusive and often illegal buccaneer practices were spurred by the sizeable profits to be made, as by 2005 a normal mortgage loan in the Barcelona metropolitan area was easily between €200,000 and €300,000. The fact that they were preying on low-income and especially non-

European immigrant populations enabled them to get away with many bar-barities. I heard dozens of stories from compañerxs, both in interviews and in PAH collective advising assemblies, of outright scams. A broker swindled José, a Colombian compañero who used to work as a mechanic, upon arranging his mortgage with the savings bank Bancaja. Upon supposedly merging José's small debts in other financial entities with the mortgage loan, the broker in-stead took out a €3,000 loan made in José's name. José said, "It ends up they were colluding, I understood later. Brokers, real estate agents, they were col-luding with financial entities: 'Bring me someone and I'll give you your com-mission.'" José's powerful statement also illustrates the affective and intimate entanglements that Deville (2015) and Dawney, Kirwan, and Walker (2020) highlight as a key part of the process of becoming indebted: "They work you really hard at a psychological level, they turn your head around. You don't even realize it and you have already signed: this will be for you, this will be for you. Like when you hold out a biscuit for a dog: if you sit, I'll give you the bis-cuit. The biscuit was our keys and the thrill that you will get your apartment. The broker has told you all sorts of things and the bank director is giving you hugs and kisses."

CROSSED GUARANTORS AND CO-BORROWERS: RACIALIZED AND CLASSED CHAINS OF RENT APPROPRIATION

Conditioning mortgage lending through requirements for co-borrowers or (crossed) guarantors emerged as the other clear racialized and classed differ-ence from compañerxs in interviews and in PAH collective advising assem-blies. Spanish Mortgage Law stipulates that banks can provide only 80 percent of mortgage financing, with the remaining 20 percent secured either from a down payment or from the incomes or properties of mortgage loan signatories or guarantors. Inflating appraisal values was one strategy used to reduce the 20 percent down payment. Another was including more co-owners or guarantors in the mortgage contract, which helped ensure that the Bank of Spain would approve a mortgage application.

Three of five low- to middle-income Spanish compañerxs explicitly sought mortgage conditions that did not require any guarantors or co-borrowers and were able to successfully negotiate this condition with real estate agents or the bank. The other two were obliged to include guarantors. Fran's experience is exemplary of many young or middle-aged Spaniards who come to the PAH to fight for debt forgiveness, having signed over their parents' sole home, paid for decades ago, to cover the 20 percent loan guarantee. Fran worked as a se-curity guard in his early to mid-thirties and was the sole earner in his household, making €2,200 a month. His parents' home, purchased fifty-seven years earlier and paid for long since, served as the guarantee to obtain 100 percent financing for his €328,000 mortgage. This of course was not a problem when he could pay, but when the crisis hit and he lost his job and defaulted on his loan, the problems started. After refinancing and having paid only interest on the mortgage capital, upon default and foreclosure his home was seized by the bank. In order to cover part of his €328,000 outstanding debt, the bank tried to seize his parents' home as well.

In contrast, the bank required nine out of the ten non-European immigrant compañerxs I interviewed to include (crossed) guarantors or co-borrowers, as explained in María's story at the start of this book. José was told that if his eighteen-year-old daughter did not sign as a guarantor, their €245,000 loan in Sabadell (130 percent of the appraised price of the apartment) would not be approved. "We said, well, no problem, since the bank told us that we can sell the apartment in a few years and recover our debt, we'll take our daughter out [of the mortgage deed] and that's it, it will just be me and my wife. We'll buy a smaller apartment, and be kings of the castle." Isa's in-laws were guarantors for her €198,000 mortgage loan (108 percent of the appraised apartment's price) via power of attorney, as they were not physically present to sign the loan or its refinancing a few years later. The extensive use of (crossed) guarantors was a regular practice to make it look like the numbers were tallied properly. As Fernando, a retired bank office director at La Caixa with twenty-seven years' experience, explained to me, "The deed and purchase sale price of a home was €100,000 while the mortgage granted was €130,000, and the Bank of Spain didn't meddle. How was this done? Making it look like there were four guarantors. . . . It looked as if they bought the apartment with a friend, but they had no relationship or anything. Just to balance the numbers. That one earned €800, his/her friend €1,000, so that makes €1,800. The thing is, they believe you because you're buying."

This points to perhaps the most nefarious subprime practice: crossed guarantors (*avales cruzados*) or crossed mortgages (*hipotecas cruzadas*), where friends or even just acquaintances—as Fernando says, "they had no relationship or anything"—introduced to each other by real estate agencies or savings banks signed each other's mortgages. Real estate agents and financial entities did this to ensure that the mortgage loans of "high-risk" borrowers—almost exclusively non-European immigrants—would be approved. Speed was often of the essence when closing a crossed mortgage operation, to beat the two-month lag time between signing a mortgage loan and its official registration in the Bank of Spain's risk information center, known as Cirbe. In other words, if the operations took place within the same week or two, the debt was not registered on either signatory's state-monitored credit record, meaning that the Bank of Spain would almost definitely approve both applications.

Carlos, an Ecuadorian compañero, was obligated to have two guarantors and another co-borrower to purchase his apartment in the periphery of Barcelona in 2000 with a 100 percent loan, amounting to €136,500, despite having a permanent employment contract as an office worker in an infrastructure company and earning over €2,000 per month. The two guarantors were friends and the co-borrower was only an acquaintance, whose mortgage he also signed as a guarantor; all were from his home country of Ecuador. As Carlos said,

> In this day and age, so many cases arrive each day at the PAH, cases that are difficult to solve because they are crossed mortgages. They told me, to sell me the mortgage, well you were a guarantor for him so he'll act as yours. Or they put you as co-borrowers, so it was a web. . . . In my case I am the guarantor of the person that is the co-borrower in my mortgage. Yes, she is in the same situation I am, we are all in the same situation. . . . They told me that I had to be her guarantor but we signed in different entities. I signed in Caja Madrid and she has a loan from Caixa Catalunya. It's like a chain. All banks did the same thing, they all operated in the same way. They accepted that you were someone's guarantor, and that this person could also be your guarantee.

Crossed guarantors are the ultimate example of the unequal differentiation of human value (Melamed 2015): the lower and more unstable salaries that characterized many non-European immigrant family units in Spain at the time meant that their lives and labor were "not enough" to obtain a mortgage loan, even in some cases when they demonstrated stable and higher incomes. Unlike upper-middle-income Spaniards, they did not have current or past properties to act as collateral or, unlike low-income Spaniards, family who could guarantee their mortgage through property paid off long ago. Because of the unequal differentiation of human value, multiple lives of non-European immigrants were needed to "count" the same as upper-middle-income Spaniards. This finds echo in Kish and Leroy's (2015) writing about bonded life, showing the racialized dimensions of financialization, underscoring how all populations can be, and are made, investable. Crossed guarantors, in this light, chained non-European immigrants' mortgages and lives together into a web, as Carlos noted. During boom times, when everyone could pay, crossed guarantors were just a detail on paper, another bureaucratic step required to final-ize a mortgage loan. But when the crisis hit and a mortgaged homeowner was unable to pay, the financial entity pursued all the outstanding debt from the ensemble of guarantors, and there was a tsunami effect of default, foreclosure, and eviction.

On top of the classed and explicitly racialized practices of real estate agents, brokers, and financial entities, the latter maximized their possibilities of profit making from mortgage signatories—particularly low-income and immigrant populations—through a variety of techniques that I turn to look at now.

"Feast Today, Famine Tomorrow": Financial Entities' Drive for Profit

Despite working in entities that can be characterized as relatively prudent and conservative lenders, the four (ex-)bankers I interviewed all stated that they received immense pressure to sell mortgages during the boom. For example, Manel, who oversaw more than eight thousand notarized mortgage loan sig-natures during his thirty-five-year career at Santander, stated that especially from 2005 to 2007 it was the "total and absolute priority to sell mortgages." Office directors received calls "on a daily basis to see what you sold, what you invested, what you achieved." During this period, every day the central office received—"well we *had* to receive, because if we didn't, we had to report it"— one hundred to one hundred twenty mortgage loan applications to study from the bank branches across Catalonia. If they weren't approved upon review by the risk department, they went through a second process "where someone ended up authorizing them, surely some were denied but . . . there was an at-tempt for all mortgages to go ahead, with personal guarantees, real guarantees. Directors received a lot of pressure to sell that product."

David, the Ibercaja office director, characterized the housing credit boom and the role that financial entities played in perpetuating it as follows:

> The comparison I make is to one of drunkenness. Entities got drunk, and I say this because, damn, that little savings bank over there, smaller than me, is granting mortgages nonstop. My bank area manager even said to me at one point: "How many mortgages are you short on? You're not meeting objec-tives. . . ." I told him, "Well, I have these dossiers from this real estate agent and that real estate agent, but they really don't. . . ." The response from the area manager? "Take them. If they default, you won't be asked about it. . . ." That is, it was a strict policy of feast today, famine tomorrow [*pan para hoy, ham-*

bre para mañana]. Achieve the objectives today, any which way, thinking that the mortgage foreclosure documents won't reach you, that this will always be on the up.

Fernando and Vicky, former and current bankers at La Caixa, each spoke of an office in their zone in the Barcelona metropolitan region—l'Hospitalet de Llobregat and Badalona, respectively—that was touted as an example to follow during the boom. Fernando explained how the office of the year in l'Hospitalet "was the one that granted the most mortgages, all with the Mortgage Loan Index Reference (IRPH) + 0.5 percent and insurance not worth the paper it was written on. All the immigrants went there. How did that office turn out? Well from 2008 until 2014 it was being cleaned up, exorbitant commissions to real estate agents have emerged and everything you can imagine."[1] Vicky noted that the director of Badalona's top-ranked office was the king of the castle. He collaborated with two real estate agencies and saw his business volume increase dramatically. He was also Badalona's area risk manager, meaning that he had a greater capacity to grant higher-risk mortgages. Vicky stated that his office "grew enormously, enormously and it was always given as an example: look at that office, look at that director." When crisis hit, the once-praised office soon had a default index far beyond the average for all forty offices in Badalona.

Several bankers detailed the importance of the nature of mortgages as a product. Vicky explained that a mortgage is "a powerful product to make an office grow" because upon selling one, a bank's assets increase by hundreds of thousands of euros in just a day, on top of a 1 to 1.5 percent arrangement fee: "Of course 1 percent of €300,000 is €3,000. Having a €3,000 commission breeze in on one day, to make €3,000 now or before without granting a mortgage, how many credit cards do you need to sell in a year, you know? Besides, you bind a customer forever. In principle, they marry you."

In this way, mortgages are a flagship product for financial entities. Manel went further to say that this was the case because they enabled cross-selling: "Cross-selling means that you asked for the salaries of mortgage holders to be directly deposited at the bank, that bills are direct debited, that they contract home insurance, which is obligatory [by law], but you tried to add fire insurance too, and credit cards. This was cross-selling. As you did the numbers you conditioned the granting of a mortgage by a series of requirements, and the person who intended to buy an apartment said: what difference does it make to have a credit card in one place or the other. Cross-selling allowed you to sell products, and that was a good way to foster customer loyalty and to bind the customer."

Securitization—packaging and selling mortgage loans on secondary markets—was another important tool to generate more capital inflows and extend lending. Manel underlined how his remit was to approve and securitize as many mortgage applications as possible at Santander, focusing on primary home mortgages that had not been refinanced. Especially in 2006 and 2007, he noted that all mortgages were required to have insurance from AIG, a company that provided nonpayment coverage in favor of the bank and received a U.S. government bailout in 2008 for $182 billion because of its extensive subprime loan insurance (Massad 2012). All (ex-)bankers I interviewed stated that securitization was managed through each financial entity's central office. The minimum requirements for any given mortgage to be securitized at their entities included up-to-date home insurance, regular paid monthly mortgage installments, and complete economic documentation that was properly notarized. Ibercaja was described as being very scrupulous in terms of oversight and control of this process (David). La Caixa prioritized the securitization of shops, industrial warehouses, and medical centers, with housing being last on the list (Fernando). At the same time, the secondary literature points to the critical role that savings banks played in securitization during the boom, issuing 85 percent of covered bonds and holding over half the live balance of all securitized bonds in the Spanish market, the remainder (40 percent) largely held by banks (Fuentes Egusquiza 2007). The fact that over half of all Spanish savings banks went bankrupt at the start of the crisis reflects their deep exposure to high-risk mortgage lending and extensive use of securitization.

Mortgaged compañerxs experienced these processes in different, and in some cases racialized, ways. First, all compañerxs were unaware if/when their mortgage was securitized. This was not an issue that affected or even concerned them until default, foreclosure, or eviction. In many cases mortgage securitization affected how they struggled for debt forgiveness, as I explain in detail in the next chapter. Second, all the immigrant compañerxs I interviewed who were granted mortgages by savings banks through real estate agents or brokers explicitly noted that they were obliged to accept a series of products and financial relations to obtain their mortgage. In other words, cross-selling conditioned their mortgage loan. For example, Sara was required to sign life insurance and job insurance upon contracting her mortgage, the latter in case her husband lost his job. Yet the coverage was not valid when he lost his job, and despite arguments to get the €5,000 back, the savings bank refused. When Patricia and her husband started to have trouble paying their mortgage, they tried to cancel the life insurance they had contracted. Caixa Catalunya told them if they did, their monthly mortgage installment would increase. Upon looking at her mortgage deed, signed by her husband while she was in Colombia before the family reunification process, Patricia explained that "all of it was in the mortgage deed, we couldn't say no, because the deed stated that you were obliged to pay life insurance, if not the mortgage installment increased 0.5 percent, to pay house insurance otherwise the installment increased, to use credit cards. . . . When I read the deed, I said, my goodness, what have you signed? It was all there, and now there was no escape."

Isa and Marta, two Ecuadorian friends I interviewed together, took out mortgage loans in two different savings banks through two different real estate agencies. They acknowledged that upon signing their mortgages they did not fully understand what they were getting into:

> ISA: You do not realize that you are getting a mortgage for all your life.
> MARTA: House and life insurance.
> ISA: And the obligation to contract insurance with the same bank.
> MARTA: And the debit cards.
> ISA: The debit cards, one for each. You had to have all of your regular
> expenses set up as direct deposits and debits.
> MARTA: Your salary and bills.
> ISA: I mean, those were the requirements.

Seven compañerxs pointed out a final way that banks appropriated rent: abusive mortgage clauses. These were either excessive default rate fees or "floor clauses" (*cláusulas suelo*), where the latter refers to a clause in the mortgage deed that prevented monthly mortgage installments from dropping below a stipulated minimum interest rate. In a survey administered by the Bank of Spain in 2009 to forty-nine credit entities whose aggregate portfolio was representative of the sector, it was found that 30 percent of mortgages granted up to 2004 had floor clauses, while 42 percent did in 2008, with the average minimum rate set at 3.12 percent (Banco de España 2010). In a critique of this report, ADICAE (2010), the Association of Bank, Savings Bank, Financial Product and Insurance Consumers and Users (Asociación de Consumidores y Usuarios de Bancos, Cajas, Productos Financieros y de Seguros), estimated that financial entities granted close to two million mortgages with floor clauses between 2005 and 2008. This enabled entities to earn somewhere between €3.3 billion and €6.7 billion in 2009 as the Euro Interbank Offered Rate (Euribor)—the interest rate at which European credit institutions lend money to each other, used to benchmark mortgages—dropped below 1 percent.

In 2010 the first court ruling of its kind in Spain declared floor clauses null and void due to their abusive nature, and in February 2013 the EU Court of

Justice ruled that abusive mortgage clauses could be contested through law-suits. While changes to Spanish Mortgage Law in 2017 removed floor clauses and prevented other elements like cross-selling, at the peak of the crisis most mortgaged households were negatively affected.

Maintaining Homeostasis:
(Differentially) Regulating and Disciplining the Population

The experiences of housing and life becoming financialized during the Span-ish housing boom, considered through the experience of a cross-spectrum of mortgage-affected compañerxs as well as a handful of (ex-)bankers, uncover several fundamental biopolitical dimensions of mortgages and how they op-erated to differentially regulate and discipline the population. I highlight the key dimensions here, before concluding the chapter.

While the previous chapter illustrated how homeownership was normal-ized historically—where normalization is understood as the procedures, pro-cesses, and techniques that establish behaviors dividing the normal from the abnormal, making the "normal" acceptable (Foucault 2007)—this chap-ter shows how *mortgaged* homeownership was normalized. Homeownership through mortgage debt came to be implicitly inscribed as a self-evident and normal way to access housing, backed by legal and regulatory mechanisms and the material reality of nonchoice, through discourses and options compañerxs faced when accessing housing. Media, government, and financial sector nar-ratives pointed to owning a home as a natural preference, a genetic compo-nent embedded in the Spanish DNA and Spain's social environment. Buy-ing a home was expressed by Spanish compañerxs as being instilled in them through deep-seated norms—"I always have heard that housing, you have to buy it" stated Pepe—and by immigrant compañerxs as something communi-cated by real estate agents, brokers, bankers, friends, and even acquaintances.

Critically, the normalization of mortgaged homeownership occurred alongside unprecedented easy access to credit, as Spain's adoption of the euro in 1999 made investing in the country appear to be safe and secure from all fronts. Financial entities' aggressive advertising campaigns to capture clients made mortgages appear simple, easy, and completely ordinary. José expressed this when he said that everyone was getting a mortgage, that "it was like go-ing to buy bread," as did Joan, who noted that "banks were looking for peo-ple to give mortgages to." This normalization was deepened by trust in the advice and guidance of "experts" in financial entities, the real estate sector, and government who encouraged mortgaged homeownership, advancing the dominant belief that housing prices would never fall, renting was throwing money away, and homeownership increased wealth and security. Seeing such dynamics as "normal" meant that mortgaged homeownership became the logical choice, obscuring the reality both of the creation of nonchoice other than homeownership to obtain housing stability and of indebtedness amid falling real salaries and job precarity for many. Perhaps these even became the "normal" conditions of life. Normalization was thus fundamental to create a situation wherein despite one-third of work contracts being temporary and 60 percent of the workforce living on an average annual salary of €10,935 per year in 2007—with non-European immigrants and women proportionately holding more temporary contracts and gaining lower salaries—households sought mortgages and financial entities granted them extensively.

This chapter also made clear the regulatory and disciplinary power of mortgages, serving to maintain and expand homeostasis, a specific political-economic system and "state of life" (Foucault 2003, 246), as they acted to bolster capital accumulation and economic growth. This power operated most visibly through the immediate and long-term rents appropriated through extensive taxes for the state at multiple levels and generous commissions and benefits for brokers, real estate agents, and financial entities. The latter in particular ensured their benefit through time, resonating with what Lisa Adkins (2018) calls a logic of speculation that operates as a rationality, a mode of accumulation, and a mode of social organization. Financial entities did this by using floor clauses in mortgages so that when interest rates dropped below a given level, monthly mortgage payments did not; the clauses thus ensured a minimum payment each month. Securitization commodified risk as life was capitalized through "translating contingency into risk and risk into a tradable asset" (Dillon and Lobo-Guerrero 2008, 268). That is, securitization ensured extended processes of capital circulation into global flows, betting on the future value generation of mortgaged homeowners over the coming decades, while it regulated a shifting population of (securitized) mortgaged homeowners. These techniques sought to secure the present and future rent stream from all mortgage borrowers and, when necessary, guarantors. They created added levels of security for financial entities vis-à-vis future profits and growth, and deeply tied the lives of mortgage holders—plus in many cases their guarantors—into this process.

Furthermore, this chapter made clear how the mortgage process operated with and through racialized, gendered, and classed realities to differentially maintain, monitor, and regulate a human population's—mortgaged homeowners'—productive and reproductive flows. In other words, racialized and classed mortgage conditions acted as a security apparatus to cover the contingencies of life, ensuring that all households met their debt payments and financial entities continued to collect rents far into the future. Thus, the mode of social organization that Adkins's (2018) refers to through the logic of speculation moves along with and reinforces existing socioeconomic inequalities at multiple levels. For example, both working-class Spanish and non-European immigrant compañerxs obtained worse mortgage conditions from financial entities and also tended to have less direct relationships with them than did upper-middle-income Spanish compañerxs. Immigrant compañerxs almost always found their homes through real estate agencies or brokers, whose buccaneer and predatory tactics were of value to financial entities and ultimately the state to expand mortgage lending. Financial entities ensured mortgage loan repayment from immigrants and low-income Spaniards through (crossed) guarantors and co-borrowers, be they family, friends, or sometimes mere acquaintances. Cross-selling often conditioned the mortgage loans of non-European immigrant compañerxs, providing further income streams for financial entities through insurance products, direct salary deposits, and automatic bill payments. The clear racialization that took place in many cases illustrates the unequal differentiation of human value (Melamed 2015), where non-European immigrant bodies don't count as much as European Spanish bodies, and women's paid and unpaid labor (both remunerated and invisible, unrecognized social reproduction tasks) matters less than men's paid work. More extensive guarantees were thus required especially for non-European immigrants to ensure the smooth operation of the system.

These dimensions begin to make clear the racial/postcolonial, moral, and economic referent of the subprime that, as Paula Chakravartty and Denise da Silva (2012, 365) note, "resolves past and present modalities and moments of economic expropriation into *natural* attributes of the 'others of Europe.'" The differential mortgage terms and conditions are apparently required for non-European immigrants because of their origination from outside Europe. Since they are "unrooted" and exist in an "impersonal social context"—with no direct property or other similarly reliable guarantees possible—their financial "inclusion" into Europeanness and modernity through mortgaged homeownership necessitated multiple guarantees from their compatriots. These compatriots were often required by financial entities to guarantee each other's mortgage loans, despite in some cases not even *knowing* each other, as the ultimate goal was to have a stable home and be included in the booming economic system, which was sold as extremely secure. Again, after all, Spain had obtained modernity and was completely part of the European project. While the moral and economic implications of subprime loans at the time were financial in-clusion, when crisis hit, mortgage holders became non-performing loans and thus non-performing people.

It is important to underline that through these racialized and classed dy-namics, *all* mortgaged compañerxs were ultimately proletarianized. That is, the *differentially* indebted person was the reality that emerged. Lives unwit-tingly became dependent not only on the continuation of unreliable job con-tracts but also on the performance of global financial markets and the rise and fall of interest rates. Labor exploitation continued through the primary circuit in processes of expanded reproduction, especially through lower-paying and precarious jobs, which were the most common condition for non-European immigrant and low-income Spanish populations, especially women who bore a double burden as they were also largely responsible for reproductive and caring tasks in the domestic sphere. But *all* mortgage holders' lives became as-similated into the financialization of housing and the expansion of secondary circuit through capital circulation. This occurred through the promise of fu-ture value creation by the mortgage holder (or co-borrower or guarantor) over the coming thirty-, forty-, or even fifty-year duration of a mortgage loan. Fi-nancialized housing meant that compañerxs—and their co-borrowers and/or guarantors—were objectified to ensure the circulation of capital, in essence fi-nancializing life itself. As long as people could pay their mortgage and housing prices were buoyant, this was not necessarily a problem, but the realities of fi-nancialized housing-life became evident when the speculative cycle came to a halt, as detailed in the next chapter.

Conclusions

Looking at the biopolitics of Spain's 1997–2007 financialized housing boom, I uncovered some of the mechanisms, processes, and relations characterizing mortgaged homeownership in the Barcelona metropolitan region. Building from the historical dynamics explained in chapter 1, I showed how mortgaged homeownership was normalized at multiple levels during the boom, despite falling real wages and precarious job contracts for the majority and especially for non-European immigrants. Through the experiences of mortgage-affected compañerxs and several (ex-)bankers we saw how compañerxs' racialized and classed relationships unfolded with real estate agents, brokers, and banks.

Several key theoretical points and reflections emerge from this analysis. First, the role of security is critical. Here I refer to security in terms of main-taining the system and status quo, but also the security and stability of families in terms of being able to ensure their own reproduction. Many compañerxs became mortgaged homeowners to provide stability and security for their children or for themselves in old age, or in the case of immigrants for family reunification, the latter requiring a stable residence that could not be provided by rental property. While on the one hand this shows that reality is "messier" than what are often oversimplified dichotomies between active and calculative investors or passive savers (e.g., Hall 2016; Pellandini-Simányi, Hammer, and Vargha 2015), on the other hand it brings to light a perverse reality: the principal option for stability and security was mortgaged homeownership. In other words, the experiences during the Spanish housing boom suggest that if a person wanted a stable and long-term housing solution—considering that renting was precarious and expensive, and little to no social housing exists—the most logical, commonsense option was buying a home. This reinforces a conclusion from the previous chapter: there was a political construction of nonalternatives, or the building of economic and sociocultural nonchoice, to homeownership and economic growth in the evolution of housing in Spain in the twentieth century, from the historical and ideological pressures during Francoism through to legislative changes encouraging homeownership under democracy, neoliberalism, and European modernity. Furthermore, Foucault (2007, 69) notes that while "the law prohibits and discipline prescribes," security essentially functions by responding to a reality in a way that cancels out, nullifies, or limits the reality to which it responds. This suggests that the drive to develop the construction sector and create a nation of modern homeowners became operational not only in terms of material options but also, as expressed by compañerxs, at the subjective level.

The findings in this chapter also showed the racialized, gendered, and classed terms upon which financing was accessed, particularly through abusive real estate agents and brokers, and banks both cross-selling mortgages and obliging the presence of (crossed) guarantors or co-borrowers in mortgage loans. While in the end all compañerxs were proletarianized—that is, objectified through being inserted into the circulation of capital to maintain and expand urban capital accumulation—it is clear that in terms of maintaining the security of the system some were deemed to have more "value" than others (Melamed 2015; Pulido 2017). Upper-middle-income Spanish compañerxs were not required to have guarantors, since their incomes and properties were deemed as sufficient in case they defaulted. Low- to middle-income Spanish and non-European immigrant compañerxs, however, had to provide an extra level of security—family most often in the case of Spaniards, friends or even just acquaintances for immigrants—in the form of guarantors or co-borrowers. Thus not only the compañerxs I interviewed but also their co-borrowers and/or guarantors became objects in a larger process of rent appropriation, as their current and future labor became packaged into financial products and vehicles of financial speculation in the form of debt repayments to secure the positive performance of the global financial system. This process, in the broader Spanish historical context, can be conceptualized as a shift from the dictatorship's drive to create a country of upright Spanish homeowners, not of proletariats—paraphrased from the first minister of housing José Luis Arrese in chapter 1 (*un país de propietarios, no de proletarios*)—to the (unwitting?) creation of a differential nation of proletarianized homeowners under European democratic modernity.

Finally, the chapter laid bare the financial or investor subject (Langley 2006) and the *differentially* indebted person (Lazzarato 2012) as two sides of the same coin. Beyond meeting needs for security and stability, mortgaged homeownership was sold by the state, banks, and real estate sector as a way for people to secure their own (financial) future. In other words, investment operated as a "technology of the self," where being a responsible and moral individual meant being a rational economic actor (Lemke 2001) in an otherwise irrational economic and financial world. Buying housing was widely seen as an investment that would grow to realize returns (Langley 2007), rooted in the widespread belief that the price of housing would never fall. But the reality underlying mortgaged homeownership was deepening indebtedness amid precarious employment, even more so for non-European immigrants and women. As long as people continued to earn a sufficient salary to pay monthly mortgage installments and interest rates did not rise, this was not directly experienced as a problem. Yet when crisis hit and households became unable to pay, compañerxs clearly saw their reality as an indebted person, as the deeply affective and intimate dimensions of indebtedness (Dawney, Kirwan, and Walker 2020; Deville 2015; Han 2012) that spurred capital accumulation and growth emerged in everyday life. We will see the way this process operated in depth in chapter 3.

As the financialization of housing seeks to (temporarily) overcome the fundamental contradiction between the spatial fixity of real estate and the need for capital to be in motion to create value, here I have shown how the financialization of life is a fundamental part of this process. The way in which contemporary processes of financialization intermesh and intertwine with the politics of life itself (Rose 2007) and produce distinctive capital/life/subject relations, what French and Kneale (2009, 2012) call biofinancialization, becomes clear. The important addition we see here is the racialized, gendered, and classed ways in which this occurs, generating differential debt ecologies (Harker 2020): debt shapes the movement of different bodies differentially through space, entangling financial, geopolitical, economic, and cultural processes. The capital-labor process (expanded reproduction) differentially proletarianizes lives and subjects' bodies, but so too does the circulation of capital in the (mortgage) debt relation. The financialization of life depicts a situation where a differential speculation with life itself lies at the heart of economic and political strategies and decision making (Rose 2007), with further disciplinary mechanisms that also operate at the level of the body that fully rear their head once people are unable to pay their mortgage. The next chapter turns to look at the lived political economy of the housing crisis, focusing on how defaulting mortgage-affected compañerxs were intimately enmeshed in its consequences.

CHAPTER 3

Maintaining Mortgaged Lives

Approaching mortgages as a "technology of power over life" (Foucault 2003, 236), a tool to regulate and discipline the population, the previous chapter exposed the differential processes used to mortgage life at the peak of the housing boom in the Barcelona metropolitan region. I illustrated how a racialized, gendered, and classed secondary form of exploitation occurred through the mortgage debt relation in the sphere of circulation. The current chapter turns to unpack both the continuities and consequences of this financialization of life during the post-2008 crisis. I weave together the deep-seated restructuring of the Spanish financial system with the shifting relationships compañerxs we met in the previous chapter had with financial entities as they struggled to pay their mortgage debt amid widespread unemployment, increasing monthly mortgage payments, and plummeting housing prices. I illustrate how—and with what consequences—mortgaged lives became even more deeply enmeshed in a financial maelstrom once the conditions facilitating the supposedly ever-rising housing prices and creation of fictitious capital stopped. We see how, why, and under what conditions non-performing loans are equated to non-performing people.

In 2012, Spain's financial system was rescued and restructured with €61.5 billion in European and Spanish taxpayer funds, although Spain's Court of Auditors estimates that assigned public funds sit closer to €108 billion, a figure in line with estimates from Brussels.[1] As the loses were socialized onto the public's shoulders, the gains were privatized to benefit a reduced elite of Spanish banks, foreign investment funds, and their local intermediaries. In this chapter I show how mortgage-affected people lived through the public bailout of the financial sector as they were forced to choose between life and getting—oftentimes unbeknownst to compañerxs—more deeply indebted through mortgage refinancing, grace periods, or credit offers from the bank in order to keep paying monthly installments. In this chapter we clearly see how complex debt ecologies (Harker 2020) can become as mortgages are caught up in financial sector restructuring processes, having been securitized and/or sold to foreign investment funds, leaving mortgage-affected people in the dark about whom to negotiate with or how to seek a solution. Finally, this chapter underlines the lived experience of the treatment of life, and the body, as an accumulation strategy (Harvey 1998). We ultimately see how life, relationships, livelihoods, and the body are deeply subjected to debt servicing practices.

I now turn to look at why compañerxs stopped paying their mortgage as the government first denied the burst of the housing bubble then floundered with the onset of the financial crisis, after turning to consider financial entities' responses to households on the brink of default.

Crisis Hits:
Household Mortgage Defaults and Financial Sector Bailouts

Difficulties in paying monthly mortgage installments began with the onset of economic crisis in 2008 for over two-thirds of the mortgage-affected compañerxs I interviewed in-depth. Sixteen compañerxs became unemployed, as in their household either the sole income earner, one of two income earners, or both income earners lost their job. Those who worked in construction and related sectors such as infrastructure development, electrical installation and repair, and house painting were among the first to be laid off in 2009 or 2010. But compañerxs working in restaurants, trucking, or factories or as a mechanic also lost their jobs soon after, as did the upper-middle-income compañerxs I interviewed who were entrepreneurs, an information technology worker, and a business manager. During this time, total unemployment steadily climbed from its historic minimum of just over 8 percent in 2006–7 to more than 26 percent in 2013 nationally, with similar figures of 6–7 percent to 23 percent, respectively, in Catalonia during the same period. These differences were even more pronounced for non-European immigrants, or non–European Union foreigners, as the category is officially called by the Spanish National Institute of Statistics (Figure 3.1). Unemployment statistics for non-European immigrants went from a minimum of 9.3 percent in the third trimester of 2006 in Catalonia to a peak of 45.3 percent in the first trimester of 2012. This peak was 5 percent higher than the Spanish one, reflecting the greater presence of non-European foreigners in Catalonia. If we consider these statistics in relation to gender, Figure 3.2 illustrates that non-European immigrant men suffered the highest unemployment rates at the peak of the crisis, followed by non-European immigrant women. The former peaked in 2012 at 51.4 percent and the latter in 2013 at 42.2 percent.

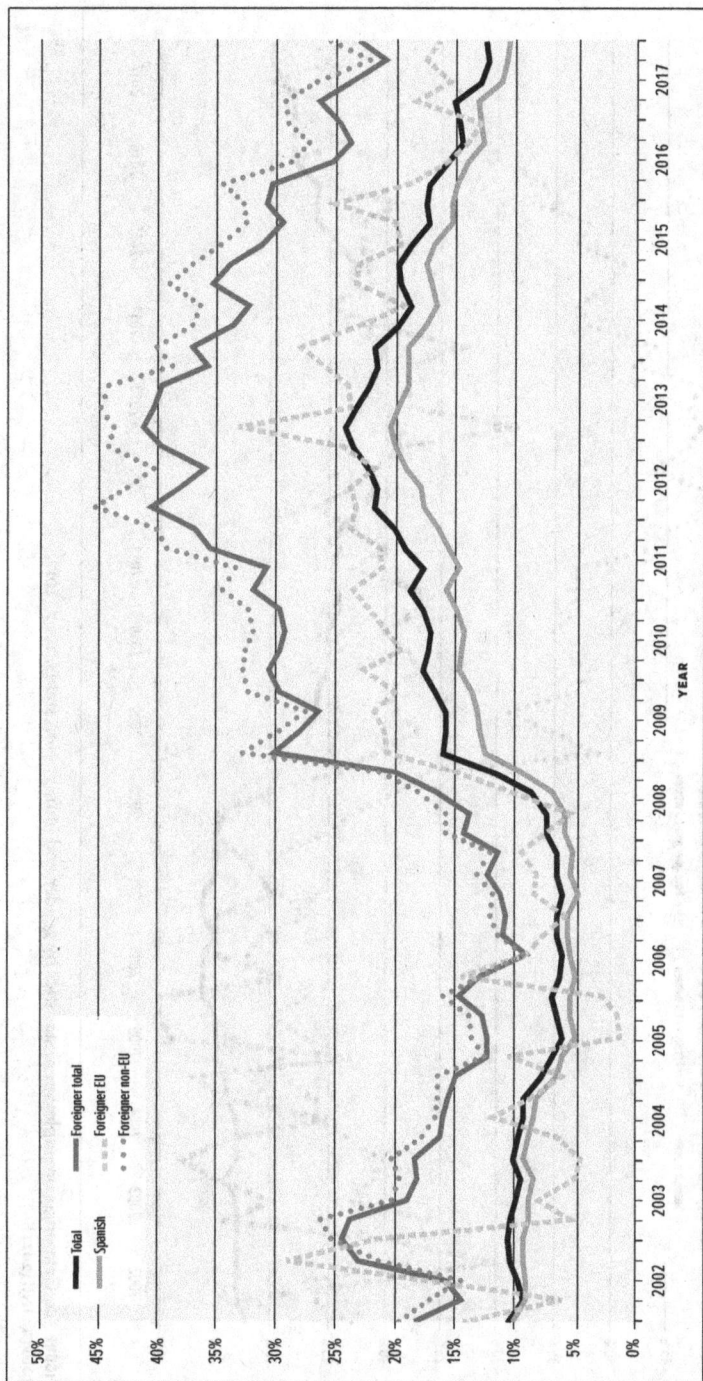

FIGURE 3.1. Catalonia's unemployment statistics by immigration status, 2002–2017.

SOURCE: INE (2021).

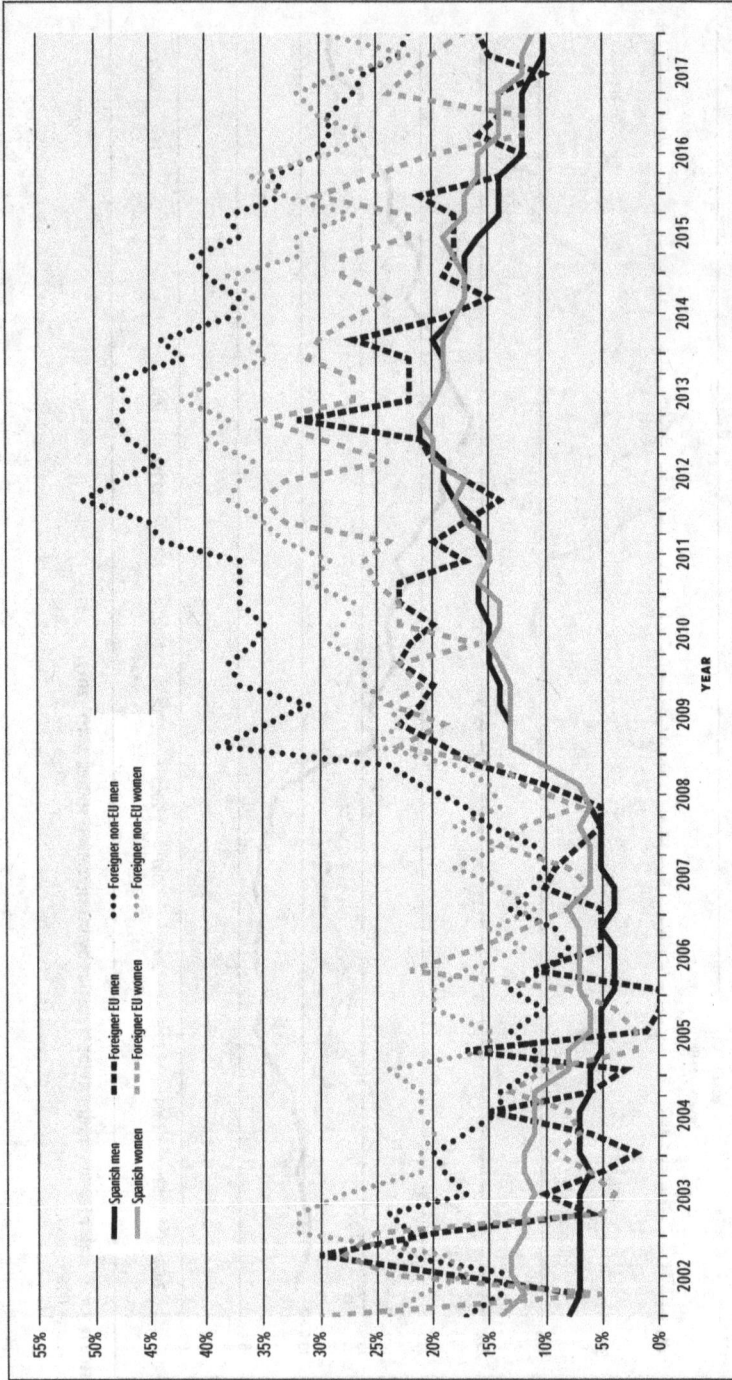

FIGURE 3.2. Catalonia's unemployment statistics by gender and immigration status, 2002–2017.
SOURCE: INE (2021).

Either splitting up with a partner, illness—a child born with a disease requiring constant care, a long-term colon disorder flaring up and demanding months in hospital—or a significant reduction in salary forced the remaining compañerxs into default. After separating from her husband, Joana, a Spanish office worker in her late fifties, went to La Caixa to negotiate a €600 monthly mortgage installment, an amount she could comfortably pay with her own salary. "Don't worry, don't worry," she was told. "You know what we can do? We need a guarantor. It could be your son." At the first meeting they said a guarantor was needed for €40,000, but on the following day it was €50,000, and La Caixa finally called her again to say they needed a guarantor for life. "For €50,000 my son said yes, but a guarantor for life, I'm the one who said no, I'm not mortgaging my son." Unable to find another solution, she stopped paying. Yet the reasons to stop paying a mortgage were in most cases multirelational, moving between strict categorization, echoing findings in the United Kingdom and United States that people's problems paying their mortgage stem from multiple socioeconomic lived realities (Fields, Libman, and Saegert 2010; Nettleton and Burrows 2000). For example, there were several cases where job loss and an inability to pay mortgage installments were exacerbated by health problems or breaking up with a partner whose salary was critical to making monthly payments.

The increasing cost of monthly mortgage installments was another factor affecting people's ability to pay. The Euribor rose steadily from the end of 2005 (2.1 percent) to the end of 2008 (4.85 percent), but then even when it later fell below 1 percent in 2009 and again in 2011 many mortgage floor clauses, explained in the previous chapter, meant that monthly installments remained at a higher fixed rate. Five compañerxs experienced a significant jump in monthly installments when their mortgage grace period (*carencia*) expired, that is, when their reduced monthly mortgage payment for anywhere between one to five years upon signing a mortgage loan finished. Grace periods were commonplace during the boom among all financial entities. Most compañerxs who had a grace period didn't worry at the time, as they were reassured that mortgage installments would not significantly increase when it ended. But when grace periods finished, five compañerxs saw their installments increase between €300 and €410 per month.

The fact that official recognition of a housing bubble was taboo meant that decisive state action to address the socioeconomic meltdown started at a snail's pace. The two Spanish ministers of housing serving between 2004 and 2008, both from the Socialist Party, underlined how voicing the word "bubble" was an "irresponsibility," as Spain had "the best real estate sector in the world"

(García Montalvo 2010, 58). Similarly, a former Catalan secretary of housing explained to me that when his superior, a minister in the Catalan Parliament, spoke publicly of a housing bubble in 2008, he received a call from an executive in a powerful real estate association to say "please, do not use that word because it is considered to be a jinx, it's being, as [the economist] Paul Krugman says, a spoilsport." In any case, the government and financial sector were confident that housing prices would stabilize and that the real estate sector, upon a "smooth deceleration" due to the "maturity" of the cycle (Banco de España 2007), would make a "soft landing" (BBVA 2007). Spain's sustained economic growth, standing at levels not seen since the early 1970s, was instead widely seen as evidence that the country had made it into the "Champions League of the world's economies," as Socialist president Zapatero stated in September 2007 (Elmundo.es 2007). Indeed during a visit to New York in September 2008, when the U.S. financial-housing crisis was rearing its head, Zapatero declared that Spain "perhaps has the most solid financial system in the international community" (*El Confidencial* 2008). After living the longest dictatorship in Europe, Spanish democracy and Europeanization appeared to be proof that the country had moved from the periphery to the core of Europe, and thus the world.

But despite Zapatero's declarations, by late 2008 the façade of Spanish success had already started to crumble. Don Piso, a major real estate agency chain, closed its doors in May 2008, and Spanish developer Martinsa Fadesa filed the largest bankruptcy in Spain's history, with €7 billion in debt. Inflation and interest rates were creeping up, unemployment was rising, liquidity disappeared, fewer real-estate-related loans were granted, and housing construction began to plummet. The façade dissolved completely as it soon came to light that over half the country's forty-five savings banks were reeling under the weight of billions of euros of non-performing real estate loans granted to developers and households over the past decade. In December 2011, over half of the entire Spanish loan portfolio of domestic credit assets was real estate related, 16 percent for developers, and 42 percent retail mortgages (Oliver Wyman 2012). While the extent of non-performing loans in this portfolio would not become clear for several years, increasing numbers of households and "zombie developers" (Smyth and Urban 2013) were unable to meet their debt repayments. After denying the crisis, Zapatero's reigning Socialist Party then made multibillion-euro Keynesian-style bets to counteract the economy's demise, to no avail (Salmon 2010). Shortly thereafter, Spain launched into what economist José García Montalvo (2014, 527) aptly calls "an absurd orgy of financial entity fusions with the supposed objective that public resources wouldn't be spent and the counterfactual assumption that the crisis would soon be over."

In what became a profound financial restructuring process largely occurring over half a decade, Spain went from having forty-five savings banks and eight banks in 2008 to two savings banks and ten banks by 2020 (Figure 3.3).[2] One of several key instruments to carry out this process was the Spanish Fund for Orderly Bank Restructuring (FROB), established by the Socialist Zapatero government in June 2009. The FROB, governed by representatives from the Bank of Spain and economic branches of the central government, led a three-phased restructuring and recapitalization of the banking system. The first phase included extensive fusions and liquidity injections (€9.7 billion) into various entities in 2010, while the second sought to improve solvency (€5.7 billion) and nationalize various institutions during 2011. In this second phase, savings banks unable to meet certain levels of solvency were transformed into banks to create a shareholder structure and capture external capital investment. The third phase, implemented by the newly appointed Popular Party (Conservative) majority government under President Rajoy, plugged up holes in entities' balance sheets detected by an independent stress test in June 2012 with €39 billion in European Stability Mechanism funds (Oliver Wyman 2012).

Spain's memorandum of understanding (MoU) with the European Commission made the €39 billion conditional upon the creation of an asset management company or a so-called bad bank. Pioneered during the U.S. Savings and Loan Crisis in the 1980s, a bad bank is a company that buys failed/non-performing loans and is an instrument used across the world to revive crisis-ridden real estate markets (Byrne 2015). Spain's bad bank was named the SAREB (Sociedad de Gestión de Activos Precedentes de la Reestructuración Bancaria [Management Company for Assets Arising from Bank Reorganization]) and became a highly contested entity in the restructuring of the financial system.[3]

Founded in November 2012 and 45 percent owned by the state through the FROB, the SAREB became Spain's largest real estate agent overnight, holding €51 billion worth of debt and property (Figure 3.4). It is where the "toxic assets" from nine partially or fully nationalized banks were transferred at 47 percent of their original price; these assets included developer debt above €250,000 and properties of foreclosed households or unfinished construction projects valued above €100,000. This transfer happened in exchange for bonds guaranteed by the Spanish government and European rescue funds destined to rebuild semi- and fully nationalized banks (Eurostate 2014; International Monetary Fund 2014). The SAREB's objective is to obtain at least a 15 percent

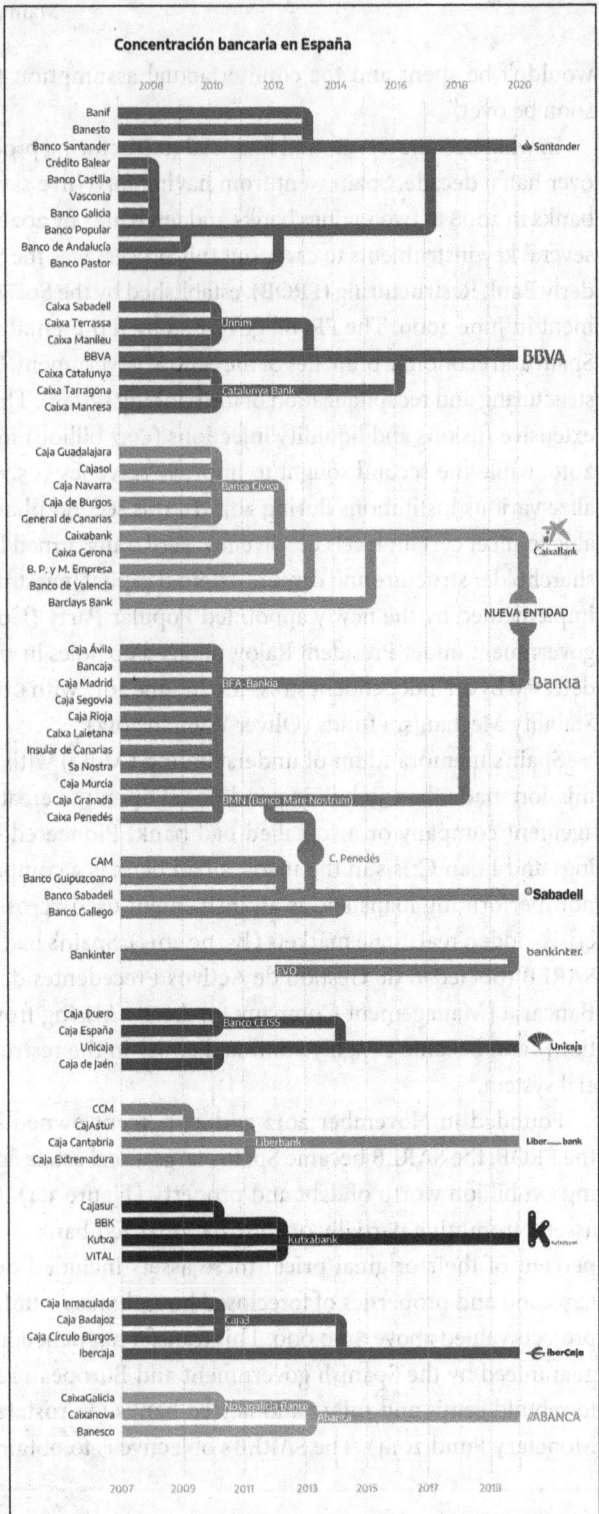

FIGURE 3.3. Spanish financial system restructuring, 2009–2020.

SOURCE: Ponce de León (2020).

(a) Who forms part of the SAREB?
Shareholders (by percentage)

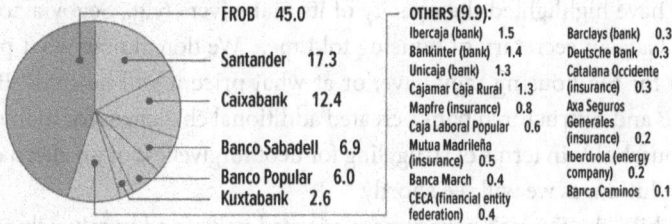

FROB 45.0
Santander 17.3
Caixabank 12.4
Banco Sabadell 6.9
Banco Popular 6.0
Kuxtabank 2.6

OTHERS (9.9):
Ibercaja (bank) 1.5
Bankinter (bank) 1.4
Unicaja (bank) 1.3
Cajamar Caja Rural 1.3
Mapfre (insurance) 0.8
Caja Laboral Popular 0.6
Mutua Madrileña (insurance) 0.5
Banca March 0.4
CECA (financial entity federation) 0.4

Barclays (bank) 0.3
Deutsche Bank 0.3
Catalana Occidente (insurance) 0.3
Axa Seguros Generales (insurance) 0.2
Iberdrola (energy company) 0.2
Banca Caminos 0.1

(b) What the SAREB has bought

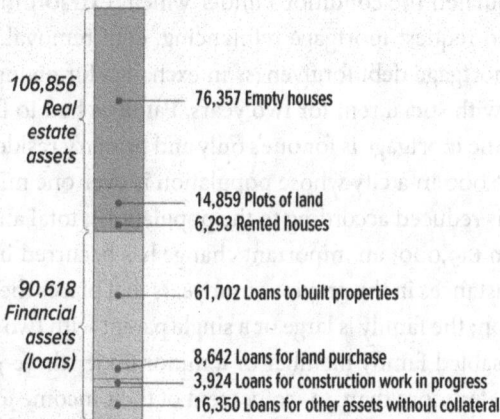

106,856 Real estate assets
76,357 Empty houses
14,859 Plots of land
6,293 Rented houses

90,618 Financial assets (loans)
61,702 Loans to built properties
8,642 Loans for land purchase
3,924 Loans for construction work in progress
16,350 Loans for other assets without collateral

(c) Financial entities purchased and the cost of each
(billions of Euros)

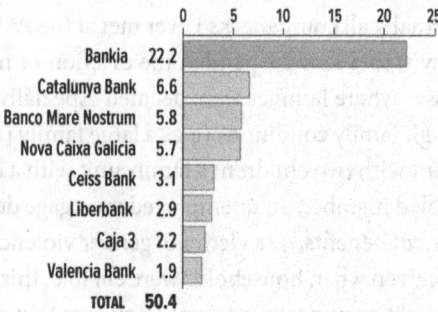

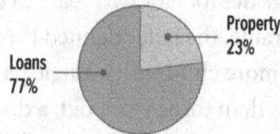

Bankia 22.2
Catalunya Bank 6.6
Banco Mare Nostrum 5.8
Nova Caixa Galicia 5.7
Ceiss Bank 3.1
Liberbank 2.9
Caja 3 2.2
Valencia Bank 1.9
TOTAL 50.4

Property 23%
Loans 77%

FIGURE 3.4. Characteristics of Spain's bad bank, the SAREB.
SOURCE: Méndez (2013).

profit through the sale of these assets over its fifteen-year lifespan (2012–27). While the SAREB touts a discourse of transparency, many journalists and researchers have highlighted the opacity of its maneuvers (e.g., Segovia 2014). A former Catalan secretary of housing told me, "We don't know what price they paid for the housing they have, or at what price it will be sold." Both the SAREB and restructured banks created additional challenges for many defaulted households in terms of struggling for debt forgiveness or an alternative housing solution, as we will see shortly.

Meanwhile, the Spanish government adopted paltry and purely voluntary measures to help mortgaged households facing default. The Good Practices Royal Decree 6/2012 stipulated the conditions under which "extraordinarily vulnerable families" could request mortgage refinancing, debt removal, and finally *dación en pago* (mortgage debt forgiveness in exchange for giving the home back to the bank) with social rent for two years. Families had to fulfill all the following criteria: the mortgage is for one's only and primary residence, which cost less than €200,000 in a city whose population is over one million people (maximum price is reduced according to the population); total annual family income is less than €19,000; an important change has occurred in the family's economic circumstances in the previous four years that places them in a more vulnerable situation; the family is large or a single parent with two children; the family has a disabled family member or a minor under three years old; and the family dedicates more than 40–50 percent of their income to pay monthly mortgage installments. Furthermore, mortgage co-owners or guarantors must also fulfil all the previous criteria. The fact that most housing at the peak of the boom cost well over €200,000 in the Barcelona metropolitan region automatically excluded virtually all compañerxs I ever met at the PAH. In the subsequent year, the 14 May 1/2013 Law suspended the eviction of mortgage debtors for two years in cases where families were deemed especially vulnerable, the latter defined through family conditions (e.g., a large family [three or more children]; a single parent with two children; a family unit with a child less than three years old, a disabled member, an unemployed mortgage debtor no longer receiving unemployment benefits, or a victim of gender violence) or a range of economic conditions. Even when households were eligible, this program was almost always just a politics of postponement (Roy 2017). In other words, eviction remained imminent.

Choosing between the Mortgage or Life:
Refinancing and Not Being Able to Pay

As factors including job loss, health problems, relationship breakup, salary reduction, and/or increased monthly installments came together, all compañerxs found themselves unable to pay their mortgage, the situation of virtually everyone who came to the PAH in the early 2010s. "No one stops paying all of the sudden," Bea, a Spanish factory worker, underlined. "Everyone will explain that they've done the same as me, first letting up the installment, trying again, asking for money, giving it. . . ." Part of this process involved seeking a solution from the bank, where over three-quarters of those I interviewed were offered mortgage refinancing or a grace period, an extremely common offer I heard discussed in well over a dozen PAH assemblies.[4] "We're going to help you," Marta was told by Caixa Catalunya, "until your husband finds work, we're going to help you to pay, you won't be paying the €1,250 monthly installment." Over three-quarters of compañerxs I interviewed who received these offers accepted, becoming more deeply indebted and ultimately defaulting. Two who signed a refinancing agreement or grace period were unable to get to the end of it before they defaulted. Isa, an Ecuadorian supermarket worker then in her late twenties, explains her experience as follows: "I did not want to stop paying, it's difficult for you to accept what is happening. . . . I said to my husband: 'Look, you are going to find work, I am going to keep going with the €800 I earn.' We had to pay €600 per month after refinancing. My husband said: 'But its €600, we're left with €200 for the rest of the month. . . .' Then comes a moment when my husband says: 'I don't know, I can no longer support you on this because we don't even have enough to eat. Either the mortgage, or we live.'"

When Isa returned to the bank to explain that she was unable to pay, they said, "Look, I can't offer you further help. The only thing I can do is give you a grace period for two years. You won't pay anything and then when your husband finds work you start paying the mortgage again. We'll make the mortgage twenty years longer [from a thirty-year mortgage]. You are young, you can extend it ten or twenty more years." She signed again and continued to pay until it again became impossible to do so.

At the end of the refinancing agreement or grace period, compañerxs found not only that their economic situation had not improved but also that their monthly installment increased significantly, up to €1,350, €1,400, or in one case €1,643. The latter was Julian's case. As the only household income earner who brought his family to Spain from Ecuador under family reunification, here he explains what happened after losing his job at a cleaning company that shut down in 2009, where he was earning up to €3,000 a month as a temporary worker: "I restructured my mortgage and signed a refinancing agreement, thinking that the crisis would last two or three years. So, there I was, playing with the bank. But I never imagined that the bank was going to play with me, right? I thought, well, at least this way I stay calm, I keep paying, I am earning a bit from little jobs, I have my unemployment payment, I'm keeping my chin up (*voy tirando 'palante*). And a time arrives where you go work in another restaurant, then another, for six months, part-time. Then I'm fired, once again I return to work as a waiter in another restaurant. Six months later that restaurant fires me and after that, I was left . . . with nothing. Just collecting €253 per month in government assistance."

Upon returning to Caixa Catalunya, the office director offered Julián another proposal: to pay €190 per month over five years, while the debt he owed—now at €300,000, from a €280,000 mortgage loan paid during almost six years—would be frozen. "And after those five years?," he inquired. "'Well look, Julián, you might win the lottery, maybe policies will change, it could be that the savings bank soon decides to gift you the house. . . .' And so on and so forth. So I said, no." When Julián later began to insist on dación en pago, the bank told him that so much money was at play that they were not willing to lose.

The implications of signing refinancing or grace periods, furthermore, were not made clear to many compañerxs. This was the case for Sara, the Moroccan chef, who signed a grace period for two years with Nova Caixa Galicia in 2008, during which time she would pay €700 a month. Sara had no idea the grace period involved a change to her original contract: "They didn't tell me that if you owed €228,000, you will pay over two years then owe €242,000. They didn't explain to me that when you pay less, it's like you are accumulating debt." Patricia's mortgage contract stipulated her and her husband's eligibility for up to five grace periods, since they had always paid their insurance and monthly installments on time. Before signing the grace period agreement, she insistently inquired about what would happen to their overall debt. Caixa Catalunya told her that "nothing will increase, not even one euro, you'll pay less for one year and by then for sure you'll find work. Keep paying." At that point her and her husband owed €223,000 of their original €250,000 mortgage loan, after having paid close to €100,000 in mortgage installments over six years, excluding insurance products. Patricia was working the morning that her husband and brother-in-law (a co-borrower on the loan) went to sign the new contract, and when she read the contract later that day it stated their new balance in 2013, when they would start paying the full installment again, as €234,200—increasing their overall debt by €11,200.

Such increasing indebtedness upon signing refinancing agreements or grace periods occurred in the context of not only rising unemployment but also plummeting housing prices. From their peak in 2008 to the trough in 2014, housing price indices point to average prices falling 30 to 45 percent across Spain (García Montalvo 2015). Decreases were even more pronounced for compañerxs—who were largely low-income Spaniards or non-European immigrants—living in the periphery of or just outside Barcelona and Sabadell. For example, Patricia's apartment in Cornellà, ten kilometers from Barcelona, was worth €250,000 in 2006 but €90,000 in 2013, a 65 percent decrease. In the most extreme case, Bea's apartment in Torre Romeu, a working-class neighborhood in Sabadell, was appraised at €275,000 in 2007 but €60,000 in 2014: a 78 percent plunge. The drop in housing prices was closer to the reported averages by García Montalvo (2015) for those who contracted a mortgage closer to the start of the housing boom, such as Ahmed, whose apartment in Badalona cost €108,000 in 2003 and was appraised at €71,000 in 2014, or Carlos, whose apartment in Bon Pastor was €136,500 in 2000 and valued at €90,000 in 2014. But Patricia's and Bea's situations were not uncommon among those who signed their mortgage between 2005 and 2007, when housing prices were at all-time highs. In these cases, the overall debt load was even starker when the loan granted was over 100 percent of the home's appraised price. For example, while Julián's debt increased to €300,000, from an apartment in l'Hospitalet de Llobregat priced at €240,000 in 2005 and financed with a 116 percent loan (totaling €280,000), the same property was appraised at €90,000 in 2013.

Four compañerxs offered refinancing agreements or grace periods were aware of what signing entailed and thus declined. Bankia offered Carlos, an Ecuadorian compañero in his late thirties who worked in an infrastructure company, both a refinancing agreement and a grace period, but he saw them as "solutions at their convenience." Bankia proposed that he pay €350 per month over three years, after which he would pay €1,200 per month, double his original mortgage installment. And while he had seventeen or eighteen years left on his thirty-year mortgage, the new mortgage he'd have to sign would be for forty years: "Imagine the swindle, how terrible that could be. Unbelievable." Similarly, Amira knew her overall debt would increase with a grace period, seeing it as a vicious circle, so she insisted on coming to an agreement to lower the monthly installment. Nova Caixa Galicia said that a grace period was the only option: "No, no, such is life. If not, here's what we can do: we'll give you a €10,000 loan and with that money you can pay your monthly installments and repay the loan."

Like Amira, many financial entities offered loans to households in order to meet their mortgage debt payments and not enter default. Ángela was offered a €12,000 loan with 12 percent interest rates upon her third month of nonpayment and was told that she needed to sign it immediately: "They play with being in a hurry, they play with your fear, that you don't know what to do, and that you don't have time to consult anyone." After his apartment was auctioned, Bankia offered Pepe a personal credit, "but with guarantors, guarantors with salaries and with paid properties, because we're not going to let you get out of this. It would be a loan with 11 percent interest, that could be 12 percent." Bankia told Pepe that he had twelve years to pay the €100,000 loan. Pepe exclaimed that it was "€1,400 per month, when I stopped paying the apartment for €1,200 per month." Loans are an attractive option for financial entities because aside from avoiding default, if a debtor is unable to meet loan repayments, the minimum income repossession rate is €645. This compares to the €967 income repossession rate for mortgage loans: if a debtor earns below this amount the bank is legally unable to seize their salary, although I heard a handful of cases in the PAH where despite their earning below this amount the bank automatically withdrew the money from their account.[5]

The push by restructured banks to refinance mortgage loans, offer grace periods, sell a new loan, or otherwise find a way for defaulters to not be in the red—at least in the books—was driven by their obligation to reduce their exposure to real-estate-related debt and assets. This action was driven by two connected developments. The first was the result of a study conducted by private consultants Oliver Wyman for the Bank of Spain in June 2012, finding a €52 to €62 billion capital shortfall in an adverse scenario. Banks were thus pressed to restructure their capital investments and improve their solvency because if the financial system took another beating some entities might not survive. The second was stricter requirements for banks to account for restructured and refinanced debt, requirements dictated by the MoU signed by Spanish and European authorities in July 2012 to improve information about the status of real-estate-related loans. Stricter requirements were also set to respond to the European Commission's worries over "hidden defaults" in March 2013 (Banco de España 2014). As reported in the *Wall Street Journal*, the extensive refinancing of mortgage loans in Spain made banks' loan books look "healthier" than they really were, helping banks bury risk in their credit portfolios (Brat and Bjork 2013). In other words, refinancing was "hiding reality," as a banker explained to me in an interview. In April 2013, the Bank of

TABLE 3.1. Spanish Banks' Real Estate Platforms Sold to Foreign Real Estate Investment Funds

Real estate platform	Sold by	Sold to	Sale price (€)	Value of assets managed (€)	Sale date
Aktua	Banesto	Centerbridge	100 million		November 2012
Servihabitat	CaixaBank (La Caixa)	TPG Texas Pacific Group (51%)	185 million	>22.0 billion	September 2013
BankiaHabitat	Bankia	Haya Real Estate (Cerebus)	40–90 million	>12.2 billion	September 2013
Aliseda	Banco Popular	Kennedy Wilson and Varde Partners	815 million	>15.0 billion	December 2013
Altamira	Santander	Apollo (85%)	664 million	11.4 billion	January 2014
CX Inmobiliaria (Anticipa)	Caixa Catalunya (CX)	Magic Real Estate and Blackstone	40 million	7.8 billion	April 2014
Inmare	Banco Mare Nostrum (BMN)	Centerbridge	50 million	7.0 billion	April 2014
Cimenta2	Cajamar	Haya Real Estate (Cerebus)	225 million	7.3 billion	June 2014
Grupo Neinor	Kutxabank	Lone Star	930 million		May 2015
Inmobiliaria Portugal—RECBUS	Banco Popular	Quarteira (Carval)	72 million		June 2015
Anida	BBVA	Cerebus (80%)	4 billion	13 billion	November 2017
Solvia	Banc Sabadell	Oaktree	882 million	1.3 billion	August 2019

SOURCES: García Montalvo (2015); Martínez (2017); Lafraya (2019).

Spain stipulated that to classify credit as being of "normal" risk, banks needed "objective and verifiable evidence making highly probable the recovery of the total outstanding amount due." Otherwise, entities had to reclassify debt as substandard or doubtful as per the true repayment capacity of loan holders (Banco de España 2013a).[6]

While the SAREB served to absorb troubled assets from the balance sheets of partially and fully nationalized banks, all banks were forced to carefully study their debt, that is, to reclassify loans and to divest noncore real estate assets and non-performing loans. Shortly after the Bank of Spain's official communication, refinanced real estate loans classified as doubtful or substandard increased from €119 billion in 2012 to €148 billion in 2013, out of a total of €208 billion in refinanced loans, 27 percent being developer and 27 percent household mortgage loans (Banco de España 2013b, 2014).[7] While mortgage loan default rates, peaking at 6.3 percent in the first quarter of 2014, are proportionately much lower than developer-related defaults (reaching 34 percent in the fourth quarter of 2013), according to the Bank of Spain total defaulted mortgage credit increased from €24 billion in the fourth quarter of 2012 to a peak of €36.2 billion in the first quarter of 2014. Similarly, sales of credit portfolios and real estate assets increased dramatically in 2013, with the nominal value sold from November 2013 to mid-2015 sitting at €28 billion (García Montalvo 2015).

A final step that many banks took to reduce their exposure to real estate risk was selling their real estate platforms. All banks have sold part or all of their platforms, largely to foreign investment funds (Table 3.1). Three of these funds—Apollo, TPG, and Cerebus—became the servicers of the SAREB's asset portfolios in December 2014. While funds now manage asset sales, in most cases the real estate and credit assets remain on the balance sheets of the originating banks. The latter have raked in at least €2 billion from the sale of the management of these platforms (Ollero 2013).

Pay, or Be a Debtor for Life: Interactions with Financial Entities

Mortgage-affected people, as explained in detail to me by compañerxs in interviews and as I heard in countless assemblies, received a range of responses from financial entities when they stopped paying their mortgage. Three were the most common. The first was being told to "pay what you can," despite the reality—underlined in PAH assemblies—that a debtor automatically enters into default if the *full* monthly mortgage installment is not paid. The second was spurring defaulters into payment through instilling guilt or fear in person (at the bank), by telephone, or by mail. These are commonplace strategies to exploit affect through debt collection processes (Deville 2015). The third most frequent response from the bank was threating mortgage holders when they stopped paying. It was not uncommon for bankers to speak to immigrants in blatantly racist terms, illustrating how the racialized "others of Europe" emerged into spoken space. For example, Ahmed explained how when he went to the bank, the office director always yelled at him, "'You better pay!' She told me ridiculous things not in the law or in books. They were 120 percent racist." Immigrant women oftentimes also faced threats to their family, as bankers used not only their reproductive and caring roles but also their immigration status as scare tactics. When Sara stopped paying, Nova Caixa Galicia told her, "'We are going to take away your kids, they are going to inherit the debt. We're going to kick you out of the country. Why did you buy the apartment if you can't face the debt? This is not a game.' ... He said everything, everything, everything. That we are Moors [*moros*—a derogatory term for Moroccans]. Everything, everything."

Several low-income Spanish compañerxs reported abusive behavior. Pepe, a Spanish former electrician in his early thirties, explained the bank's reactions as follows: "When I stopped paying, I went to inform the bank, buff. 'No, what you have to do is pay, you have to pay because it is your right. You shouldn't have gotten yourself into this. We're going to take away your apartment *and* you'll have to pay more, and. . . .' Hey, no, I've come to look for solutions, I already have problems, I want solutions. 'Well now you need pay, pay and pay.' I already saw that I couldn't pay the full installment [€1,200], the next month I sacrificed myself, and the next month, getting by, getting by." Pepe stopped paying, and his apartment was foreclosed and auctioned. He left before the court-ordered eviction, moving in with his girlfriend. When he went to speak with the bank a few months later he was told there was no way he would get the apartment back. Pepe owed the bank €100,000, which he was offered to pay with a personal credit. When Pepe firmly refused, the bank told him either he could pay or his salary and goods would be seized for life.

The bank or debt collectors hounded five compañerxs to pay through telephone and mail. Isa and Marta, two Ecuadorians who forged a deep friendship in the PAH, explained how they were overwhelmed with phone calls and letters, at the receiving end of a relentless pursuit to recuperate the outstanding debt. Daniel, a Spanish former house painter in his late thirties, noted that it is common to receive calls "where they tell you, pay, you must pay, you must pay. They call your father. They call your mother. They call everyone, that's what they do. The majority of banks do it, because it is really the majority of them that do telephone harassment."

Of all compañerxs I interviewed, María, whom we met at the start of the book, was the sole person whose bank director advised her to stop paying. In her case, her ex-partner refused to pay his half, and she was unable to pay the full monthly installment on her own. A few months later she received the foreclosure documents, and the bank director said they would look at her situation to see what solution was possible. The bank proposed that she and her ex-partner sign a notarized certificate enabling the bank to sell the apartment—for which she paid €215,000 in 2005—at whatever price they could and that María and her ex would be indebted with the difference. "I told them that this can't be, I can't give them authorization to sell my apartment without knowing its sale price. . . . I asked that they take the apartment and give me the possibility to rent it, if not then just taking the apartment and leaving me without debt would be fine. He said no, that their offer was the only option." Shortly after, María's apartment was auctioned off, and she fought for four years—one alone and three with the PAH—to get her debt forgiven. The bank has always told her that debt forgiveness was out of the question because the debt was for a lifetime and they can pursue her ex-partner and their four mortgage guarantors.

Entering into mortgage default when a mortgage loan was from a bank being rescued and restructured left several compañerxs uncertain about exactly how much debt they owed and to whom. Take Isa, who contracted her mortgage from Caixa Penedès in 2005, refinanced it in 2009, and stopped paying in 2010. The year she stopped paying was when Caixa Penedès was absorbed into the nationalized Banco Mare Nostrum, a bank "cleaned up" with €916 million in public funds. While the president and director of Caixa Penedès stepped down over a scandal related to the bank's multimillion-euro pensions in 2011, in March 2012 Isa received an eviction order. Her court-appointed lawyer, in typical fashion, told her there was nothing to be done and advised Isa to abandon her apartment. Frightened about a possible eviction, Isa obeyed. Shortly thereafter her mortgage guarantors started to receive letters claiming Isa's debt, which spurred Isa to go to the PAH. Meanwhile, in 2013 Banc Sabadell bought Caixa Penedès from Banco Mare Nostrum. Banc Sabadell insisted that Isa owed €13,500, but when she went to the Bank of Spain to confirm this, they said she was €10,000 in debt. But Banco Mare Nostrum said she also owed them €25,000. If this tale seems dizzying, confusing, and contradictory, this is an apt characterization of Isa and other compañerxs' experiences of being caught up in some of the more complex financial sector restructuring.

Meanwhile—in sharp contrast to the whirlwind of foreclosure, eviction, and a lifetime of indebtedness that increasing numbers of mortgage-affected people faced—a handful of Spanish banks reinforced their dominance in the domestic market, purchasing nationalized entities and publicly rescued assets at symbolic or massively discounted prices. For example, BBVA and CaixaBank both bought fully nationalized entities (Unnim and Banco de Valencia, respectively) for the token price of one euro. BBVA also bought the nationalized Caixa Catalunya for €1.1 billion only three years after it was rescued by the state for €12 billion.[8] Spain's doors have also been opened to distressed debt and other corporate investors who see a wealth of opportunities in the Spanish market, thanks in large part to legislative changes to attract foreign investors to the burgeoning rental market (García-Lamarca 2021). Meanwhile, as of 2019, the state has recovered only €5 billion of the €65 billion in European and Spanish funds used to rescue the financial system.

As compañerxs struggled with the bank for a solution, both before and with the PAH, many were told that nothing could be done because their debt was securitized. Four compañerxs found themselves in this situation, and I came to know of at least a dozen other cases through assemblies and conversations with people struggling for debt forgiveness. For example, Carlos and six others in PAH Barcelona with mortgages from Bankia were told that their mortgage debt had been securitized and that while dación en pago may be possible, obtaining a social rent in the same apartment was not. Similarly, a man came to an assembly to ask what he should do because his bank, Caixa Catalunya, had told him, "Don't come talk to me because your mortgage has been securitized." Banks often used the fact that a mortgage was securitized as a way to wash their hands of responsibility or the possibility to take any action, although others used it to condition possible solutions.

The bank furthermore told some compañerxs that their debt had been sold, an experience I heard mentioned and discussed by mortgage-affected people in over half a dozen assemblies. For example, Ibercaja sold María's debt to Global Finance, which was a key factor dragging out the length of her struggle for debt forgiveness over four years. As a banker explained to me in an interview, a mortgage is often sold in its entirety when the originating bank sees that the attempt to recover the debt will cost more than the debtor owes. "Clearly, that's not profitable." So they sell the debt to funds or investors who buy it for 20 percent of its original cost: "The assets we had accounted for as failed and irrecoverable now give a 20 percent return," he told me. These loans, and thus mortgage holders, have ultimately been categorized by the bank as doubtful, substandard, or non-performing, and better to be pawned off to investment funds specialized in such "investments."

Daily Life Caught Up in the Tsunami of Capital Flowing into Real Estate Debt

Aside from clarifying the logic behind banks deleveraging non-performing loans and thus effectively making mortgage-affected people financial pawns, the sale of doubtful, substandard, or non-performing mortgage debt creates deeply convoluted debt ecologies (Harker 2020), especially in terms of their entangled spatial and temporal formations. The experience of a Honduran family I met at the PAH exemplifies this complexity. Hector and Scarlett purchased their apartment on the outskirts of Barcelona in September 2007 with a €266,000 mortgage from GMAC, the financial arm of General Motors, which began operating in Spain in 2005. After GMAC was bailed out by the U.S. government with over €12.6 billion because it was one of the largest subprime housing lenders (Davidoff 2012), the company closed their administrative centers in Spain in 2009. Their mortgage loans were thereupon sold to the American financial company Fortress Investment Group, and in November 2011 Fortress sold them to Banco Pichincha (Hernanz 2009; KPMG 2013).[9] During these sales Hector and Scarlett kept paying until a few years later, like hundreds of thousands of other families, they were unable to do so. Pichincha is an Ecuadorian entity, operating in Spain since 2010 and purchasing portfolios of mortgage debt from other entities. Despite Hector and Scarlett having paid almost €70,000 of their loan—which considering the fall in housing prices is likely not far off its current price—Pichincha flatly refused to negotiate any solution and proceeded with foreclosure. The entity has not adopted the Good Practices Code Royal Decree 6/2012 nor the 14 May 1/2013 Law. Although they are voluntary, with criteria that are too strict and overall insufficient for the scale of Spain's mortgage problem, especially in large cities, both decrees have largely been adopted by Spanish banks. This meant that as of 2014, most Spanish banks would at least examine requests for dación en pago. Despite Hector and Scarlett's continuous attempts, including actions with the PAH, Pichincha would not budge.

Pichincha is only one example of the influx of dozens of foreign financial entities and capital into Spain. In the midst of Spain's financial sector restructuring, real estate magnate-cum-former U.S. president Donald Trump declared that "Spain is an amazing place, it's a great country and it's got a fever, and this is the time to take advantage of it" (Cox 2012). The massive devaluation of housing and real estate debt more broadly enticed increasing numbers of private equity and institutional investors, who are snatching up the assets being disposed of by the SAREB and other banks at hugely discounted prices and with significant fiscal incentives. Critical to underline again here is that Spanish household mortgage debt can be of particular interest to investors because once the loan is non-performing and the debtor is foreclosed and evicted, the investor keeps the asset (the home) *and* the debtor still owes all the outstanding debt.[10] Thus the purchaser of household mortgage debt not only keeps the asset but also has the legal right to continue claiming debt payments from the formerly mortgaged homeowner and guarantors, plus any fees incurred through legal proceedings.

As Spain's subsecretary of economic affairs and competitiveness made clear at a private equity fund forum on Spanish real estate in May 2014, Spain's bad bank the SAREB aims to "make the Spanish real estate sector an attractive place for investors." But the SAREB's analysts scrambled to understand the details of the properties they suddenly had in their hands (*Financial Times* 2013). This was confirmed by the Catalan secretary of housing, who underlined in an interview that the extensive fusion and restructuring of savings banks has left "significant disorder" in many nationalized entities, as they don't know if their properties are habitable, already rented, or currently home to squatters. "The problem with the SAREB," a real estate broker told me, "is that it's impossible to know [what's in] a €43 billion asset portfolio." For this reason, he continued, the SAREB decided to auction its asset management to large venture capital funds "that are used to managing them because they have done it in all crises, in all countries." These funds "then transfer part of the management to smaller companies like mine. . . . We are an expert in the markets we operate in, and we transfer all this knowledge and know-how to the SAREB and its management companies." Three of the four winners of the bid to manage and sell the SAREB's assets are servicing companies owned by U.S. venture capital funds, also known as vulture funds: Apollo, TPG, and Cerebus. Through commercializing and selling €41 billion worth of real estate assets bailed out with public funds, they got commissions and insight into the Spanish market (Neumann 2014).

The Spanish state also created new financial vehicles to attract foreign investment in real estate, the most significant in terms of its use and market impact being real estate investment trusts (REITs). Known in Spain as SOCIMIs (Sociedades Anónimas Cotizadas de Inversión Inmobiliaria), REITs are companies that own or finance rental properties and are listed on stock markets. According to investors I heard speaking at a Spanish real estate investment fair in 2014, the Spanish SOCIMI model is one of the most attractive REIT schemes globally, structured in a way to purely and simply attract as much foreign direct investment as possible. In 2013 the majority Conservative government liberalized the legislation first created by the Socialist Zapatero government in 2009 to tax them at zero percent, and promises of future liquidity once SOCIMIs go public on the Spanish stock market have stimulated increasing amounts of investment in the rental sector. SOCIMIs were pioneered by the international vulture fund Blackstone in Madrid through privatized social housing (Janoshcka et al. 2020), and Blackstone is also leading the way in SOCIMI creation in Catalonia, which has more recently shown signs of reinforcing urban sociospatial inequality (García-Lamarca 2021).

Signposted by articles in September 2013 with titles like "Who's Buying Spain?" (Méndez and Pellicer 2013) or "How Vulture Funds Feed Off Spanish Banks' Rubbish Credits" (Blázquez 2013), devalued real estate debt and assets made an increasingly attractive market for distressed debt investors. While still far from its peak during the housing boom in 2005, foreign investment in real estate doubled from its minimum in 2009 to €8.6 billion in 2014 (Ministerio de Fomento 2014).[11] The burgeoning interest in Spain was summarized by one of PricewaterhouseCoopers' 500 real estate industry expert respondents in their 2015 Emerging Trends in Real Estate report: "Spain was a no-go area but now it is a let's-all-go area." As the report (2015, 21) continues, "A tsunami of capital has washed over Spain, much of it global. U.S. opportunity and hedge funds, global investment banks, European fund managers, Chinese real estate magnates, and even Warren Buffett, the sage of Omaha, have all piled in. So whether Spain is still good business is hotly debated among opportunistic investors. Views range from 'the train has already left the station' to 'Spain is still very much an opportunistic play.' There is very little core activity because debt is quite difficult and the domestic banks are still not lending."

While devalued real estate and non-performing loans were a bonanza for investors, the lives of mortgage-indebted people were caught up in the tsunami of capital flowing into the country. The experience of Hector and Scarlett was echoed, but on a mass scale, in July 2014 when the FROB sold forty thousand residential mortgages from the fully nationalized CatalunyaBanc (formerly Caixa Catalunya) worth €6.4 billion to the American multinational vulture fund Blackstone for €3.6 billion (Munoz 2014). Due to the complexity of the purchase, the sale took many months to be finalized. Meanwhile, with the utmost secrecy, CatalunyaBanc began offering a "waiting agreement" to households trying to negotiate a solution to their mortgage problem or extend social rental contracts that were soon to expire. The "agreement" allowed households to stay in their home for a few months by paying €300 to €400 per month, under the condition that they commit to not take any direct or indirect action against the bank during this period (Rusiñol 2015). Households were ultimately offered short-term concessions to "wait" for Blackstone, who subsequently took over their mortgage debt or social rental contracts and proved impossible to contact or negotiate with for any real or stable solution. Even while writing this text, countless numbers of people continue to struggle with Blackstone in PAHs across Catalonia, many of their stories crystalized in a report created by the PAH (2019) on Blackstone. A final note worth underlining: distressed mortgage debt sales to vulture funds are not unique to Spain but have also been under way in the United States and Ireland (Byrne 2016; Goldstein 2015). The "non-performing people" that are attempting to live with non-performing mortgage loans are increasingly forced into uncertain and unexpected situations, as vulture funds seek to squeeze everything they can out of their new investment—the mortgaged homeowner, their guarantors, and the property.

Failing to Be a Financial Rent Appropriation Strategy: Impacts on Everyday Life and the Body

What happens to everyday life as people—who have been deemed non-performing, a failure in the eyes of the system—as they are unable to pay their mortgage, formally falling into default, facing foreclosure and eviction, and a debt for life? All compañerxs suffered emotionally, physically, and mentally from being exhorted to pay, as they struggled to make mortgage payments, many not knowing what to do and feeling impotent. My constant engagement with the PAH and the in-depth interviews mortgage-affected compañerxs illustrated very clearly how this process eats into people's mind and flesh. I was deeply struck how the vast majority of compañerxs—without being asked—divulged being riddled with deep-seated feelings of guilt, fear, and shame as well as a wide range of physical and mental health problems. Their stories echo experiences of foreclosed households in England in the late 1990s (Nettleton and Burrows 2000), pointing to the individualized and individualizing experiences of foreclosure and eviction. Living the process of losing a home either provoked or deepened a range of family and health problems and led many to depression, suicidal thoughts, and even suicide attempts. This illustrates how despite the historic shift away from the body as the ultimate material guarantee of unpaid debt (Deville 2015), profound mental and physical health impacts remain. People in essence are, as Seigworth (2016) conceptualizes, wearing debt more and more deeply in their body and psyche, with deeply gendered dimensions closely connected to space and social relations (Harker, Sayyad, and Shebeitah 2019). Before turning to reflect on what non-performing loans and non-performing people mean, the next subsections share the experiences of compañerxs whose lives were deeply disrupted as the financialized housing model fails.

GUILT, SHAME, AND FEAR

Feelings of guilt were prevalent among compañerxs when they stopped paying their mortgage and were unable to find a solution to their situation. Lawyers or bankers often fueled these feelings. Lawyers told them nothing could be done, and the bank declared that they hadn't tried hard enough or threatened to seize the assets of their mortgage guarantor(s). Guilt appeared to be most powerful the earlier in time compañerxs stopped paying, since in 2009 and 2010 mortgage defaults and foreclosure were nascent and there was virtually no social awareness of the phenomenon. María, who stopped paying in 2010, explains this very clearly:

> At the beginning when I consulted several lawyers, they all told me that it is my fault, that since I signed the bank was in the right. . . . I went around asking different lawyers how I could solve my problem and they all said, "Look, you can't do anything. It is your fault for having signed without reading." . . . In the courthouse they also told me the bank was right: "I know that it's rotten luck, but that's what you signed, it is fair. We can't do anything. You are guilty for having signed." In other words, everyone sunk you psychologically, telling you that you are guilty, you signed, you didn't read, always, everyone. . . . So I went about feeling guilty, and I couldn't even sleep anymore [chokes up]. I had no hope of solving my case.

Other compañerxs explained feeling like they had failed, that they had not tried hard enough, "feeling like a big mess when I have been a man that never threw away money." Sebas, formerly an entrepreneur, contrasted his past and present lives. He was born in a shack in the shantytowns covering Barcelona's Montjuïc mountain and decades later bought a home in a middle-class suburb north of Barcelona, giving his children a university education and cars: "I arrived [at the PAH] broken, with a feeling of guilt I thought would never leave."

Many compañerxs openly expressed how they felt deeply ashamed for not having been able to pay. Bea explained how "you see yourself alone, you know nothing of other people, you think that you have failed. How are you going to tell people: I don't pay my mortgage. . . . Look at this one, it's because she doesn't want to pay. And you're going to tell people your problems?" At her first assembly in Sabadell in 2013, she shared that she felt foreclosed for life, living without a future. Shame was also felt in relation to family members, for not having been able to "succeed." Others underlined Bea's sense of being alone. Joana, for example, cried "for the shame I had inside. It's not exactly shame, it is for one's self, you cry, you cry. . . . But yes I felt ashamed."

Finally, half of the compañerxs I interviewed spoke of deep-seated fear: of what would happen once they stopped paying, of their home being repossessed, of what would happen to their guarantors, and, in general, a broader fear largely driven by not knowing what to do. Daniel noted that the situation "drove me to the depths of despair because there are things you don't know. . . . And it's due to a lack of information. Because you stop paying and the bank says they will take your kids or your house. It's not legal. But what happens is that we are deeply scared (*tenemos el miedo en el cuerpo*)." The literal translation from Spanish is telling: "We have fear in our bodies."

Half a dozen compañerxs voiced their fear of being evicted, one noting that "I was always afraid that one day I would come home and be outside, on the street." Many people are struck so deeply by the fear of a possible eviction, in particular once their apartment is auctioned, that they abandon their home of their own free will. This was the case with three compañeras, who, before coming to the PAH, left their apartment just after it was auctioned by the bank. Sara said, "I didn't want to be evicted, not with minors in my home. I was afraid that my children would be taken away; now that you don't have a house, they'll take them away, they don't think twice." Isa was similarly afraid to go to social services because they would take her children away if they knew she was facing eviction or later squatting. Aside from all being women, all were mothers, plus two of the three compañeras are from Morocco and Ecuador. Fear was further stoked by both gendered and racialized realities: consider, for example, the banker telling Sara that her kids would be taken away and that she would be deported to Morocco if she didn't pay her debt. Despite the fact that she grew up in Catalonia and speaks Spanish and Catalan as a native speaker, Sara's form of dress and skin color marked her as other. The PAH always explains to compañerxs at assemblies that their children can't be taken away and that staying in their home is ultimately their best weapon. "If I would have known what I know now," Sandra told me, "I would not have left my home."

"YOU'VE SCREWED UP MY LIFE":
PROBLEMS WITH PARTNERS OR FAMILY MEMBERS

Serious tension between compañerxs and their partners and/or families was commonplace when they stopped paying their mortgage and were struggling with the bank for a solution. Sebas noted that "the married couples in the PAH are almost all broken, or on the point of breaking." Four compañerxs told me that they split up with their partners or were about to do so due to their mortgage problems. Ángela said that if her and her husband hadn't had children, she "for sure, absolutely sure" would have separated from him. He is ready to bow down and accept any offer from the bank, while Ángela is the one at the PAH every week insisting they must keep fighting to be debt free. It is not uncommon for women to be shifted into a double role of social care and reproduction within the household as well as fighting for its (debt-free) survival with the collective support of the movement. Julián told me that his family "was disintegrating due to this situation. My wife and I had never argued, ever, and we argued over the mortgage. That was when the alarm bells went off in my family and we said, 'Damn, what is happening?'"

Tension within families also tends to emerge when parents, siblings, or other family members are mortgage guarantors or, as was frequently the case of racialized mortgage conditions for immigrants, signed on unbeknownst as mortgage co-owners. Patricia, a Colombian compañera, explained her husband's suffering due to problems with his brother, whom the bank surreptitiously signed on as the mortgage co-owner: "He went with his brother to the bank and in front of the banker they would start arguing, 'It's your fault because of this, because of that.' It was always like that." Her brother-in-law was enraged because he was working but was never meant to pay his brother's mortgage, which is what the bank insisted that he did. Isa's sister and brother-in-law guaranteed her mortgage. When they were foreclosed and the apartment was auctioned, she went with her husband and their small child to their home with their heads bowed, asking for help: "You have two people behind you that are paying for your apartment. They are family but you don't have the same relationship. When you used to go to their place you said hello, gave them kisses and hugs. Now it is more indifferent, it's not the same because they think that it is your fault, that you don't want to solve the situation. In my case, it is my brother-in-law: 'Look, you've screwed up my life. I have my mortgage, my job.'"

Sometimes these conflicts between family members are painfully visible when people, seeking collective advising, come to the PAH, where, for example, I saw the palpable frustration between Spanish middle-aged mortgage holders and their now elderly parents, the latter having guaranteed their children's mortgage with their only home paid through blood, sweat, and tears decades ago. Other siblings who lost their jobs compound the situation, as it is not uncommon to have no other option but to return to the family home and get by thanks to a parent's pension. The pain and anxiety experienced in the face of their parents losing their home and the anger and blame some parents feel toward their children can be incredibly intense. While indebtedness in itself can generate tensions in the home and deepen already quite gendered social relations (Harker, Sayyad, and Shebeitah 2019), the inability to pay absolutely disrupts domestic life economically and emotionally. Many stories I heard echoed lived experiences of indebtedness and care under neoliberalism by Clara Han (2012) in Chile and Johnna Montgomerie and Daniela Tepe-Belfrage (2017) in the United Kingdom. And similar to these cases, being unable to pay triggers severe mental and physical health impacts.

MORTGAGED HEALTH:
NERVOUSNESS, INSOMNIA, STRESS, DEPRESSION, AND SUICIDE ATTEMPTS

Health problems, often overlapping, were extremely common among compañerxs. These included pain and depression, stress, irritation, insomnia, nervous breakdowns, suicidal thoughts, and suicide attempts. These reflect the deeply affective and intimate entanglements of defaulted (mortgage) debt, as conceptualized by Dawney, Kirwan, and Walker (2020). Bea explains what it felt like when she kept trying to find a way to pay her mortgage but couldn't: "It's like getting on a conveyor belt. You're running, you run, you run and you don't stop. You're exhausted and you get nowhere. I was spent, physically and psychologically, worn out and terrible. I was going for everyone's throats, I felt awful."

After refinancing twice and trying almost half a dozen times to obtain dación en pago, which Caixa Catalunya always rejected, Julián's monthly installment was €1,643: "We said this is unviable and unpayable. . . . We cried that day because it hurt us to have practically lost our apartment, the hope we bought it with, the dreams we had made, we had imagined ourselves growing old there. That causes you immense pain, it's agony to see yourself so impotent, to see no solution." Similarly, upon hearing the options Bankia offered him—a personal loan or being a debtor for life—Pepe said he felt utterly impotent: "Well, what can I do? I'll hold out and endure. I went to a court-appointed lawyer to inform myself, and upon looking at the documents he said they are going to screw me to the limit. That if I had a property, a car, something in my name they could take. . . . Oh, I completely freaked out. I lived depressed, depressed. What have I gotten myself into?"

Cobralia, a debt collection company that was hounding María, made her incredibly nervous, clearly illustrating how debt collection "depends on and feeds off people's lives" (Deville 2015, xii). A debt collector would make her an offer one day, then another day would say that same offer was impossible: "They made me crazy, making it seem like I'm a liar." Struggling for four years to get her debt forgiven, upon countless accompaniments and actions at the bank, I heard María share more than once in a PAH assembly that she was sick from nerves (*estoy enferma de los nervios*). In one of these same assemblies in Sabadell, I sat next to a middle-aged Spanish woman with curly brown hair who at one point, as we both were looking at our laps, held out her hands toward me to show her splotchy, red, irritated skin. She whispered that her psoriasis was related to stress and that the doctor told her there was nothing she could do because it was psychosomatic.

Sara, a Moroccan compañera, underlined how her mortgage brought her trauma and poor health:

> Before I didn't have any problems, I didn't owe anyone, I didn't owe any-thing. . . . When someone [at the bank] tells you that they will take away your children, that your children will inherit the debt and they begin to foam at the mouth, looking like a dog with rabies, how do you react at that moment? That's what they want, to provoke you, so something happens. Well, due to that, I had a nervous breakdown and was hospitalized ten days. Since then I've been to many different neurologists because I can't see out of my left eye and they don't really know what is wrong. . . . The mortgage has turned my health into a knot, I don't know when but it is exploding bit by bit. Right now, my feet and hands are numb. It is a sense of distress you can't imagine.

Preexisting health problems are almost always exacerbated by the stress, strain, and pressure of foreclosure and/or eviction. Daniel had a colon disorder that subsided for close to a decade, but the stress from his mortgage difficulties triggered a relapse: "I was hospitalized and needed an operation. . . . Well, it all happened due to this, I couldn't pay and my nerves were on edge, every day I had to go this way and that way. My wife also got depressed, she had bulimia, and then when my second daughter was born, I don't know if it was my wife's nerves or what happened, but she was born and nine months later got child epilepsy. Then things really got very very complicated. And people hounding you, because there were continuous telephone calls: you have to pay."

This exchange that occurred in an interview with two friends from Ecuador, Marta and Isa, illustrates how nerves, stress, insomnia, guilt, fear, and impotence come together:

> MARTA: Above all, they [the bank, debt collectors] destroy you morally and physically because you become terrible, nervous. . . . For example, I didn't know what to do, I walked dim-witted down the street, not knowing what to do, because receiving phone calls, being told you have to pay, you can't sleep.
>
> ISA: You can't answer the phone.
>
> MARTA: You become afraid of everything. With my friend [mortgage cosignatory], we were classmates in school and we have become enemies, we no longer have a good relationship because she says: get me out of this, get me out of this. . . . Psychologically they [the bank, debt collectors] make you bitter because now I am nervous, sick from stress, my stomach, everything. Always distressed, you can't sleep, you walk down the street badly, absent-mindedly. . . . Besides having finished my life here, leaving all our work, all the money that we have earned stays there.
>
> ISA: The lost years.
>
> MARTA: And it is a favor, we still have to show gratitude to the bank. When they forgive your debt in exchange for your apartment: thank you. Thanks for what, if you have made my life bitter?

Suicidal thoughts and suicide attempts were discussed in depth with a handful of compañerxs.[12] Upon receiving her foreclosure documents, Marta went to the court, but her request for a court-appointed lawyer was denied and she was told nothing could be done. Feeling terrible and alone, on her way home she recounted how she was on the verge of throwing herself in front of an oncoming train: "It ends here. What did I come [to Spain] for, to spend all my money? My work has been wasted. What was all my sacrifice for? Working day and night to pay, because my husband didn't have a work permit so he couldn't contribute. I had to work all day, on the weekends until two in the morning to cover that money, on Saturday working extra hours wherever to be able to pay, and sometimes even then we didn't make it."

People often arrive at the PAH "on the edge of the abyss, with no desire or will to live," as Carlos articulated and I witnessed at many assemblies. The situation they are living is fundamentally overwhelming. As elaborated by Julián, "The people who are not fighters, well look at how it finishes, they end up committing suicide, it finishes below the train tracks. They have nothing left, because no, there is no other alternative according to them. Because this is something that makes you feel impotent, it is something that marks you for life. If you don't solve it, it will be there." Suicides are acknowledged with a moment of silence in PAH assemblies. Someone always declares that the compañerx did not take their own life, but rather the bank took their life from them.

Non-Performing Loans, Non-Performing People

This chapter uncovered how mortgaged and financialized lives were maintained during the post-2008 crisis, both through the lived experience of mortgage-affected compañerxs and at the political-economic level in relation to the restructuring of the Spanish financial system. Here I reflect on how the findings illustrated several fundamental shifts in the biopolitical dimensions of mortgages during the housing crisis and how they functioned to regulate and discipline the population, more deeply entrenching financialized housing-life relations.

Upon being unable to pay their mortgage, the experiences of mortgage-affected compañerxs suggest that the options offered by the bank—to refinance, sign a grace period, pay what you can, or contract another loan to pay mortgage installments—were the principal attempts to regulate the homeostasis mortgages had provided, that is, to maintain the current political-economic system and "state of life" (Foucault 2003, 246) based in financial speculation with indebtedness and financialized housing-life. This appeared to be particularly true at the start of the crisis when, on the one hand, the crisis was broadly depicted as something temporary, while on the other hand banks "hid reality," as retired banker Manel explained, to make their balance sheets look better. Critical in sustaining this dynamic was the deep-seated subjective role of debt and (mortgaged) homeownership, as expressed, for example, by Isa when she stated, "I did not want to stop paying, it's difficult for you to accept what is happening." The deeply instilled nature of this indebted subjectivity underlines the critical role it plays in enabling capitalism to bridge the past and present with the future (Lazzarato 2012), to ensure the stability and continuity of capital circulation. This indebted subjectivity occurs through both racialized and classed relations.

Furthermore, the majority of compañerxs I interviewed, similar to countless numbers who came to the PAH, agreed to refinancing agreements despite extensive unemployment, increasing precarity, and plummeting housing prices. The latter reinforced existing sociospatial urban inequality: the fall in housing prices in the peripheries of Barcelona and Sabadell, where most low-income immigrant and Spanish mortgage-affected people purchased during the peak of the housing boom, was even more pronounced than average housing price decreases in the rest of Catalonia and Spain. These are sites already characterized by a history of marginality, where working-class Spaniards immigrating from southern Spain during the dictatorship settled, then in the 2000s sold their properties for a pretty penny. The experiences explored in this chapter show how mortgage indebtedness operates as a sociospatial relation at multiple levels, connecting life to global financial flows and reinforcing existing urban sociospatial inequality (Harker and Kirwan 2019; Wyly et al. 2009).

At the same, it became clear that real-estate-related debt and risk, the latter having been commodified through securitization (Bryan, Martin, and Rafferty 2009; Dillon and Lobo-Guerrero 2008), became *too* risky, penetrating the entire Spanish financial system. The EU-backed public rescue and restructuring of the Spanish financial system was conditioned by obligations that illustrate Spain's peripheral role in the European configuration. These conditions included siphoning off "toxic" debt and assets from semi- and fully nationalized financial entities into the SAREB, conducting stress tests, and obliging all Spanish banks to reclassify non-performing debt. Losses were socialized and gains privatized, as systemic losses, and systemic risk, were severed in an attempt to establish a new homeostasis in the context of mass devaluation. Financial tools created or reconfigured by the Spanish state to maximize investor profit attracted international capital and large corporate investors to buy up non-performing "toxic" debt and assets appearing on the market, restarting economic growth.

In considering the conditions and realities behind "toxic" debts and "non-performing" loans, they can be conceptualized from their flip side: "toxic" or "non-performing" people. In other words, a defaulted mortgage loan is held by a defaulted person, who is broadly seen as someone who has failed to "tighten their belt" in order to pay their loan. Pressure and threats from the bank or debt collectors to pay serve to stake creditors' claims on the current and future labor enshrined in mortgage loan contracts. The embodied feeling and lived reality of being a defaulted person manifested in the guilt, fear, shame, serious mental and health impacts, family problems, and suicidal thoughts or attempts triggered in compañerxs upon becoming a "failed" debtor, reflecting the extensive quantitative evidence of the causal links between debt and mental health (Davies, Montgomerie, and Wallin 2015). I propose that these are the lived, bodily experiences of people who have been objectified or proletarianized by the financial system but "fail" as avenues for financial rent extraction. In other words, they are the impacts on the body when life fails to be an accumulation strategy (Harvey 1998). The fact that these impacts have clearly gendered and racialized dimensions reinforces the importance of research such as that by Montgomerie and Tepe-Belfrage (2017) and Harker, Sayyad, and Shebeitah (2019), to name but two studies that unravel and understand the multiple forms of oppression (Charusheela 2013) ever present in debt relations.

But in the case at hand, as the process of proletarianization advanced—as mortgage-affected people were "used up" (Dean 2012) as financial objects of speculation—they were not "discarded" because they owe the debt for life. In other words, rather than forgiving or writing off the debt as unrecoverable, either the bank that originated the mortgage loan or the financial entity that bought it maintained a hold on the mortgage holder and guarantors because the mortgage relation gives them the right to claim a portion of any future value produced. This substantiates Lisa Adkins's (2018) claim that debt not only is a social relation but fully reconstitutes the social.

Furthermore, a hierarchy in the proletarianization of mortgaged life became clear, illustrating the uneven unfolding of debt ecologies (Harker 2020). At the top, upper-middle-income Spanish compañerxs directly had only their lives to account for, since due to their previous properties and income, the bank did not require guarantors on their mortgage loan. Then, low-income Spanish compañerxs often had their parents sign as guarantors, enrolling them and often their long-ago-paid-off property into the debt collection process. At the bottom of the hierarchy were low-income non-European immigrant compañerxs who sometimes had family or friends—either mortgaged or living as renters—who could act as co-borrowers or guarantors, or acquaintances introduced to them by real estate agencies or financial entities whose mortgage loans they also signed in return. These people also became objects to be proletarianized if the main mortgage signatory was "non-performing." This was clearly expressed by Ecuadorian compañera María: "I have always asked the bank to forgive my debt. They have told me that they won't do it because even if I were insolvent and have nothing, the debt was for a lifetime. They have six people they can charge, because there were four guarantors and two owners." While all compañerxs were proletarianized both despite and through racialized and classed relations, the findings here underline how the life of most low- to medium-income signatories alone was not enough. These signatories needed to add other lives on top of their own—the present and future goods of guarantors or co-borrowers—to guarantee the security of the system. This finding underlines how classed and racialized realities operate in order to protect "valued" lives (Bhattacharyya 2018; Mitchell 2010). In sum, some (low-income and non-European non-performing) life is worth sacrificing—

or *making* foreign and shutting out, as Goldstein (2014) underlines in analyzing the etymological source of the word "foreclose"—to ensure the continued securitization of valued, performing life and debt.

The process of proletarianization that unfolds as banks or investment funds attempt to recover "non-performing" rent extraction avenues—be it through refinancing mortgage loans or selling mortgage debt—underlines an experience enunciated by compañerxs and in countless assemblies: how the bank treats people like they are numbers. Narratives of foreclosed households in the United States and England also employ this same language (Fields, Libman, and Saegert 2010; Nettleton and Burrows 2000). The following statements exemplify being proletarianized by mortgage debt, being reduced to a number in the system to advance financial speculation: "The bank is a moneymaking machine," said Nuria in a collective advising assembly, "we are numbers." Or as a young Spanish couple who have defaulted on their loan and whose parents guaranteed their refinanced €220,000 mortgage loan stated in an assembly, "You are a number, a product, the bank really couldn't care less." Julián articulated in an interview, "They [the bank] have no consideration for society, they're after what they're after: money, money. The banker doesn't talk to you about anything else but numbers. That is, seeing how they can ... benefit. How they can get a slice for the bank." Finally, Joan underlined how when people's mortgages were securitized their lives were essentially turned into numbers, sold to financial entities to speculate with. Once a family is unable to pay, Joan said, the entity in effect "manages the portfolio classified as 'junk.' So what are we? Rubbish. Scum." Life is devalued to the status of junk bonds.

This chapter made clear how instruments like the SAREB and SOCIMIs that have emerged through financial sector restructuring are examples of tools the state creates to enable new markets and counteract the illiquidity of real estate assets (Byrne 2015). The legislative and policy changes accompanying these instruments, as Gotham (2006, 268) explains, "create new political and economic conditions that allow powerful class segments to tap into new sources of capital available for market transformation and market building." These tools echo financial innovations in securitization—particularly residential mortgage-backed securities—developed by the United States' bad bank called the Resolution Trust Corporation (RTC), created after the U.S. Savings and Loan Crisis in the late 1980s. It was from this context that securitization emerged and shaped a multibillion-euro market to maximize the disposal of non-performing loans by integrating them into larger capital markets (Ashton 2009), a process being extended through the rental housing market via rental backed securities (Fields, Kohli, and Schafran 2016). As tools like SOCIMIs act

to deeply intertwine local real estate with global flows of capital, in attempts
to overcome crisis, they may lead to another—albeit different—financialized
housing-life cycle and ultimately another crisis as fictitious capital is attracted
en masse to secondary markets and sparks another speculative bubble.

Conclusions

This chapter considered the continuities, changing strategies, and consequences of maintaining mortgaged lives during the post-2008 crisis in the
Barcelona metropolitan region. From the celebratory declarations about the
success of the Spanish economic model and its financial system in 2008, Socialist and subsequent Conservative governments adopted EU conditions to
spend at least €63 billion to rescue and restructure the financial system. I connected this political-economic handling of the 2008 crisis to the experiences
of mortgage-affected compañerxs to consider why people stopped paying their
mortgage loans, the responses from financial entities, and the impacts people
experienced in their lives and bodies. Some important broader theoretical reflections emerge from the way in which the set of regulatory and disciplinary
techniques underlying mortgages were reconfigured in the post-2008 crisis
period, as financial entities—and subsequently distressed debt investors and
other vulture funds—attempted to maintain rent extraction from mortgage-
affected (under/unemployed) households and in turn generated profound impacts on people's everyday life.

First, maintaining or disposing of mortgaged lives equates to, above all,
maintaining the circulation of capital and/or the security of the system. The
findings in this chapter illustrate how the actors changed—from forty-five savings banks and eight banks during the boom to fifteen banks and a myriad
of international vulture funds during the crisis—but the goal to appropriate
as much rent as possible from mortgaged households, albeit through different strategies, remained the same. The nature of mortgages as a technology
of power shifted in this period to ensure the circulation of capital, as the disciplinary mechanisms became more pronounced through pressuring and/
or threatening mortgaged households to pay their debt. "Circulation," as Michael Dillon and Luis Lobo-Guerrero (2008, 268) remark, "is concerned with
flows, but flows have to be monitored and regulated." When it became clear
that mortgaged households had defaulted, that loans were non-performing—
that people, and their co-borrowers and/or (crossed) guarantors, were non-
performing and that the costs for the bank outweighed the benefits—the debt
was sold for a fraction of its value to its highest bidder. Mortgage-indebted

lives became further entrenched in the operation of financial markets and transactions. The extensive reclassification of debt that in part drove this process can be seen as a sacrifice of certain lives—with an underlying differential racialized, gendered, and classed valuation of life—to ensure the security of the collective whole, to ensure that the system continues to exist for the "correct" or "performing" type of circulatory capital flows and thus life.

Second, the deeply entangled nature of mortgage-related regulatory and disciplinary mechanisms became clear when looking at the impacts of not paying one's mortgage on life and the body, impacts that are both gendered and racialized. Foucault (1991, 26) states that "a body becomes a useful force only if it is both a productive body and a subjected body." Facing widespread unemployment, in many cases a body is no longer productive but remains subjected, enforced particularly at the *subjective* level, reflected in people feeling guilty and ashamed for not being able to pay, facing significant family problems and a range of physical and mental health impacts. These are individual and individualizing feelings, both inculcated and self-imposed, as a person has failed in the eyes of society, failed to be an entrepreneur of the self. The gendered dimension comes into play as women often bear the brunt of social reproduction tasks in the domestic sphere while maintaining very low-wage employment that enables the family to feed themselves and provide basic necessities, while they at the same time can face threats to their family's well-being if they do not pay immediately. The overt disciplining techniques of the bank or investment funds—pressure and/or threats to pay—combine with a deeply ingrained self-discipline. Critically, the entity claiming the debt uses this to their advantage, as was pointed out by Ángela: "They play with being in a hurry, they play with your fear, that you don't know what to do, and that you don't have time to consult anyone." This points to the powerful nature of debt relations in terms of the almost universally instilled morality it draws upon, integrating feelings of care for family and home.

Finally, in this context, the role of mortgages as a "secondary form of exploitation" (Harvey 1982, 285) becomes starkly visible, as housing prices plummeted and unemployment rose to around a quarter of Spain's residents and over 40 percent for non-European immigrants. Furthermore, the system continues thanks to the socialization of losses and the privatization of profits, as seen through the rescue and reconfiguration of the Spanish financial system. The debt economy thus certainly appears to be a new historical wave of proletarianization (Balibar 2013). The outcome is that former mortgage holders are becoming a homeless proletariat, evicted yet still indebted for life to their creditors due to Spain's Mortgage Law that claims their current and future goods, or an indebted proletariat who is nevertheless "in material and housing-class terms, barely distinguishable from renters ... simply paying rent to the new landlord" (Wyly et al. 2009, 338). Along these lines, a more provocative statement comes from one of the cofounders and the former spokesperson of the PAH, Ada Colau, who characterized being a mortgage debtor as "the perfect form or extortion and slavery" (Muriel 2012, n.p.).

However—fortunately—this system is not so clear-cut and is being questioned, challenged, and disrupted. The next chapter turns to look at how these dynamics have been ruptured through the stories of compañerxs and their actions and experiences with the PAH in the Barcelona metropolitan region.

CHAPTER 4

Political Subject Formation in Struggles to Demortgage Life

Shifting from a focus on the historic and contemporary underpinnings of financialized housing-life and mortgaged biopolitics in the Barcelona metropolitan region, this chapter considers what happens when people start to collectively break debt relations, both materially and subjectively. In other words, it considers the emergence of the political subject as life begins to be "performing" again—albeit in a new and disruptive way. Specifically, I look at how the status quo that maintained differentially valued states of life rooted in the financialization of housing and of life itself is ruptured when people refuse to do what is "expected" of them, as they accept their inability to pay and see the housing boom as a scam, fight for debt forgiveness, and undertake collective action to enact housing equality.

When people stop paying their mortgage, they are seen as defaulters and "bad" debtors: their non-performing loan equates them to being non-performing people. Mortgage defaulters are an "outcast" in the eyes of the dominant system, "denied an identity in a given order of policy" (Rancière 1992, 61). Here I explore how these "outcasts" both reclaim and reconstitute their position through engaging in housing rights struggles in the Barcelona metropolitan region. In considering Spain's renowned and most extensive housing rights platform, the Platform for Mortgage-Affected People (PAH), I use the lens of political subjectivation to understand how mortgage-affected people's positions and identities are reconstituted through assemblies and action. Political subjectivation is explored here as "the enactment of equality—or the handling of a wrong—by people who are together to the extent that they are between" (61). By "between," Rancière refers to being between existing, named statuses or identities. As mortgage defaulters and debtors, PAH members begin challenging their proletarianization by finance capital through engaging in collective struggles for their and others' liberation from mortgage debt and for housing equality. The processes they engage in reconfigure the field of experience (Rancière 1999, 40) and disrupt the expert-led, hierarchical, and patriarchal system that tells one to do certain things and act a certain way in given spaces, what Rancière (2001, Thesis 7) calls the "partition of the sensible." At the same time, the racialized dynamics underlying the mortgage relation, and ever present in broader society, are not openly addressed by the movement, meaning that some more fundamental, structural elements of the partition of the sensible remain explicitly unquestioned.

To develop these arguments, I unpack the PAH's main activities during the movement's peak in 2013–14, specifically weekly collective advising assemblies and regular direct actions: blocking evictions, disrupting/occupying banks, and occupying/recuperating empty bank-owned housing. These co-constitutive activities turn mortgaged financialized subjects into political subjects as they disrupt the regulatory and disciplinary power of mortgages, fundamentally challenging their underlying dynamics of financial rent appropriation. In other words, people "refuse to be the population" (Foucault 2007, 66) that was to be regulated and disciplined by the relations and norms underlying their mortgage and enact housing equality themselves. This process, however, is not uniform and has challenges and tensions. A nonlinear sequence of liberating life from debt emerges in this chapter, and I thus argue that political subjectivation is not just an event or act of disruption, as proposed by political theorists like Jacques Rancière and Alain Badiou, but an accumulation of collectively learned practices. I also reflect on the contradictions at the heart of Ananya Roy's (2017) powerful notion of dis/possessive collectivism, specifically the relationship of poor people's movements, of which the PAH is one, to the apparatus of property.

The PAH: Origins, Emergence, and Demands

The PAH is an open, non-party-affiliated movement that emerged in Barcelona in 2009 amid growing and unanswered mortgage default, foreclosures, and evictions. It both denounces the reality that has made hundreds of thousands of families unable to pay their mortgage, facing foreclosure and eviction, and seeks to ensure the right to fair and affordable housing for all. Similar to both the Chicago (United States) and Western Cape (South Africa) Anti-Eviction Movements (Miraftab and Wills 2005; Roy 2017; Salo 2015), the PAH employs the language of the human right to housing with the spirit of enforcing this right themselves.

Several of the antiglobalization activists who founded the PAH in Barcelona participated previously in a group named Miles de Viviendas (Thousands of Houses) that sought to popularize squatting around 2003, albeit unsuccessfully and amid differences and conflicts within the squatting movement (Mir Garcia et al. 2013). The PAH's direct precursor, V de Vivienda (H for Housing), grew out of Miles de Viviendas as a militant sector of the Spanish-wide Platform for Dignified Housing, demanding the fulfilment of Article 47 of the constitutional right to housing. In 2006, it mobilized thousands of people in Barcelona and Madrid in protest under the emblematic slogan "you'll never own a house in your whole fucking life" (Prieto Serrano 2014). Yet despite sit-ins, protests, and parodies over the following years, Susana Aguilar Fernández and Alberto Fernández Gibaja (2010) underline how V de Vivienda's communication, framing, and tactics largely mobilized youth and students, not reaching immigrants and others facing difficulties accessing housing during the boom. It was furthermore, as two of the PAH's cofounders Ada Colau and Adrià Alemany (2012) note, a minority movement pushing against a largely homeownership-based society who, during the boom, saw its patrimony (housing) steadily increase in value.

But the burst of the real estate bubble changed these conditions. It also obliged V de Vivienda to reinvent itself, on the one hand to respond to the wave of mortgage evictions and on the other hand to point out the failure of the model that created it (Colau and Alemany 2012). Colau and Alemany and activists worked with a handful of others to organize the first PAH assembly in Barcelona in February 2009, attracting forty people—largely non-European immigrants—facing mortgage foreclosure via posters plastered on telephone boxes and in government social service centers (Blanchar 2014). Yet PAH Barcelona's founders noted that it was hard going for the first while because in workshops or sessions led by lawyers, people were almost elbowing each other to be able to talk about their own problem. What finally worked was "collective and open assemblies to generate a space of confidence, where people lose their fear, empower themselves and verify that alone they can't but together they can" (Domingo, as quoted in Blanchar 2014, n.p.). Rather than providing expert advice, the PAH was thus built upon the principle of collective learning and knowledge generation through uniting activists and mortgage-affected people as equals. This is illustrated in a phrase from the basic guide to the PAH: "We are all affected by mortgages: the housing policies of the real estate boom, the mortgage scam and bad banking praxis are at the origin of the crisis that today condemns millions of people to unemployment and precariousness" (PAH 2014, 6).

Feminist-inspired practices of care (Santos 2020) also undergirded the development of the movement. Collective advising assemblies soon started to take place weekly, alongside a coordination assembly and mutual aid (*ayuda mutua*) meetings, the latter serving to discuss feelings of loss, fear, or shame in a more intimate and unstructured format. Different types of collective spaces were thus created where compañerxs could learn practical information but also share their experiences, feelings, and emotions with different degrees of intimacy, a sharp contrast to the individualizing and mathematical logic of mortgage relations and the top-down imposed "solutions" they had received to date. The PAH's feminist-inspired practices are also reflected in the strong presence of women in the movement, in part because the dominant patriarchal culture means that many men are not willing or able to ask for "help" and are furthermore uncomfortable talking about their experiences of indebtedness, as this suggests their failure as the family provider. This also means that women are often in more complex situations in terms of maintaining low-paid employment (if employed), handling reproductive and caring responsibilities, *and* leading the fight for their household's debt forgiveness. The predominance of women in the movement is sometimes reflected in language, where in some PAHs people always speak the plural feminine (*compañeras*) instead of the standard generic masculine (*compañeros*), the latter used in the Spanish language as default when referring to a group of people.

Street-based actions also began in the face of silence from the government and banks. Meanwhile the PAH articulated its three nonnegotiable demands: first, retroactively changing Spanish Mortgage Law so that during foreclosure proceedings the bank cancels all outstanding mortgage debt in exchange for the house (dación en pago); second, halting all evictions of principal and sole homes; and third, transforming empty houses held by financial institutions into social housing. The last demand seeks to expand an alternative modality of property (Blomley 2004) in the form of social rental housing managed by the public sector. At present, such housing makes up a small fraction of the 2 percent that constitutes Spain's social housing stock.

The PAH's local assembly model spread as increasing numbers of families across Catalonia and Spain faced foreclosure, eviction, and debt for life. Plummeting housing prices and the inability to declare personal bankruptcy meant that once the bank auctioned their homes, former homeowners owed significant debt that also included interest and legal costs. A smattering of PAHs existed in the Barcelona metropolitan region until 2011, but they mushroomed across Spain after the 15M Indignado plaza occupations in May 2011, the latter inspired by the Arab Spring and a precursor to Occupy Wall Street. Coordination among PAHs occurs through monthly assemblies of the 74 PAH groups in

Catalonia and a quarterly meeting of over 220 PAH nodes across Spain, with email lists and other online tools used by those on Catalan and Spanish PAH coordination commissions to communicate and organize between assemblies.

It is important to underline that each PAH grows out of a specific context and dynamic. The conditions, experience, and capacity in each place, alongside the specific needs that emerge within each PAH, affect its way of organizing and involvement in campaigns and actions. In some places mortgage-affected people themselves establish their local PAH, while others grow out of already existing movements. For example, the PAHC in Sabadell—where the "C" stands for crisis—was born in March 2011 out of an anticapitalist network that brought together feminist, squatter, and socialist pro–Catalan independence collectives in the city. As articulated by a former spokesperson, the PAHC Sabadell saw powerful political possibilities in the PAH's process of organizing for legislative reforms. In particular, he underlined how if institutional reforms were not made, conditions could be generated in the future to exert the use value of housing over its exchange value through disobedience, generating a squatting movement of a new order. PAHC Sabadell's structure was consciously integrated into a unitary assembly—with movement coordination and collective advising on the same afternoon rather than on two different days like in Barcelona—to ensure mortgage-affected people engaged in a broader politicizing process.

While they are among two of the strongest PAHs in Catalonia and Spain, Sabadell and Barcelona illustrate the heterogeneity of the movement arising from specific material conditions, urban configurations, and organizing strategies. For example, during my engagement with the PAH as a researcher in 2013–14, PAH Barcelona advised only mortgage-related cases, while PAHC Sabadell advised all housing-related problems: mortgage, rental, squatting, and others. Indeed, PAHC Sabadell shifted from three-quarters of its cases being mortgage related in 2013 to less than half in 2014 (PAHC Sabadell 2014). This trend has since grown more pronounced. PAHC Sabadell is also more racially diverse, with proportionally more Moroccan and other African mortgage- and housing-affected members than Barcelona, while in Barcelona most non-Spanish members are Latin American. These two differences—around the type of housing problems addressed and racial makeup of compañerxs— in part reflect the metropolitan dynamics in which these two PAHs are situated and in part reflect their organizing strategies. Finally, these two platforms have political positions that are often in tension: Sabadell is openly anticapitalist, with a clear working-class and antifascist discourse, while Barcelona does not explicitly position itself on these issues, although arguably it has a more feminist approach reflected, for example, in language use (the feminine plural *compañeras* is regularly used in assemblies rather than the standard masculine *compañeros*). The tension reflects the long-standing relationships of several founders of both platforms, who have interacted—and sometimes collided ideologically—in broader squatting and antiglobalization activism in the 1990s, as well as Barcelona's dominant role in regional and national coordination networks.

Local specificities and broader tensions aside, all PAHs are united in their struggle for the universal right to dignified and affordable housing, not conditioned on extreme indebtedness, the precariousness of rental markets, or the extreme difficulty in accessing social housing. Their overarching strategy is to pressure the administration to implement the PAH's three demands, and in the face of insufficient structural and practical responses at all levels, to collectively enact them through various actions. In this light, they echo the dual-pronged legal action approach followed by the Chicago Anti-Eviction Campaign, with a clear view on both the importance and limitations of engaging with broader national and international (human) rights frameworks (Roy 2017). The PAH's most emblematic national legal campaign successfully collected 1.6 million signatures to support a Popular Legislative Initiative (ILP) presented to the Spanish Congress in April 2013, seeking to embed the PAH's three demands in the Spanish legal framework. Albeit unsuccessful, this process was repeated in early 2015 with the Catalan government, also including measures to address energy poverty. The Catalan ILP was unanimously approved in July 2015, although part of it was later repealed by the Spanish constitutional courts on the (ironic) grounds that it created territorial inequality. The PAH also petitions and pressures local government. Simultaneous to institutionally directed legal actions, periodic actions like street mobilizations, denouncing politicians at public acts (*escraches*), real estate fair occupations, and city hall occupations take place alongside more regular actions. The three most common direct actions during the height of the PAH's activities, described in detail later in this chapter, include blocking evictions, occupying empty bank-owned housing, and disrupting/occupying banks to demand mortgage debt forgiveness.

Despite widespread popular support, the PAH has been demonized in particular by the Conservative Popular Party (PP), a party that held a majority in national government from 2011 to 2015. Accusing the PAH's former spokesperson of supporting pro-Basque terrorist groups (ETA) and of taking a "radical political strategy" (*ABC.es*, 2013), the president of the PP in Madrid denounced people who participate in escraches as "imitators of the thuggery of ETA followers in the Basque country," as "violent stalkers" who use "the tactics of the worst totalitarianisms of the past century" (*Público.es* 2013). This was echoed among others by the PP's secretary-general, calling escraches "pure Nazism" (Manetto 2013). Such statements illustrate how, in the eyes and discourse of the PP, the PAH exemplifies the Rancièrian part-of-those-who-have-no-part, who do not "belong" in the existing order.

Collective Advising Assemblies: Setting the Stage for the Political Act

People with mortgage problems, in different stages of default, foreclosure, or eviction, usually first come into contact with the PAH through a weekly collective advising assembly. In these spaces, PAH members outline the three phases of foreclosure and the steps to take in each phase (Box 4.1), followed by a process of collective advising where mortgage-affected people explain their situation and receive support and guidance from the assembly. In most cases, like the compañerxs I interviewed, over three-quarters of the anywhere between 80 and 160 people who attended assemblies each week found themselves in one of the three phases of housing dispossession: unable to pay their mortgage (either having defaulted or on the brink of doing so), in foreclosure, or with an immanent eviction. Especially since 2014, increasing numbers of people come to the PAH with rental or squatting evictions, the latter largely being those left with no other option but to squat after rental or mortgage evictions. The remaining attendees, less than a quarter of the total, are non-mortgage-affected activists and mortgage-affected people who have solved their case and continue supporting others in the PAH.

At welcome assemblies the PAH is briefly introduced and its collective process, where people advise and help each other, is underlined and enacted. The purposeful spatial arrangement of assemblies in Barcelona and Sabadell emphasizes this, where the circular or ovular shape of the seating with an empty center reinforces the notion of an interchange among equals. There is no individual advising, PAH members often explain, because the PAH is not based in a handout mentality (*no es asistencialista*). In other words, people are seen not as clients, customers, or objects but as active agents who can solve their own case, through struggle that is supported and strengthened by the collective. This is reflected in common phrases such as "the only way to win is to fight" and "you have to insist, insist, be a pest [to the bank]," and it is constantly reinforced in assemblies that there is no one in the PAH who has fought and not achieved what they sought. People who share what the PAH terms "little big victories" each week—obtaining mortgage debt forgiveness, a social rent

BOX 4.1. The PAH's Advice during the Mortgage Foreclosure Process

PHASE 1: PROBLEMS BEGIN AND YOU CAN'T PAY YOUR MORTGAGE

When to stop paying your mortgage? You decide. But the bank will not start negotiating until you stop paying. Paying only a part of the monthly instalment is like throwing money away. Most important is first to buy food and cover your family's basic needs.

Before starting to negotiate with the bank, the PAH can advise you but you need to know what you want: *dación en pago* (debt forgiveness in exchange for the home), partial debt removal (*quita*), social rent (rent set at maximum 30 percent household income).
Check to see if you meet the government's Good Practices Code requirements, although a very small proportion of people fulfil the criteria.

From the PAH's "useful documents" web page, download and adapt the PAH's form requesting *dación en pago* (and social rent if desired). Print two copies and hand one in at your bank; both should be signed and stamped. Keep one copy for yourself.

- Insist, insist, and insist. The bank will often not accept the form. If they refuse to sign it, ask for the Generalitat's (Catalan government) complaint form. If they don't give you the form, call the police. It is your right to be given a complaint form.
- If problems persist, request an accompaniment at a pah assembly.
- Once the form is accepted, be patient. The bank can take weeks or months to respond. Go to the bank weekly and ask how your case is progressing.

Open a bank account in a new entity, pay your bills and spend from there. Although they are not allowed to do so the bank where you contracted your mortgage sometimes automatically withdraws whatever you have in your account to pay your mortgage instalment.

Exhaust all institutional paths "to show public authorities the scale of the problem":

- Go to Social Services; ask for a report that verifies your socioeconomic situation
- Go to Ofideute (Generalitat's office that mediates between mortgage-affected people and banks)

If you stop paying your mortgage, try to keep paying your building's resident association fee and water and electricity bills. If you can't pay the association fee, offer to clean the stairs in the building. It helps make the case for your *dación en pago*, but also to keep good relations with the neighbors, as you want them to support you if you face eviction. If you can't pay your water and electricity bills, the Alliance Against Energy Poverty (an activist platform fighting for the right to basic energy supplies for all) can support you.

PHASE 2: FORECLOSURE DOCUMENTS ARRIVE

Before foreclosure begins, you will receive an official fax stating the total quantity of debt you owe and a time period for its payment. When you do not pay, the foreclosure order is sent.

Upon receiving the foreclosure order, you have 10 days to request a court-appointed lawyer. This is important as it delays the foreclosure process. You can also denounce abusive mortgage clauses at this point.

The court sets an auction date for the apartment and provides a minimum twenty-day notice. When it is auctioned, the bank keeps the apartment for 70 percent of its appraised auction value (a price set in the mortgage contract).

Keep negotiating and pressuring the bank for *dación en pago*. "The apartment is your best weapon. Stay there." If you have not already gone, go to Social Services and Ofideute.

PHASE 3: RECEIVING AN EVICTION ORDER

Once auctioned, the apartment is the bank's property and they can claim the remaining debt: the difference between the bid price at the auction and the total debt, plus default interest fees and judicial costs.

The auction does not mean an immediate eviction or repossessed salary; both are notified in advance.

Once you receive an eviction order:

- Request a court-appointed lawyer
- Present an appeal using Article 704 from the Civil Indictment Law, which can delay the eviction a month or more, depending on the ruling of the judge
- Demand debt forgiveness from the bank (insist!)

Social Services can help get a temporary suspension of the eviction.

Go to the Housing Office to apply for a social emergency apartment.

If we can't stop the eviction, we can participate in the Obra Social campaign, recuperating bank-owned housing for people who have exhausted all housing possibilities. No one in the PAH ends up on the street.

SOURCE: Field notes, 2014.

---

contract with the bank—stress how they constantly pressured the bank for months, sometimes years, through individual weekly visits, accompaniments with other PAH members, and collective actions when necessary. For example, a person who had fought for one and a half years for debt forgiveness and social rent in the same apartment explained in an assembly, "You have to come each day, to be in the struggle, that's how you can do it." When people who solve their case thank the PAH, others are quick to jump in and say "thanks to the PAH is thanks to them too," directly connecting those struggling into a collectivity. In other words, the PAH is not "other." It is us/we.

In interviews and assemblies, compañerxs explained their attempts to solve their mortgage debt problems through government services or privately contracted lawyers. In terms of the former, all overwhelmingly expressed that the Catalan government's mortgage debt mediation service (Ofideute) and the housing service (Habitatge) do not solve anything. Nonetheless, the PAH encourages people to register themselves with these services to make public authorities aware of the scale of the problem. Payments to lawyers are also commonplace, and I heard accounts of compañerxs paying lawyers up to €3,000 to solve their situation. Legal battles are however virtually impossible to win because the Spanish legal system consecrates the principle of universal patrimonial responsibility through Article 1911 in the Civil Code, which states that "the debtor responds to the fulfilment of obligations with all their goods, present and future" (Ayuso 2011). In practice, this means that, as was explained in one assembly, not even the best law firms can secure mortgage debt forgiveness or stop evictions. Or as stated bluntly in another, "A lawyer will not be able to do anything for you. The law is made for your current and future goods to be appropriated. That's how it is." Instead, the experiences shared by PAH members illustrate that solutions arise through collective struggle, with assemblies playing a key role in initiating a process of political subjectivation. Three key processes occur in these assemblies: mortgage-affected people realizing they are no longer alone; shedding fear, shame, and guilt; and gaining knowledge.

NO LONGER BEING ALONE

After coming to the PAH many compañerxs explained feeling relief, and over half explicitly expressed how they no longer felt like they were alone. They became reenergized and injected with hope. Such experiences are exemplified by Amira, a Moroccan compañera, who noted how "before coming to the PAH I thought my world had fallen apart, that I was the only one who has this problem. However, no, when I went there [to an assembly], well millions of us are affected and we are in the same boat, fighting for the same things, because there is strength in numbers."

Similarly, compañerxs' experiences in the PAH were commonly explained as a process of rebelonging. This occurred, for example, through being able to relate with other people or developing compassion for and solidarity with others whom they encountered in the same, or an even worse, situation. Joan and Pepe express these sentiments: "My house was supposed to be auctioned on 22 October [2013], I'm going to fight. But how can I fight, if I barely knew what was going on? I came to the welcome assembly and it was like a collision. I arrive and see something I will remember my entire life, a widower who said, 'We used to earn €4,500 a month in my house,' and I thought, 'Me too!' She became a widow and here she is today. €4,500! And here I thought that, sure, there were many South Americans, not that I came dressed up, but I was expecting to find very humble and modest people. And someone says they earned €4,500." As Pepe explained, "I saw many cases, many people really in need, but there were so many people that were truly worse off than me. I thought my situation was a world of its own, then I realized that it was but not so much in comparison to other people. Yes, they [the bank] had committed atrocities with me, but with others they committed atrocities and then some."

Sebas noted that the great success of the welcome assembly is "calming people, giving them a bit of affection, making them see that they are not alone—since the law doesn't defend them, the police don't protect them." It is common to hear the phrase "you are no longer alone" (*ya no estás solo/a*) in assemblies, and I witnessed remarkable gestures of generosity and solidarity on countless occasions.

SHEDDING FEAR, SHAME, AND GUILT

In assemblies, emphasis is placed on getting rid of fear, shame, and guilt, through sayings like "they should be the ones who are ashamed" or "there is no reason to feel ignorant, we've been scammed." People often underline the need to turn the relationship with the bank on its head, where instead of feeling tormented by the bank the compañerxs need to become the bank's worst nightmare. Furthermore, lies that mortgage-affected people are told by the bank, especially to racialized compañerxs, are dispelled in assemblies. For example, children won't be taken away if they stop paying their mortgage, and the government will renew tax identification numbers for immigrants even if they default.

It is not uncommon for new arrivals at the PAH to be terribly upset, having trouble verbally articulating their situation when it is their turn to speak. When this occurs, calls like "Chin up!" and "You are no longer alone!" ring out in the assembly, and in solidarity people share and socialize their lived experiences. This was exemplified in one situation where a newcomer, so choked up she held the microphone and stared at the floor in an attempt to gather strength to continue to tell her story, was comforted by different people as they explained, "I couldn't sleep, I couldn't eat, we've all been down that path" or "I haven't paid in one year and I am as happy as ever!" I heard relative newcomers to the PAH explain how they experience "fear and desperation when you don't come to the PAH, but that coming to listen and talk changes it." Carlos, an Ecuadorian compañero, underlined this: "I've seen people arrive [at assemblies] on the edge of the precipice, with no will to live. They think their life is over, that they have failed, why have they had to go through this. You feel for them, it really moves you, you go and tell the person: 'Don't worry, hey listen you are not alone, this is how it works. Be calm, we're going to help you with this.' That person's attitude, well they realize that they aren't alone, that there are people who value them and that they don't have to feel guilty.... You do it for the future, for the collective. It's worth it."

This process of losing fear, shame, and guilt through engaging in assemblies was very clear in the narratives of virtually all compañerxs I interviewed.

Several underlined how in a very short period of time people who were barely able to speak upon arrival, ridden with fear and guilt, gain amazing strength and become rejuvenated, even appearing to grow taller. I have also seen this astonishing transformation take place, which can be considered as the beginning of liberation from the self-imposed disciplinary techniques and indebted subjectivity racking minds and bodies when they are deemed to be "nonperforming." As Raquel, a Spanish compañera in her late forties, exclaimed, "If you would have told me a year and a half ago that I would be talking, letting loose and making a fuss in front of two hundred people [in an assembly], I would've said, you, you're being mental! I had never been in an assembly, I had never belonged to any collective. . . . You grow, the word that we have on our lips: empowerment of people, the way you see them grow day-by-day." Similar to Raquel, all but a few compañerxs I interviewed had never been involved in any type of social or political movement before joining the PAH.

MORE KNOWLEDGE, LESS FEAR

The learning that takes place during collective advising assemblies is fundamental, as virtually all mortgage-affected compañerxs felt uninformed and uncertain about how to solve their situation. As Patricia, an Ecuadorian compañera, put it, information gives her "more grounds to argue. . . . I didn't have information about the foreclosure process, I had no idea what it was about. The PAH gives you the weapons and you try to use them." Compañerxs begin to learn from others in the same situation and understand that constant struggle is needed to solve their case. For example, Isa noted that "people cheer you up, you see how they talk, what the banker will tell you, what he will say and how you need to respond, and that you need to insistently fight every week, every week." On the flip side, several compañerxs underlined that the bank was able to make them weak because they lacked information. Daniel underlined how "information is power, if you don't have information they can finish you off, you are sunk." As was stated in one assembly, "The more knowledge you have, the less you fear." The fundamental role that knowledge plays is similarly critical in the tactics of postponement to slow down and find loopholes in the legal process in other housing movements like the U.S.-based Chicago Anti-Eviction Campaign and the South African Western Cape Anti-Eviction Campaign (Miraftab and Wills 2005; Roy 2017; Salo 2015).

Mortgage refinancing was a question that commonly emerged in the PAH's welcome assemblies. As explored in the previous chapter, three-quarters of compañerxs I interviewed were offered refinancing agreements from their bank upon being unable to pay their mortgage. Three-quarters of those offered signed them. Refinancing is often framed by the PAH as "feast today, famine tomorrow" (*pan para hoy, hambre para mañana*), underlining that "everything the bank offers you is to benefit them today, tomorrow and in the long term." When newcomers ask about refinancing, PAH members share their experiences of becoming even more indebted with no hope of repayment, expressed through phrases like "I didn't want to stop paying, I refinanced and spent all my savings. Now I have nothing"; "Signing a refinancing agreement is like putting a smaller noose around your neck. Refinancing is a mistake"; and "Signing only extends the agony. You won't take your apartment to heaven."

Giving and sharing information in this way goes against "expert" knowledge, in both its content (doing what you are told by "experts" not to do) and its delivery (collective, caring, and assembly-based). While the PAH's accumulated knowledge points to individual empowerment through collective learning and struggle as the most effective way to solve housing problems, it sharply contrasts with the mind-set of some people who seek advice at the PAH. For example, in one assembly Antonio, a fifty-year-old Spaniard, stood up and explained that he had been unable to pay his mortgage for the past two months after a six-month spell of unemployment. The bank told him he signed the mortgage contract—"Such is life," they said—and Antonio expressed frustration that the bank was not helping him. Upon receiving advice from half a dozen PAH members on how he could proceed—for example, knowing what he wants or how the situation changes with collective struggle—Antonio finally declared, "I've always paid what I owe." His response was met with a collective groan from the assembly. While not frequent, this situation is important in pointing to the uneven nature of and challenges behind shedding indebted subjectivities. In other words, people move through different processes in accepting, reclaiming, and vindicating their inability to pay their mortgage—while some never do. The PAH works to normalize not paying one's mortgage debt, just as it works, for example, to normalize squatting in empty bank-owned apartments for people with no housing options. But taking on, identifying, accepting, and living these ideas is by no means a smooth, easy, or even process.

Assemblies as Places to Disidentify with the Existing Order

Collective advising assemblies set the stage for political acts on the streets, where people unable to pay their mortgage begin to disidentify with their position in the dominant configuration. Upon arriving at the PAH, people had been labeled a "failed" mortgaged homeowner, a non-performing person, someone who should be guilty and ashamed of being a defaulted debtor. Existing as a widespread social norm, this position is bolstered by their experiences with the bank, government services, and lawyers. It is also reinforced by statements such as the one uttered by the PP's secretary-general: "Voters for the PP adjust their belts but they pay their mortgage" (Izquierdo and del Riego 2013), and more subtly through assertions like that from the president of the Spanish Banking Association, stating that evictions are a consequence of the economic crisis, "not Spain's credit model or Mortgage Law which seek to give mortgages so that the population can buy housing" (Europa Press 2012). The logic behind these two statements is that "good people" pay their mortgage no matter what and that the current problem is conjectural, not systemic. In other words, once the crisis is over and things return to "normal" everyone will be fine, with mortgaged homeownership continuing to reign as the appropriate mode of housing provision.

Assemblies trigger a process of disidentification with this logic, often beginning when mortgage-affected people arrive at the PAH. Disidentification is by no means a smooth, even, or easy process since, as we saw in chapter 3, people experience tremendous emotional, health-related, and family problems upon foreclosure and eviction. But when individuals finally accept their inability to pay their mortgage and begin to struggle with the PAH, a process of subjectivation is initiated. Refusing to be the population (Foucault 2007), mortgage-affected people begin to question their position as indebted people and the credit-debtor relationship it is embedded in, that is, "the specific relations of power that entail specific forms of production and control of subjectivity—a particular form of homo economicus" (Lazzarato 2012, 30). They also start to question other dominant societal and governmental housing-related relations. These relations are embedded in the struggle over the supposed right to dignified and affordable housing for all, not contingent on extreme indebtedness, the precariousness of rental markets, or the extreme difficulty in accessing social housing.

Assemblies are spaces where mortgage-affected people, rather than seeing their situation as an individual, solitary problem and personal failure, begin to see the housing boom and bust as a collective scam and to understand that they were an object in this process, a number in the system. That is, they begin to understand how they have been proletarianized (Dean 2012) by the financial system. Indeed, virtually all compañerxs explicitly expressed the classed—although not racialized—dimension of the proletarianization process in different ways. The most common remarks signaled that there are people who are responsible for the current state of affairs, who actively created it. Most mark a division between an "us" and a "them," creating a situation where "we" suffer and "they" benefit. This is exemplified through the words of Pepe, Sara, and Daniel:

> The bank gave you the credit. Considering that the bank keeps your apartment why do you have to pay more when they have been the ones speculating? They were the real speculators. Why? Because the guy sold you the apartment probably for €60,000, then two months later €90,000, then a few months after that €100,000, €150,000. And you said, what a boom! And wow, this works. Things are going well in Spain, people are working, people are earning money, going on holiday, buying cars. But then you realized, oh, this speculation I think the banks did it. . . . They are the ones running the country. . . . And all this made me think that yes there are rich people, and when the rich people saw that the poor workers starting to lift up their head, wanting to get ahead, they were the ones who said no. No way. Rich people and poor people. No people in the middle or anything. (Pepe)

> We are distressed while people are going to the Bahamas or to countries where they've taken money, leaving people in poverty. . . . Who increased [housing prices]? It was the politicians, not us. The price of housing went up as if it were a grain of caviar, the best in the world. What us poor people ask for is a house, we are not asking for anything, just a dignified house where we can keep living, working. We keep being your slaves but at least don't take away our housing, let us breath a bit. We are their slaves and we are waiting for them to toss us something. Like a dog, when you bring it food it is happy. When you have work you are happy because you can pay, you can live, but if you have a debt and you are a defaulter, you can't even buy a secondhand washing machine. (Sara)

> I saw life like any other Spaniard. You have to pay the bank, that's how I saw it. . . . But when you have a serious problem like this you really understand what is behind it. That is, all the people who don't care: they just want your money, you don't matter. If you live in the gutter it makes no difference to them. I knew about being materialistic but it has made me see that it is much worse and that most people have their eyes closed. A lot of people undervalue us, or they say, damn the PAH, out of shame or whatever. They walk by and look at you but say, "Don't look at me." Join us. You are the same but you really don't know it. (Daniel)

Furthermore, three of the four formerly upper-middle-income compañerxs shared experiences that can be interpreted as a process of declassing or recognizing one's (perceived) former class position. This is illustrated by Sebas, who explained, "I consider myself from a class that no longer exists, that has been wiped off the map. Middle. Now it is no longer middle, now we are nothing." Ángela also expressed this as follows: "My father-in-law once said to me: 'What a shame that you have to find yourselves in this situation.' I said, what a shame, no. Thanks to seeing myself in this situation I'm seeing reality for what it is, because otherwise I lived my life earning a good salary and in circumstances where you probably didn't realize that people are having a really tough time. You know what I mean? It's not that it makes me happy, but it has opened my eyes."

Many mortgage-affected people thus begin to see themselves as outcasts in the existing classed order that was made for winners and losers, the rich and the poor. The racialized nature of the status quo order is not explicitly addressed through PAH discourses, discussions, or practices, as these focus on unifying all mortgage-affected people no matter their origin through a shared experience of the housing and mortgage scam. In this process, people slowly start to recognize their position as "the part of those who have no part" (Rancière 1999, 11) or, as Jodi Dean (2012, 70) says, "the people as the rest of us." Yet as they start struggling to enact equality, they adopt a new name, mortgage-affected (*afectado/a por la hipoteca*); this name does not exist in political action but emerges through it (May 2008). In other words, it is a misnomer, a name that "inadequately refers to the anonymous multitude that has no title in the police order" (Rancière 2004a, 92). Through action, as Musfata Dikeç (2005, 178) frames it, "they constitute an order with another conception of the whole": the true right to dignified and affordable housing for all. Here the political moment unfolds, as Dikeç continues, when the logic of the police and the logic of equality meet in the creation of a common space addressing a wrong and demonstrating equality. For example, as explained by a PAH member in a focus group, the movement "breaks the tool the bank uses against us, which is fear. The PAH helps break this fear." The encounter between the logic of the police and the logic of equality occurs in collective assemblies as well as a variety of spaces generated by the PAH. I now turn to look at how this operates in direct actions that subjectively, symbolically, and materially disrupt financialized housing-life and biopolitical technologies of mortgage power.

Direct Action: Making Visible Claims of Equality and Solidarity

With regular, weekly support from the assembly as a base, mortgage-affected people engaged in collective action and began their struggle for debt forgiveness, in some cases including social rent. In the PAH's early days, protests held in various urban spaces—outside real estate agencies, the court, banks, city halls—were key to make mortgage problems visible, continue to lose fear, shame, and guilt, and build collective struggle. Then, as the PAH faced insufficient responses from all levels of government to their three main demands—retroactive dación en pago, a stop to all evictions, and turning empty bank-owned houses into social housing—they began to address urgent material needs themselves. Making visible a wrong, they took action that interrupted "the natural order of domination . . . by the institution of a part of those who have no part" (Rancière 1999, 11). These are sites where two different worlds meet and where the political takes place. The following three subsections explain the PAH's most prominent actions, and the next section analyzes them in detail.

STOPPING EVICTIONS: "WE WILL NOT LET ANYONE PASS"

Amid chants like "Today it's him, tomorrow it's you!" and "Don't watch us, join us!," physically stopping evictions by creating a human shield to block the entrance to the apartment of a family facing eviction is the PAH's most emblematic form of mobilization. The Stop Evictions (Stop Desahucios) campaign started in 2010 when a mortgage-affected person in Bisbal de Penedès, Catalonia, found out that if his eviction proceeded, he not only would be left living in the street with a €100,000 mortgage debt but also ran the risk of losing custody of his nine-year-old son. He wanted to fight back, and dozens of PAH activists came to support him by physically blocking the entrance to the property. The judicial retinue (*comitiva judicial*) was unable to deliver the eviction order as the PAH successfully turned them and their police escort away. As physically stopping an eviction in this way provides only temporary respite from eviction—what Roy (2017) aptly terms the politics of postponement—the PAH supports the compañerx in negotiating a social rent with the bank, in the meantime pressing government agencies to provide a solution. By doing so they make visible the need for, yet the inability of, the government to take action. The PAH continues to mobilize its members to block the delivery of any subsequent eviction order until a medium- or long-term solution is established, which might be occupying empty bank-owned housing through participating in the Obra Social campaign, discussed subsequently. Over two thousand evictions were estimated to have been stopped from 2010 to 2017 across Spain through the PAH's Stop Evictions campaign.

The frequency and nature of blocking mortgage-related evictions shifted in the Barcelona metropolitan region around 2013–14. This was in part the result of the PAH-initiated collective negotiations with banks at the end of 2012, when the PAH established points of contact higher up in several banks' administrative hierarchies—specifically in debt recuperation offices—to enable the negotiation of multiple cases. Mortgage-affected people, at the same time, fought to solve their own cases. Collective negotiation agreements were signed with many banks, enabling the PAH to stop evictions and sometimes apartments from being auctioned upon foreclosure. When I was engaged with the PAH conducting this research, no mortgage-affected compañerx in the PAH got evicted. Furthermore, in Sabadell the PAHC's court commission was in contact with the city's public servants who deliver citations and notices from the court's Official Notice Service (SAC). If the bank did not respond to demands to stop a mortgage-related eviction, a member of the PAHC's court commission called the SAC and was often able to halt the eviction. Ultimately these processes meant that calls to physically block mortgage evictions became less frequent because, through collective negotiations or the court, many evictions were stopped before actions were required. Since 2015, the Stop Evictions campaign has blocked the evictions of people holding defaulted mortgages sold to financial companies as well as rental and squatting evictions, the latter two of which remain all too frequent.

Blocking evictions is seen as an important action by compañerxs because evictions are deeply unjust, often discussed with outrage and frustration. As Amira told me, "It's a very deep feeling, it touches you profoundly . . . when you see people who have fought for their house and in the end they [the bank] evicts them just like that: I keep your money, everything you have paid, I keep your house and evict you. The bank sees the person as if they were money, they don't see humanity, only the economic side. Once they suck you dry, they are no longer interested nor do they care to think about your intentions or how you suffer. . . . It's enraging and makes you feel impotent. Thanks to the PAH, every time we are there we have always been able to stop the eviction." Similarly, Joan exclaimed,

> How can we systematize evictions? On Monday at 9:00 a.m. a judicial retinue in a taxi convenes the police, all paid with our taxes, to evict someone. . . . Evictions have to be the first things that are nonnegotiable. They should be stopped, by law! In fifteen days [the government] adopted a law where the country's deficit is prioritized above all other things. They do it in a hurry, running during the summer, boom, the constitution was changed! By law, evictions are over. "Oh no, it's that the bank. . . ." The bank?! "The bank has the legitimacy to. . . ." No, no, no, the bank does not have any legitimacy to

evict people from their homes. Look at what I do with your paper: I wipe my ass with it. We have to wipe our ass with all the mortgages and judicial proceedings. I'm not Marxist, Leninist, communist nor separatist nor pro-independence. That is, I'm interested. This. I'm interested in this.

Half of the compañerxs I interviewed underlined blocking evictions as critical illustrations of mutual aid and the fact that the family facing eviction is not alone, demonstrating unity and solidarity. For example, Pepe noted, "There is unity, there is a lot of unity. . . . I think it's important, because it has been shown that one person alone can't do anything, alone no." Elena underlined how blocking evictions "demonstrates solidarity despite being in such an individualized and grim system." Isa's story about going to block an eviction demonstrates solidarity, collectivity, and the anger at the underlying injustice: "We were supposed to meet at 9:00 a.m., I arrived at 8.30. . . . I went upstairs and the woman was there, smoking a cigarette, her eyes swollen and filled with tears. I said to her, 'Excuse me, you are the woman facing eviction?' 'Yes child, but no one is going to come, I'm desperate. I sent my kids to school.'" Isa comforts her, sits with her, cries with her. More and more people arrive, as do the police, and Isa is alone with the woman facing eviction in her apartment. Isa becomes emotional as she tells me, "But here either they'll have to hit us or whatever, but we will not let anyone pass. . . . She had already given her apartment [to the bank], her mother's apartment was paid off and [the bank] also took it. You see how they took the woman's working years, she was already older and should be at peace. . . . We stopped the eviction, she was happy but at the same time said: but they've taken everything away from me. You are joyful but you also feel confident and want to go hit [the bank], to tell them, but this woman has worked so many years and you're taking away all her life." Isa's narrative also underscores the double burden women often face, as defaulting, foreclosure, and eviction deeply impact caring responsibilities—where, for example, women often decide to send their children to school so they will not witness the eviction attempt or its possible execution—and generate profound despair about domestic stability and futures.

CONFRONTING THE BANK:
INDIVIDUAL ACTIONS, BLOCKING BANKS, AND BANK OCCUPATIONS

Especially during 2013–14, banks were the target of multiple types of actions. Mortgage-affected people first engaged in their individual and collectively supported struggle against the bank as they insisted that the PAH's dación en pago or debt forgiveness papers are accepted. In the PAH's early years, most banks refused to process this paperwork, as doing so committed them—even if quite loosely—to study the request and provide a response. If the documents are accepted, something that has become easier over the years due to the PAH's collective pressure, the bank's answer often cites the government's Good Practices Code, which is often a smokescreen since it excludes virtually everyone living in the Barcelona metropolitan region due to high housing prices.[1]

With weekly support and encouragement from the assembly, most mortgage-affected people continuously visit their bank branch, handing in their dación en pago or debt forgiveness paperwork multiple times and demanding that it be studied until the bank eventually makes an offer. This process can last months or even years, depending on the complexity of the case. This changed in 2014 due to the PAH's collective negotiations with banks, solving some cases within months of a person's arrival at the PAH, a process that has its own implications and challenges for both the movement and processes of political subjectivation, as discussed later in this chapter. If the person encounters problems—for example, the bank rejects their documents, does not respond, or, once an offer is made, refuses to make a better one—an accompaniment can be requested at an assembly, where one or two experienced PAH members visit the bank with their compañerx to firmly speak with the branch director.

All compañerxs interviewed either received accompaniments or accompanied others. Half explicitly underlined how in the presence of the PAH the attitude of bank directors changed dramatically. The racist treatment that many non-European immigrant compañerxs reported disappeared. Sara, a Moroccan compañera, explained how the way the bank treated her was "very different. They are very polite, not rude, not wolves. They are like rabbits trying to eat a carrot. When I went alone, they told me atrocities: your children will be taken away, they'll inherit the debt, all kinds of things." Three compañerxs explained how going to the office accompanied by the PAH shifted the physical nervousness from them to the banker. Isa, an Ecuadorian compañera, described how "when I go alone or with my husband, I'm the one who shakes, but when I am with the PAH the banker starts shaking and says, 'Why don't you go there, why don't you try this.' But when I am alone, no, he pressures me, makes me nervous, lowers my morale. You leave worse than when you came in."

Several compañerxs explained the importance of helping others as they were helped, because the others will have the same sensation that they did: "Releasing the biggest bonds of your life, taking off your chains. Starting to walk, knowing where you are putting your feet—moreover, now with wisdom and intelligence" (José). Accompaniments can reverse the relationship of fear, as expressed by Carlos: "When we have gone in and put on our T-shirts, with the PAH logo, their attitude changed. It changed 100 percent. You can tell that the PAH exists and it is something that terrifies [the bank], they fear it." Without the information backed by collective support and pressure from the PAH, compañerxs I interviewed underlined that it would have been otherwise impossible to get any positive results from the bank.

Yet when the bank refuses to budge on its offer, as often occurs, accompaniments are not enough. Most compañerxs resort to one or more bank actions to wring out a better solution. Depending on the objectives—previously discussed and agreed upon in an assembly—and the (un)willingness of the bank to respond, three types of actions can be organized. The most common at the peak of the PAH's activities were daytime bank branch occupations. Here, anywhere from thirty to one hundred or more compañerxs storm into a bank branch and raise a ruckus, paralyzing business activities until the director or a senior banker negotiates a solution. Such actions are festive moments of disruption: chanting, using noisemakers, banging on garbage bins as drums, dancing, plastering PAH stickers on the bank's windows, walls, and ATMs, and creating impromptu confetti from the bank's advertising brochures. The second type of action is a bank block, aimed at hindering the normal operation of a bank branch or the bank more generally by collapsing its services through phone calls, emails, ATM use, and dozens of PAH members posed as clients lining up in front of one or multiple bank branches to ask banal questions. Finally, there are multiday occupations. PAHC Sabadell pioneered these actions in early 2013, staying four days and nights in a bank branch until Ahmed's dación en pago and social rent were approved. During my fieldwork such occupations became more common, with PAH Osona setting a record of over eighty days camped out in front of the bank to obtain dación en pago for a family. Multiday bank occupations sometimes also group together multiple cases in the same entity, such as when PAHC Sabadell organized a joint action at a BBVA branch for ten cases that had similar characteristics and were stuck in negotiations with no solution in sight in March 2014. The compañerxs refused to leave the office until all cases were solved, and the occupation lasted nineteen days, with solidarity actions against BBVA organized during this period by over thirty PAHs in other cities and extensive support from local collectives and unions in Sabadell.

Five compañerxs needed one or multiple daytime bank occupations because the bank refused to budge on its offer. José organized several daytime occupation actions with the PAH, finally obtaining his dación en pago with zero debt. He remarked that "showing them that we are united, and that there is strength in numbers," the office director "was terrified when we went to the office, he was scared shitless when the PAH used to come in for an action." Two of the five compañerxs had more complex cases, as their mortgage loan either was with a foreign bank or had been sold to another financial entity. In the latter case, Ibercaja sold María's mortgage debt to Global Finance, an entity with no offices in Spain. Despite over a dozen accompaniments and several actions at Ibercaja, the bank kept repeating that "we can no longer do anything"—although after four years of struggle María finally had her remaining debt forgiven and obtained social rent. In the other case, Bea's mortgage was from a French bank, whose sole office in Barcelona is staffed only by salespeople who grant loans. After several daytime actions occupying the office, she was finally able to meet with the director and sign an agreement whereby €50,000 of her mortgage debt was forgiven and she would pay a €150 monthly installment over four years. Bea said, "The fact that I had to barge in there, stage what I had to stage to speak with him when he should have been the first to say, 'Hey, look, you are a client, we're going to sit down and negotiate. . . .' The bank really doesn't give a damn about us, you see it most when you go to do [bank actions], they treat you terribly. That is, when you go to sign your mortgage, 'Oh please sit down Ms. so-and-so, sit here.' But just don't come with a problem."

OCCUPYING EMPTY BANK-OWNED HOUSING: "TAKE AND DO INSTEAD OF ASK AND WAIT!"

The PAH's Obra Social campaign originated in the autumn of 2011, when, as one of its founders explained to me, "it was born in the street in a very intuitive way," responding to "the pressure of the judicial machinery" that began to issue open eviction dates as the PAH blocked increasing numbers of evictions in the streets. Thus the "natural reaction of the PAH was, well, we can't stop the eviction, so we will rehouse" the household. The first occupation took place in September 2011 when the PAH was unable to stop the third eviction of a family with an open eviction order in Montcada i Reixac, a city in the Barcelona metropolitan region, and the City Council provided no alternative. The family occupied their former apartment then owned by the bank. Collective occupations of empty bank-owned housing blocks to rehouse multiple households started in Terrassa, a city in the Barcelona metropolitan region, at the end of 2011, when the Obra Social campaign was officially launched.

Aside from its principal goal of meeting an immediate housing need, the campaign aims to recover the social function of housing by ensuring that families engaged with the PAH who are facing eviction and have exhausted all housing options—meaning that they can't afford to pay rent and have received no solution from social services and the government housing department—are not left living in the street. In both collective and individual occupations, the PAH seeks to regularize a family's situation by negotiating a social rent with the bank in the same apartment or another, in this way pressing an alternative modality of property (Blomley 2004). Over fifty-five buildings have been collectively recuperated across Spain, rehousing well over twenty-five hundred people.

Empty bank- or investor-owned apartments or entire housing blocks are the exclusive targets of the PAH's occupations. Occupying this housing asserts use value over the exchange value and profit-driven focus of these entities, disrupting the core dynamics of urban capital accumulation and financialized housing relations that they hope to (re)instigate (García-Lamarca 2017). By "recuperating" or "liberating" housing (Gonick 2016), as it is framed by some in the PAH, the movement attempts "to give [squatting] a language, new in the sense that we don't focus on the house but rather put what has happened at the center: they have robbed rights and housing from us, so we recover them; they've evicted us so we rehouse." This echoes the Chicago Anti-Eviction Campaign's language of "home liberations," language used to convey legitimacy and positivity (Roy 2017). In contrast, some PAH nodes use the term "squatting" (okupar) as a way to both recognize the history of the squatting movement and reposition the term in the current economic and social configuration, toward normalizing and positivizing it as a legitimate practice.

The process of liberating/recuperating/occupying housing signals wrongs and makes visible several realities. First, recuperated buildings are symbols of the paradox of the current system—that only 2 percent of Spain's housing stock is social housing and there are millions of empty apartments across the country at the same time that hundreds of thousands of people are being evicted and have no housing alternative. The campaign thus, as its former spokesperson explained to me, "lets us illustrate the contradictions of systemic accumulation and domination more than other campaigns." As expressed on PAHC Sabadell's Twitter feed in September 2014, it is an act of "recuperating dead capital, remaking connections of social solidarity, without fear." Second, liberating housing shows how despite the PAH's efforts to pressure local, regional, and national governments through campaigns and meetings, government action at all levels has been limited and insufficient. As the campaign's former spokesperson framed it, "It's like the end point of a process to accumulate legitimacies grounded in objective conditions." Upon pressing the government and receiving no response, the PAH takes matters into their own hands to enact the right to housing. As Carlos said, "If the political authorities think they are in their right and we elect them to represent us, and they don't represent us, they don't do what they need to do, well then we have to do it!" It is also clearly illustrated by the eloquent slogan of an Obra Social in Madrid: "Take and do instead of ask and wait!" Both statements echo the words of a Chicago Anti-Eviction Campaign activist: "housing is a human right and we're gonna enforce it ourselves" (Salo, cited in Roy 2017, A4). The Obra Social campaign illustrates the absolute contradiction between the PAH's collective solidarity-based practices and the values of the capitalist liberal democratic system grounded in individualism, competition, and personal benefit (Jiménez 2013a). In many ways this questioning of the commodification of housing and life can be seen as a decolonial ontology (Roy 2017) in the way that it rejects and reframes the Franco dictatorship's deeply instilled obligations of property.

Compañerxs commonly saw the Obra Social campaign as important and necessary and as a logical action. This was expressed by Sebas, who noted that he "sort of tolerated" squatting before but now sees it as clear as day: "A parent, with children, on the street, without housing? It makes one million times more sense to squat." Many, furthermore, highlight it as an action responding to an urgent need. For example, Ángela noted that now she and her husband can afford to feed their two children but rhetorically asked what they will do when her husband stops receiving his unemployment payment and how they will make ends meet living off a €420 monthly government subsidy with two young children. Amira stated that the Obra Social "has to be that way," in the sense that for many people there is no other option, but she felt it is important that everyone living in collective occupations "truly is in a precarious situation."

One compañero living in a collectively recuperated housing block in Sabadell successfully fought long and hard for his dación en pago. José was put on a waiting list for social housing, and various estate agents kept rejecting his rental apartment applications because he, his wife, and his daughter, who were all mortgage co-owners, were still officially registered as defaulters, with €245,000 in outstanding debt. When he explained his situation in an assembly, people suggested he live in the PAH's housing block until his situation improves:

> What happened with this apartment? I had to stay here due to the situation I'm in. I've never wanted to be given anything nor to keep anything that is not mine, but the situation has forced me do so, that they say to me: oh, you're the squatter that lives there. You can say whatever you want, but my family has

a roof over their heads, a roof supported by the PAH. I'm José from the PAH and we'll get this apartment and all that are needed but no one will go without housing in this city, and if that's the case, in this entire country. . . . Through the Obra Social we are showing everyone that there is a housing problem in Spain, that here there was a mortgage bubble, that here they really robbed and evicted everyone. By reclaiming housing, occupying housing blocks, we are telling the world: they built this and left it empty, they filled their pockets. Look at the people on the street. Why do we have people living on the street? The PAH is not going to leave anyone on the street. We squat and in we go, to provide a housing solution. It has been one of the biggest weapons to show the whole world what is really happening here.

Similar to José, half of mortgage-affected compañerxs I interviewed framed the Obra Social as an action signaling a wrong and enacting equality, one that makes evident a nonsensical situation. During a group interview with two residents and a PAH solidarity activist in an occupied housing block in Sabadell, it was underlined that the Obra Social is about "recovering a space for social use," in this case a new building that stood empty for four years, and "dignified housing for all families, regardless of their social position or race." Fran discussed both Stop Desahucios and the Obra Social as "the weapons that citizens have" and sees them "as the only way, the correct way to reclaim and make ourselves be noticed, that we exist, that there are very large collectives that exist and defend the rest of the people (*defienden al resto de personas*)."

"We Defend the Rights That Aren't There for Us": Actions as Political Subjectivation

The three actions discussed previously can be interpreted as processes of political subjectivation. They make visible a wrong through an act of equality that directly illustrates both a structural and everyday lived conflict that exists in society. At the very base of the wrong is the deeply inegalitarian process and relations of (financial) rent appropriation underlying housing provision and circulation. It is made visible as mortgage-affected people, the part of those who have no part as Rancière would call them, interrupt the established order toward enacting the right to dignified and affordable housing for all. The act shows that the right to housing should not be conditional on extreme indebtedness, the precariousness of rental markets, or waiting for nonexistent social housing, and that it can be made real now.

The process of subjectivation, or disidentification, of "the part of those who have no part" (Rancière 1999, 11) initiated in collective assemblies continues as mortgage-affected people engage in actions. This was illustrated through many compañerxs' narratives: "The bank sees the person as if they were money, they don't see humanity, only the economic side" (Amira in reference to blocking evictions); "If the political authorities think they are in their right and we elect them to represent us, and they don't represent us, they don't do what they need to do, well then we have to do it!" (Carlos speaking about occupying empty homes owned by financial entities). It was also exemplified in Bea's reflection on bank actions when she remarked that "the bank really doesn't give a damn about us." Financial entities are very polite and welcoming when a person signs a mortgage but make an about-face when that person is unable, and refuses, to pay. Such examples found throughout this chapter reflect an awareness of a class conflict and division, an "us" and a "them," although the differential racialized experiences are not made explicit. Through actions, equality is enacted by the subjects of equality themselves. Fran expressed this, saying that through actions the PAH "defend[s] the rest of the people"; or as José explained, "We defend the rights that aren't there for us." These statements are echoed by Lefebvre's (1968, 179) reflection on the twofold aspect of rights: "They give a legal form to inequality, and reflect the pressure of the ruling interests to turn it to their advantage. The concept of rights is thus clarified by the concept of a society that transcends them, and at the same time it throws light on the society ruled by them."

Political subjectivation can thus be seen as a fluid, ongoing, and co-constitutive process that is initiated in collective advising assemblies, circulating throughout spaces where actions unfold and back again. This is illustrated, for example, through blocking evictions, where the disidentification with the established order instigated in assemblies is reinforced by not feeling alone and experiencing solidarity and strength in numbers. Actions are spaces for the enactment of one's disidentification with the existing order—as Isa noted, "Here either they'll have to hit us or whatever, but we will not let anyone pass"—toward a material and subjective "righting" of the wrong. This connects to Todd May's (2008, 116) discussion of how "the creation of a collective subject through political action is the creation of internal connections" where sharing, trust, and solidarity are "markers of a set of connections that arise through the political process of subjectification. They indicate a willingness to expose oneself to those alongside whom struggle takes place."

Actions are moments of dissensus, the construction of a paradoxical world with the presence of two worlds in one (Rancière 2001, Thesis 8). In other words, the PAH does the opposite of what the police order states should be done—paying your mortgage—and then enacts what the police order says should not be done in specific spaces. Make an inquiry and withdraw your money at the bank but don't dare challenge the bank director or let alone physically confront the bank, despite facing indebtedness for life upon eviction and the fact that public (your) funds were used for a multibillion-euro banking system bailout. Visit an apartment for rent or purchase from a nationalized bank but heaven forbid occupy it despite being poor and evicted, while millions of bank-owned housing units lay empty across the country after being rescued by billions in taxpayer (your) funds. Compañerxs thus do what is not "supposed" to be done in certain spaces in the name of equality, creating a scene where people and objects are made visible (Rancière and Panagia 2000). Their actions echo Rancière's discussion of rights, where through staging scenes of dissensus political subjects "confront the inscriptions of rights to situations of denial; they put together the world where those rights are valid and the world where they are not" (Rancière 2004b, 304).

Through making visible a wrong, enacting equality, and creating dissensus, the PAH's actions both unveil inegalitarian logics and highlight systemic contradictions. In the case of stopping evictions, people unable to pay their mortgage or rent, or squatting because they have no other option, are being evicted after the financial system has been rescued with tens of billions of public funds. For the Obra Social, millions of apartments lay empty awaiting a new wave of profit making and speculation for the political and economic elite as hundreds of thousands of families are evicted with no other housing options, many indebted for life. Bank actions make visible that banks have been bailed out with billions of euros while a now unemployed and "insolvent" mortgage holder must repay their debt no matter what. In this way actions (re)politicize the economy by contesting what had been previously seen as neutral or "normal" political-economic decisions and showing that the state and capital act to further their own interests over those of the people.

Actions thus disrupt the distribution of the sensible (Rancière 2001, Thesis 7). They clearly illustrate the inability of expert knowledge and administration—the police, as Rancière would call it—to enact equality. This is done at a practical, day-to-day level as the insufficiencies of lawyers, government services, banks, and other actors that maintain and perpetuate the established order are laid bare and made evident. The PAH itself then initiates an "egalitarian disruption" and institutes politics by opening up spaces to verify and enact equality (Dikeç 2012, 674). It is also attempted at the level of policy as the PAH strives to change the law through Popular Legislative Initiatives and to create local government legislation such as motions to fine banks with empty apartments. In the words of one activist, this process has "served to accumulate legitimacy, to see until what point politicians in general are inoperative and short-sighted, which we knew already." Making visible this inoperativity—showing how politicians and the police order more broadly continue laws and practices that wrong equality (Rancière 1992)—then lays the ground for the PAH's attempts to demonstrate equality via rupture-based actions such as Stop Desahucios, Obra Social, bank actions, and others. These actions furthermore have a high level of popular social legitimacy across Spain because the PAH has pressed actors supposedly behind implementing "good governance" measures and then attempted to use the tools themselves for housing equality.

At the same time, some more fundamental dimensions of the distribution of the sensible in relation to the racialized nature of the broader capitalist system, which values white European (male) bodies more than others in spheres of production, (mortgage) circulation, and other dimensions of everyday life, are not questioned. I believe there are several reasons why compañerxs did not point out differential racialized realities and bring them into a larger right to housing-related distribution of the sensible. First, racialized mortgaged dynamics were never something explicitly discussed in assemblies, actions, or other spaces of the PAH; rather they emerged as unexpected—though unfortunately unsurprising—as I learned in detail about the processes compañerxs went through to contract a mortgage. So, racialized dynamics are not explicitly recognized in the movement, and to be fair there is so much emotional intensity and urgency involved in dealing with immediate housing needs (especially evictions) that makes it a difficult point to tackle. Second, my observations about Spain in general are that racism and racialized realities are largely absent from mainstream discussions, although they are growing in strength due to the work of Antifa and antiracist collectives, and also thanks to Black Lives Matter erupting across the United States in recent years. In other words, race is not a prevalent frame of analysis in general. Finally, depending on how such a racialized analysis is brought to the fore in shifting the framing of housing justice, it could divide rather than unite affected people who are ultimately struggling together to obtain housing justice for all, no matter race, gender, or nationality. This echoes how another powerful housing rights movement, the Western Cape Anti-Eviction Campaign, framed its audience for an open letter published by the U.S. alternative magazine the *Nation*, addressed to "all poor Americans and their communities in resistance" (cited in Roy 2017). How to recognize difference and intersectional realities and shift the dominant understanding of racial capitalism without alienating or reinforcing positionalities when trying to build a collective movement is a pending but critical question.

Challenges to Processes of Political Subjectivation in the PAH

As the broader lack of framing in relation to racialized relations suggests, the dynamics unfolding through the PAH's processes of political subjectivation are by no means problem free. Tensions and contradictions exist in all social processes. The main challenges I both observed and heard from PAH members were with assistencialism (*asistencialismo*) and (non)engagement, two interconnected processes. Assistencialism is a term used in the 1970s by Paulo Freire (2005a, 2005b) in Brazil's colonial context to depict treating a person as an object, not a subject, debasing popular participation in a historical process. As Freire (2005b, 12–13) wrote, "Assistencialism offers no responsibility, no opportunity to make decisions, only gestures and attitudes which encourage passivity." When used by the PAH, the term portrays how social service providers regard people as clients, focusing on the symptoms rather than the root causes of problems. The term is also used by the PAH to say what the PAH is not, because assistentialist practices are the antithesis of political subject formation and transformative change since they ultimately maintain the status quo. Assistentialism can thus be conceived as Rancière's police and as another tentacle of biopolitics: a way to regulate and control the population to maintain a state of life, as a way to keep people docile, compliant, and obedient. The fact that assistentialism has been at times inadvertently reproduced by the PAH in specific processes illustrates its deeply pervasive and ingrained position in everyday social relations.

Thus despite awareness and efforts to counteract it, assistentialism in the PAH intermittently emerged in particular through the collective negotiations initiated with banks at the end of 2012 across Catalonia, described earlier in this chapter. Previous to collective negotiations, mortgage-affected compañerxs fought for the resolution of their own case by constantly pressing the bank for a solution individually while participating in assemblies and actions, requesting direct collective support when necessary. The focus was on social and political struggle, where each affected person escalated pressure on the bank and acted as their own negotiator with the bank. While in theory this remained true after the creation of collective negotiations—and while collective negotiations have had the benefit of enabling the PAH to preemptively stop evictions and apartments from being auctioned, as well as to solve more cases—in practice assistentialist practices arose from the role of the PAH's bank interlocutors and new organizational structures in some PAHs.

The first occurred as the PAH's bank interlocutors, usually one or two people per financial entity per local PAH, began to be viewed by some mortgage-affected compañerxs as people who can "solve" their case due to their regular and direct contact with higher-ups (debt recuperators) at the given bank's central offices. In some cases, this was reinforced by certain interlocutors "taking charge" of mortgage-affected people's cases, amid disgruntlement from other PAH members, enacting the very assistentialist tendencies that the PAH is against. I saw this play out with individuals both in Barcelona and Sabadell. This occurred despite having an internal collective negotiations protocol precisely to avoid the development of assistentialist relations, by, for example, rotating the interlocutor position every six to eight months, insisting that the mortgage-affected person lead the negotiation for their case, and so on.

In terms of new organizational structures, some PAHs (e.g., Barcelona) created separate bimonthly assemblies for mortgage-affected people from specific banks, while others (Sabadell) did not because several members foresaw potential future fragmentation and demobilization if various assemblies were held on different days. While bank groups facilitated the coordination of growing numbers of cases per financial entity in Barcelona—numbering in the hundreds in some banks—this also enabled some mortgage-affected people to "bypass" the broader PAH assembly process, despite constant reminders of the need for everyone to participate in collective advising, coordination assemblies, and actions. In other words, some mortgage-affected people felt that through collective negotiations their PAH interlocutor was "handling," and would therefore find a solution to, their case. Some PAH Barcelona members felt that bank groups had diluted the collectivity and reduced belonging and group consciousness, where many newcomers instead saw the PAH as an administrative agency (*gestoría*). In PAH Barcelona coordination assemblies there was extensive discussion about dismantling bank groups, but it was actively contested by many mortgage-affected people who wanted to keep them. Based on my observation, this led to deeper tensions between some mortgage-affected people and certain PAH Barcelona members, with the former beginning to refer to the latter, behind their backs, as "the leaders" (*la cúpula*); their allegations have transformed and continued years on. While it was complex and messy, like most conflicts, this tension ultimately had to do with who had control—or was perceived to have had control—over the organization, information, and decision making in what was in theory a horizontal platform. It was also likely due to the uncertainty about what would happen to PAH Barcelona as several founding members were stepping back from their roles as they joined a new municipal political platform, one that ultimately won the elections in May 2015.

Several PAH bank interlocutors were overwhelmed by their role, and some actively addressed and fought against assistentialism. When assistentialist attitudes from mortgage-affected people (e.g., "the PAH should solve my case") arose in assemblies, there were quick rebuttals that everyone must struggle for their own case. This assistentialist attitude was clearly articulated in an interview with a Pakistani mortgage-affected compañero. When I asked him if the PAH had changed him or his way of seeing the world, he responded, "If they [the PAH] don't solve my problem, if they don't control the bank director, presenting papers, how can it change me?" The fact that this person was engaged more broadly in the PAH, attending actions to block evictions and occupy banks illustrates the complexity and unevenness of processes of political subjectivation and the deeply ingrained nature of assistentialist relations.

Debates around collective negotiations were brought in September 2014 to a Catalan-level PAH assembly, where it was decided to dismantle the interlocutor figure and bank group assemblies in all PAHs. The organizing model returned to individual struggles supported by the collective, although it still has its tensions, largely dissipated since mortgage-related housing problems have been eclipsed by rental and squatting ones. The experience is however important to illustrate how processes like collective negotiations are a double-edged sword, achieving proportionally more "victories" (dación en pago, debt forgiveness, and social rents) at the expense of disengaging some people in the struggle. This was reflected in an assembly by an impassioned plea made by a mortgage-affected compañero in Sabadell: "The essence of creating ourselves as fighters was lost. I learned to be on the street with the PAH. I am not 'using' the work of people [in the PAH], but others do. We need to involve new arrivals, so they take to the streets to fight for our lives, which are being taken away from us. People come after two to three months only because the PAH bank interlocutor says they have news about their case. We must return to struggles on the street (*la lucha callejera*). That is life [applause from assembly]." Processes like collective negotiations furthermore show the challenges that collective, horizontal processes that seek equality through rupture, in terms of both material and discursive practices, but at the same time that negotiate with the police order, constantly face.

Engagement, closely related to assistencialism, is another challenge to processes of political subjectivation in the PAH. While this occurs at different levels in the PAH, instilling and especially maintaining engagement has been a test with the Obra Social's collectively recuperated housing blocks. Some people come to the PAH expecting to be given a house, something I saw especially during my time in Sabadell, where individual and collective occupations have been extensive and openly encouraged. The Obra Social commission had to be continuously pedagogical. As one commission member explained to me, "We need to reeducate people to understand that it's not about asking for an apartment and asking for someone to connect (*pinchar*) your electricity, but providing everyone who needs it the skills to do it themselves. It is continuous work." As a way to achieve this, in 2013 PAHC Sabadell began to regularly offer workshops on squatting and on obtaining electricity and water supplies.

An interview conducted with several people living in one of the PAH's occupied housing blocks showed how the day-to-day realities of twenty-four families living together in the same building create their own problems. Some residents don't engage in the PAH's commissions, nor even actions and activities. Language and cultural differences—the building was described as a tower of babel by one of its residents—often make deeper engagement difficult. Residents emphasized the need for "pedagogy and reeducation, because many people don't know what collective struggle is, they have never moved outside their own settings." The challenges with and tensions in collective actions are also illustrated by the fact that several Obra Social buildings are steeped with problems around living together. A handful of Obra Social buildings, furthermore, have disconnected from their local PAH. These points highlight that while the Obra Social is a powerful political act—although by no means continuous or stable, as sooner or later all buildings face legal battles and eviction threats and negotiations with local and regional governments—there is constant daily work, and tension, behind maintaining such practices. Reflecting on Ananya Roy's (2017) thinking about the Chicago Anti-Eviction Campaign, as a practice of emplacement, occupation eventually becomes postponement. While in some ways the apparatus of property is somewhat disrupted through the claim of social rent from the government rather than private possession, the inevitable collective tensions and problems can come to overshadow and even surpass this political claim.

Conclusions

Based on the experiences and knowledge of the PAH in the Barcelona metropolitan region, this chapter explored the processes of, and challenges to, political subjectivation arising from collective advising assemblies and the most common forms of direct action at the peak of the PAH's activity. The contextualization of the PAH made clear how its roots grew in the historical geographical context of Spain's housing boom and emerged during its bust, with specific forms resulting in Barcelona and Sabadell that reflect the political and social relations therein, illustrating two connected but differentiated metropolitan dynamics. Collective advising assemblies, whose format was developed through trial and error and drew from feminist practices of care, are fundamental learning spaces where mortgage-affected people begin to overcome fear, guilt, shame, and loneliness. They are critical as a passage to act, instigating a process of disidentification with the existing order that classifies people in a certain way and deems certain behaviors to be "proper": for example, a mortgaged homeowner must pay or be a debtor for life. Actions, emerging progressively as a response to urgent needs and an absence of structural solutions, enact this disidentification toward "righting" the wrong and materializing housing equality for all, despite racialized, gendered, and classed housing experiences—albeit without explicit recognition of racialized experiences in particular. Together, these processes subjectively, symbolically, and materially disrupt financialized housing-lives and mortgaged biopolitical technologies of power. The chapter also highlighted some of the deep-seated challenges to processes of political subjectivation through dynamics of assistentialism and lack of engagement. Here I reflect more deeply on what these practices and their challenges mean for understanding the PAH through a Rancierian framework and vice versa.

The findings and analysis in this chapter pointed to the fact that collective advising assemblies and direct action are co-constitutive dynamics that turn mortgaged financial subjects—the indebted people—into political subjects. That is, without the subjective transformations facilitated in collective assemblies, most mortgage-affected people would likely be unable to act. As Mir García et al. (2013, 57) note, when most people arrive at the PAH they are "not the profile of a political subject ready to face a judicial committee and the police to block an eviction." Without actions, assemblies would likely not transcend a discursive process of disidentification. This has implications for the temporal dimension of political subjectivation. While according to Rancière politics and staging equality are rare and intermittent moments, the experiences of the PAH highlight that such moments of disruption can be sustained through collective processes, solidarity- and equality-based practices where mutual aid and pedagogy continuously occur. This marks the first challenge to a Rancière's interpretation of the event/act as *the* political moment. At the same time, the challenges of certain social and structural dynamics also influence this temporal dimension. In seeking to solve more cases, collective negotiations hastened solutions for some but also ran the risk of assistentialism, which in some cases counteracted the rupture of mortgaged subjectivities. Any process of subjectivation is furthermore uneven and complex because identity is built in incomplete and partial ways, so disidentification can never be total. Identity, in other words, is not static but always in the making. The long-term duration and/or ripple effects of the creation of political subjects throughout, and beyond, mortgage-affected people's engagement with the PAH is a process that continues to unfold. I reflect further upon this point in the next and final chapter of this book.

The chapter also made clear that disrupting the dynamics of mortgage biopolitics and processes financializing housing and life occurs not through an act or event but rather through what I characterize as an accumulation of collectively learned practices. That is, no single political act can be identified as the moment that creates a rupture, as suggested by Rancière, but rather this happens through time and processes that unfold in assemblies, actions, and other activities. These learned practices move directly against the dominant individualized and individualizing logic of the indebted person, which are critical elements of biopolitical technologies of mortgaged homeownership, the financialization of housing-life, and the distribution of the sensible. Collectively learned practices include not trusting the advice of "experts" (lawyers and banks) regarding one's mortgage problems; not being ashamed, afraid, or guilty and not feeling alone for not paying one's mortgage; learning how to, and being supported in, standing up to the bank to fight for debt forgiveness or social rent; piling in front of a door to stop an eviction; occupying bank-owned housing to materialize the right to housing; and occupying a bank to demand mortgage debt forgiveness on debts that were a scam. Critically, these collectively learned practices are an illustration of how the PAH is a social process that generates its own analysis, concepts, experiences, and practices. They are, as Casas-Cortés, Osterweil, and Powell (2008, 2013) propose, a situated source of knowledge. Thus, the collective knowledge and learned practices generated through the PAH—against or counterposing "official" or "expert" knowledge—are a critical component driving processes of political subjectivation.

These collectively learned practices are critical in rupturing the central mechanisms of mortgage biopolitics and the distribution of the sensible. As Davidson and Iveson (2014) note, the distribution of the sensible and bio-

politics both assign or regulate certain social positions to ensure their circulation and proper distribution and operate as implicit, often invisible, social laws. Collectively learned practices rupture circulation and distribution
at multiple levels. They rupture the process of creation and content of individualized indebted subjectivities through disrupting behaviors and "proper"
ways of saying, doing, and being in certain spaces. Collectively learned practices, ultimately, interrupt the financialized housing-life model, albeit without an explicit recognition of its racialized roots and impacts. Regarding the
financialized housing-life model, the PAH's collectively learned practices upset the normalized political economy of finance-based housing speculation.
Through making visible and enacting the political, their practices (re)polit-
icize the economy. This is absolutely fundamental considering the socialization of tens of billions of euros of financial sector losses and the subsequent
privatization of the gains at the expense of the Spanish population as well as
the primacy of the construction and real estate sectors in Spain's economic
growth model. These processes can be seen, and are often seen, as outside of
our hands, but such collectively learned political practices can become important tools in urban politics: they provide situated and grounded ways of knowing and acting to disrupt the Spanish growth model and EU imposed/adopted
austerity measures, struggles both for and against the public (Hardt and Negri
2012).

Finally, on top of their disruptive nature, the PAH's collectively learned
political practices are both nuanced according to the historic-material reality of place—as seen by the shared but different dynamics in Barcelona and
Sabadell—and propositional. By propositional, I mean that seeking housing
equality through social rent, squatting, and other insurgent demands force-
fully advances legal and institutional transformation, which could be seen
as upsetting the Spanish homeownership model, the dominant apparatus of
property (Roy 2017). Indeed, the PAH's demands for bank-owned housing to
become social rental housing managed by the state suggest tenants as temporary possessors of property through inhabitation, with the state managing this
housing for the collective Spanish population. It echoes, in some ways, Gretta
Krippner's (2015) notion of possessive collectivism. The propositional nature
of collectively learned practices furthermore goes beyond a Rancierian reading that focuses on rupture as the basis of politics and constitutes another challenge to limiting the understanding of the political to an event/act. The PAH's
proposals push the boundaries of Spain's current political-economic housing
context by challenging the roots of the financialized housing-life dynamic that

the banks and government seek to reinstigate. In other words, turning close to a million empty bank-owned apartments across the country into social housing could disrupt the larger model based on financialized circuits of housing speculation. Where the government does not act, the PAH enacts. The political incidence and resulting configuration of these practices and actions are still in the making.

CONCLUSION

Housing Life-Debt Struggles in Spain and Beyond

This book uncovered how and why hundreds of thousands of mortgage loans became non-performing—and defaulters, in turn, became socially shamed as non-performing—during the 1997–2007 financialized housing boom and crisis in the Barcelona metropolitan region. I showed how life was differentially mortgaged in times of precarity during a housing boom and what happened when the lives of defaulting households were entangled in financial sector restructuring and a tsunami of debt-buying capital flows during the post-2008 crisis. I explored how collective struggle for debt liberation and housing equality (re)seized life from financialized housing dynamics and mortgage biopolitics. These processes were contextualized through a historical geographical look at housing and homeownership in Spain in the second half of the twentieth century. From dictatorship to democracy, and Spanishness to Europeanization, the deep-seated material, social, political, and economic transformations that took place during this period laid the framework for housing financialization and its crisis at the start of the twenty-first century.

Inspired by feminist scholars bringing the everyday into contemporary political economy, I connected a heterodox, Marxist-inspired political-economic reading with the lived experience of mortgage-affected compañerxs engaged with the PAH in Barcelona and Sabadell as well as the experiences of (ex-) bankers and former government employees. Reflecting more deeply on my compañerxs' racialized, gendered, and classed experiences pushed me to examine processes through and beyond the conceptualizations of canonical thinkers like Michel Foucault, Karl Marx, and David Harvey. Scholars thinking through racial capitalism and decolonial dynamics like Gargi Bhattacharyya, Barnor Hesse, Jodi Melamed, Laura Pulido, and Ananya Roy—among several others—helped me deepen my analysis. Thus, throughout the book I attempted to unpack racialized mortgage dynamics in the Spanish context and to decenter the Spanish case as an exclusively Global North one, in order to situate the material in relation to different geographical dynamics and moments. Doing this showed, for example, how homeownership was shaped under the fascist Francoist dictatorship not only as a form of social control but also as a path for racial hygiene and a return to the "glories" of Spanishness. Such a reading articulates how an idea as simple as a homeowner is not a universal category but is forged through historical difference (Roy 2017).

This conclusion revisits the key arguments I made in this book, reflecting on what the findings contribute to theory, in terms of both the insights and the limitations of living with and collectively liberating oneself and others from mortgage indebtedness. Through these reflections I address and elaborate on the two principal goals driving this book: to understand how financial speculation with life is both lived in day-to-day experiences and differentially embedded in the dynamics of (urban) capital accumulation, and how the financialization of housing-life and the biopolitics of mortgaged homeownership can be disrupted. Finally, in closing I reflect on the new challenges and possibilities emerging in the current political environment.

Financialized Housing-Lives

The book exposed the deep roots of Spain's 1997–2007 financialized housing model (chapter 1) and showed how this model necessarily embraced the financialization of life itself (chapters 2 and 3). The historical perspective illustrated how the production of the built environment, undergirded by homeownership as the ideal tenure option, was directly shaped by the Christian, traditionalist, patriarchal Franco dictatorship (1939–75) to be a core axis of the Spanish growth model. Under democracy and processes of Europeanization, the state fully shifted to market-based strategies to fuel real estate growth: housing policy focused on counter-cyclical market stimulation, while land and financial system frameworks were steadily liberalized. In the late 1990s, full financial ascendance to Europe upon adopting the euro, historically low interest rates, and fictitious capital fleeing the bust of the dot-com boom were some of the factors that unleashed a flood of capital into Spain's real estate sector. Despite increasingly precarious and poorly paid employment, whose conditions were markedly worse for the non-European immigrant men and women who began pouring into the country at the end of the twentieth century, mortgage lending expanded dramatically. The size of mortgage loans tripled and their duration doubled during the boom as housing prices increased over 200 percent. Securitization played a fundamental role: 36 percent of Spanish mortgage debt was packaged and sold on secondary markets by 2007, with Spain's securitization bond-issuing market occupying third place globally.

The empirical material uncovered how deeply enmeshing the population's social and economic reproduction into the financial system (Fine 2010; López and Rodríguez 2010) was at the center of financializing life. I proposed this as a dynamic akin to proletarianization, whereby life and the body were objects, albeit treated differentially, to ensure and further the circulation of capital and expansion of urban growth. The empirical research revealed two key elements in this process. First, chapter 2 exposed compañerxs' racialized and classed differences in accessing mortgage loans, with abusive (racialized) practices including outright scams by real estate agencies and the conditioning of mortgage loans through co-borrowers, crossed guarantors (*avales cruzados*), and cross-selling. All compañerxs were proletarianized, but mortgage terms and conditions highlighted that some lives were "valued" more than others (Melamed 2015; Pulido 2017). Specifically, more than one life was needed to "back up" the lives and loans of most low- to middle-income Spanish and all non-European immigrant compañerxs. This illustrates how the housing and mortgage financing system unequally extends debt and rent relations as well as how financialization is constituted through class dynamics and racialization (Fields and Raymond 2021; Kish and Leroy 2015). Building on Ananya Roy (2017), it is arguable that this racialization goes beyond racial discrimination and exclusion and relates to a foundational dispossession of those who will never be part of (white, "middle-class") European normativity. Second, while investor/financial subjects were fostered at multiple levels by promoting housing as a safe investment since housing prices supposedly would never fall, the indebted person was the reality that compañerxs communicated and lived. This occurred as life and the ability to pay became embroiled not only in the continuation of precarious job contracts but also in the end of mortgage loan grace periods, the rise and fall of interest rates, and the performance of global financial markets.

The deeply ingrained nature of financial subjectivity, as well as the broader creditor-debtor relation and its form of proletarianization, started to become visible in the post-2008 context (chapter 3) as most compañerxs refinanced their mortgage or signed grace periods despite increasing unemployment and plummeting housing prices. But it was when people were unable to pay their mortgage and defaulted that the reality of being an indebted person began to hit, with serious mental, emotional, and physical gendered impacts emerging upon becoming a "failed" mortgaged homeowner. We clearly saw how holding a "non-performing" loan was equated to being a non-performing person.

Life was demoted to the status of a junk bond. Life and the body thus not only are differentially used up in a process of proletarianization in both production and circulation but also suffer upon failing to be a rent appropriation strategy. This occurs externally—being told by bankers or lawyers that you shouldn't have signed if you can't pay, or hearing statements from ruling politicians that "good people" pay their mortgages—and internally, a type of self-punishment for not performing as one "should" perform.

These are some of the core elements that illustrate the deeply symbiotic connection between the financialization of housing and the financialization of life. The mortgaged financialization of home, "first and foremost designed to fuel the economy" (Aalbers 2008, 160), is intertwined with instilling investor/financial subjectivities but results in indebted people who are essentially differentially valued objects ensuring capital circulation. As long as the economy "works" and people can pay their mortgage, this does not appear to be a problem. But as crisis strikes, as seen in the configuration that unfolded in Spain and the Barcelona metropolitan region in particular, this (differential) proletarianization became visible and was deeply felt. Compañerxs articulated their objectification when they spoke of being just a number in the eyes of the financial system.

Chapter 3 illustrated how many mortgage-affected compañerxs' lives became entangled in the reclassification and deleveraging of mortgage-related debt once they were considered to be "non-performing," at the same time that the Spanish financial system was saved with a multibillion-euro bailout thanks to European and Spanish taxpayers. Starting in 2013, non-performing devalued debt and real estate assets attracted a range of international investment (vulture) funds, also encouraged by new investment vehicles created by the Spanish state to trigger another cycle of real estate growth. Debt ecologies (Harker 2020) became extremely complex as defaulted loans were absorbed into a new financial institution then bought by another. Since in Spain (mortgage) debt is a debt for life, people were often not "discarded" in the process of mortgage proletarianization because of the possibilities to eventually extract rent from them, their co-borrowers, or guarantors. This shows another side of the role of debt in intimate relationships (Dawney, Kirwan, and Walker 2020; Han 2012). In a historic perspective, it appears that the drive to create a country of upright, Christian, Spanish homeowners during the dictatorship was replaced by the creation of hundreds of thousands of differentially proletarianized homeowners under a supposedly modern European democracy.

The Biopolitics of Mortgage Debt

Empirical findings in chapters 2 and 3 pointed to the regulatory role of mortgages as fundamental to ensure the circulation of capital at multiple levels as the role of the state shifted from more interventionist to facilitating the rule of the market. Mortgages not only regulate a population so they have to produce now and in the future in order to pay their mortgage but also ensure immediate and long-term rent appropriation to maintain the homeostasis of the broader racialized capitalist political-economic system. These included billions of euros in taxes for the state at multiple levels, hefty commissions for mortgage brokers and real estate agents, and multiple benefits for financial entities. The latter ensured both extended and continued capital circulation through the use of guarantors and/or co-borrowers, crossed guarantors in the case of non-European immigrants, cross-selling, abusive mortgage clauses, and securitization. During the post-2008 crisis, regulatory mechanisms were stretched thin as compañerxs became unable to pay, although financial entities attempted to maintain circulation and homeostasis through refinancing mortgages, offering grace periods, or selling personal loans. These strategies served to "clean up" a bank's books by making loans look perfectly performing, appearing to continue the circulation of capital and thus creating the semblance of a stable economy.

The intertwined nature of disciplinary and regulatory mechanisms became visible through the pressure and/or threats compañerxs received to pay their mortgage, via banks selling non-performing mortgage debt, and through the profound emotional, mental, and physical health problems experienced by mortgaged homeowners when they stopped paying. The gendered dimensions became visible in many cases as women sustained caring and social reproduction tasks in the domestic sphere while holding very low-wage employment that enabled the family's survival. Intersectional realities were also exposed as banks threatened to take away the children of non-European immigrant women if they didn't pay their mortgage. Disciplinary mechanisms were both imposed and self-imposed, illustrating the individualized and individualizing nature of (mortgage) debt relation(s) and the enormous subjective power of debt. Such regulatory and disciplinary mechanisms were unfurled through shifting strategies to ensure the circulation of capital from housing boom to bust, reflecting shifts in the mortgaged population's productive and reproductive flows.

The findings in this book also point to how circulation was ensured thanks not only to the normalization of mortgaged homeownership but also to the political-economic construction of nonchoice other than that of mortgaged homeownership. The latter was actively forged as *the* tenure status that could provide stability and security. Contrary to the prevalent idea of homeownership as part of the Spanish DNA, in 1950 half the Spanish population lived as renters. Homeownership, instead, became both possible and normalized through a variety of ideological, institutional, and legal changes from the 1950s onward. Building a "nation of homeowners, not proletariats" as a fascist project of racial regeneration moved hand in glove with the promotion of the growth of the construction and real estate sector. From the legal and regulatory changes unfurled under democracy and subsequent neoliberalization upon joining the EU, mortgages became a self-evident and normal way to access housing during the boom, encouraged by "experts" like the government, the media, and the financial sector. Despite deep concerns over housing affordability expressed by the population during the boom, two Catalan secretaries of housing, in office during this period, noted that their attempts to counteract the status quo rooted in over-indebtedness and overproduction were ultimately unsuccessful.

In the era of the extensive expansion of fictitious capital and financialized housing, an insightful statement made by Foucault focusing on dynamics in the sphere of production can be extended to better characterize dynamics occurring in the circulation of capital. Biopower made possible "the adjustment of the accumulation of [people] to that of capital" not only through "joining the growth of human groups to the expansion of productive forces and the differential allocation of profit" (Foucault 1978, 141) but also through the expansion of forces of circulation and the differential allocation of rent. Life and the body thus remain important as a productive force but also become objects, also differentiated through their classed, gendered, and racialized value, in the process of capital circulation.

At the same time, between the precarity and increasing cost of the rental market, the virtual nonexistence of social housing, and easy access to mortgage credit, many compañerxs explained their decision to become mortgaged homeowners as the way to provide stability and security for themselves and their family. The stability and security of the broader economic system—based in the growth of the construction sector and the mortgage financing market—thus embedded itself within and fed off the stability and security of families at subjective, material, and everyday levels. Security functions under biopolitics, according to Foucault (2007), by responding to a reality in a way that cancels out, nullifies, or limits the reality to which it responds. The findings suggest not only that mortgaged homeownership was encouraged but also that options different from mortgaged homeownership were nullified through the political-economic construction of nonchoice.

Finally, the post-2008 crisis period made evident some deeper shifts in the players and strategies driving the biopolitics of mortgaged homeownership. Actors shifted from forty-five savings banks and eight banks during the housing boom to ten concentrated and consolidated banks and, since 2013, a multiplicity of international investment (vulture) funds during the crisis. While during the boom financial entities, alongside other actors like real estate agents and brokers, sought to benefit from enrolling lives in mortgages, during the crisis strategies changed. First, loans were refinanced and financial entities attempted to maintain rent appropriation through pressure and threats to obtain payment, to ensure maximum debt recovery. Here the disciplinary mechanisms of mortgages clearly emerged. Then, upon demands from the EU and the Bank of Spain to reclassify debt and reduce exposure to the real estate sector, certain debt was deemed as non-performing, to be sold or deleveraged at a significantly devalued price. Losses were cut—which can be equated to disposing of some (subprime) lives to ensure the security of the system—in an attempt to create a new homeostasis and begin a new economic cycle. Following the economic calculus of the market means accepting that not all life is worthy of protection. The population is, again, differentially adjusted to economic processes. Meanwhile, the bad bank (the SAREB) and legislative changes to encourage speculative investment in the rental sector have been promoted to make Spanish real estate attractive again.

Rupturing the Financial/Investor Subject: Processes of Political Subjectivation

Chapter 4 considered how financialized housing-life relations and the biopolitics of mortgaged homeownership were ruptured through mortgage-affected compañerxs' engagement with the PAH in the Barcelona metropolitan region. Beyond an event or an act, as a Rancierian reading suggests, findings pointed to processes of political subjectivation as what I term an accumulation of collectively learned practices "from below," generated through the collective knowledge and experience of PAH members, against "official" or "expert" knowledge and ways of understanding the world. These included compañerxs not trusting the "solutions" provided by "experts" (lawyers and banks) regarding their mortgage problems; not being ashamed or afraid nor feeling guilty or alone for not being able to pay their mortgage; learning how to, and being supported in, confronting the bank to fight for debt forgiveness or social rent; piling in front of a door to stop an eviction; occupying a bank to demand mortgage debt forgiveness; and recuperating empty bank-owned housing when they didn't have a home and the state didn't provide a solution.

The content and process of the PAH's feminist-inspired collectively learned political practices—which start in assemblies through sharing advice and experiences and move through direct action—contest the inegalitarian, individualized relations of (financial) rent appropriation that drive the dominant model of housing provision, at the core of Spain's political-economic configuration. Practices subjectively, symbolically, and materially disrupt the distribution of the sensible established by the biopolitics of mortgaged homeownership and propose another way of organizing housing-life relations where housing is not a commodity but rather serves to meet social needs. With a focus on equality, the movement does not articulate or contest the racialized relations at the core of capitalism and the distribution of the sensible. Yet questioning—and upsetting—the commodification of housing and life is a step toward a decolonial ontology (Roy 2017) in the way it rejects and reframes the history and obligations of property profoundly instilled since the Franco dictatorship.

Collective advising assemblies and actions to enact equality were shown to be co-constitutive spaces where processes of political subjectivation were generated. The iron-fisted grip of debt on subjectivity, the entrepreneur of the self, was reflected in how most mortgage-affected people arrived at the PAH filled with guilt, shame, and/or fear. They were the indebted or "non-performing" people who felt they had failed because they are no longer able to pay their mortgage. Assemblies provide a space and a process where mortgage-affected people can begin to disidentify with the deeply entrenched idea that they must pay no matter what the cost, although this is by no means a smooth or easy process. Assemblies, and subsequently actions, in a nonlinear and uneven fashion begin to break the individual and individualizing nature of the mortgage debt relation. Many mortgage-affected people begin to perceive a division—an "us" and a "them"—and the inability to pay their mortgage started to be seen as a collective rather than an individual problem. People become aware of their proletarianization, seeing how they were objects or numbers whose principal role was to advance economic growth during the housing boom. The "official" paths to find solutions are exhausted, usually with no resolution, further making visible the unequal and illegitimate nature of the system. Then, disidentification with the existing order is enacted through actions, manifesting systemic contradictions and incurring material disruption. These interconnected processes have proven to be an effective and highly successful practice of urban politics, reflected in over two thousand evictions being stopped by the PAH from 2010 to 2017 and well over twenty-five hundred people rehoused in over fifty-five occupied bank-owned buildings.

I also explored some of the challenges that processes of political subjectivation face. The PAH's organizational structures, created for collective negotiations with banks to channel the solution of multiple cases, inadvertently spawned assistentialist practices. This happened as the role of bank interlocutor was delegated to a PAH member, and many mortgage-affected people stopped being their own negotiator with the bank and became more passive. Despite awareness of the risks this could generate and attempts to address them, "clientelist" relationships were created between bank interlocutors and mortgage-affected people. Similarly, sustaining engagement in the movement can be difficult, particularly with residents in occupied housing blocks. Such challenges point to only a few of the problems collective political practices can face. A final broader issue is the lack of an explicit racialized analysis of housing dynamics and experiences in the PAH—and in the housing movement more broadly across Spain. It is important to recognize here, as Laura Pulido (2002, 762) notes, that "organizing around race and class is hardly new—but how to build explicitly anti-racist organizations rooted in either class or anti-capitalist politics is quite challenging." Doing this, especially in a popular way that speaks to people's lived experiences, is a pending task.

At a deeper level, challenges to political subjectivation highlight tensions between "just" solving one's mortgage problem and returning to "life as normal" or generating a broader transformative process where the people themselves are active subjects in creating more egalitarian housing relations. In other words, it is a tension between operating within—or (inadvertently) reproducing—the distribution of the sensible and continuously building new ways of doing, being, and acting through rupturing the old ones. This is by no means so simple or clear-cut but raises important realities to be considered when thinking about sustaining processes of political subjectivation and creating more profound and lasting transformations in urban society and housing relations.

Between Life and Debt:
New Ways of Thinking about Mortgaged Housing Relations

The lived experiences of mortgage-affected compañerxs provide powerful theoretical insights. First, they help understand exactly how the subjection of people to the logic of capital has been differentially extended from the sphere

of production (the labor-capital relation) to relations of circulation and reproduction (Harvey 2012) through mortgage debt. This process is clearly an extension of the historic racialized and classed logic of financial value (Chakravartty and Silva 2012; Kish and Leroy 2015). Compañerxs' experiences make
tangible the lived, everyday relations of the circulation and reproduction of
capital. Rather than financial expropriation (Lapavitsas 2013), where profits are extracted from workers' personal income in the sphere of circulation,
findings point to Fine's (2010) reading of a deeper entrenchment of the economic and social reproduction of the labor force, reinforcing an already existing classed, gendered, and racialized reality. This occurs not only through
capital "acting on" and "using up" people differentially but through the same
people's subjective embrace of technologies of the self and the entrepreneur-
ial spirit, *Homo economicus* (Aitken 2007; Kear 2013; Langley 2006, 2007,
2008; Martin 2002), a subjectivity that "hides" the reality of being indebted.
Upon nonpayment, the subjectivity of the indebted person (Lazzarato 2012)
emerges, radiating guilt, fear, and shame. Despite entrepreneurs of the self apparently acting as masters of their own destiny and indebted people being in-
validated by and subservient to the system, both financial and indebted subjectivities self-inculcate subjection to (mortgage) debt relations. These insights
underscore the need for further theoretical and empirical inquiries that critically assess subjectivities, life, and the body in political-economic and nonhet-
erodox Marxist-inspired approaches to housing financialization. Specific consideration of the racialized and the more broadly intersectional nature of this
process—that is, considering how gender, ability, class, and other forms of difference come together and interact—is particularly urgent, especially outside
the Anglo-American context where such racialized and intersectional explorations are at a very incipient stage.

The empirical material also illustrates how the biopolitics of mortgage debt
serves as a security apparatus to discipline and regulate the contingency of
life, to maintain what are deemed as "useful" economic and social reproductive flows (Dillon 2007; Dillon and Lobo-Guerrero 2008; Langley 2008). The
Spanish experience exemplifies how a homeostasis or "state of life" is built
through the creation of nonchoice, systematically nullifying or cancelling out
other options (Foucault 2007). Ensuring the continuation of (urban) capital
accumulation and the growth of market relations—the security of system—
intersects with the self-regulation of the individual (Lemke 2001) fostered
through financial and investor subjectivities. These subjects are ideal and "em-
inently governable" (Foucault 2008, 270). The security of the individual is thus
inculcated to meet the need to sustain and extend the security of the broader

system. Indeed, as Lisa Adkins (2018) notes, the logic of speculation operates as a rationality, a mode of accumulation, and a mode of social organization, ultimately reconstituting the social.

The findings also give deeper insights into biofinancialization (French and Kneale 2009, 2012), a term that refers to the way in which contemporary processes of financialization intermesh and intertwine with the politics of life itself and produce distinctive capital/life/subject relations. Following the dictates of the market and the rationale of economic calculus requires accepting the unequal effects it entails (Foucault 2008; Lemke 2001): not all life is equal. In other words, embracing inequality as an operating mechanism means, to a greater or lesser degree, not only accepting the unequal differentiation of human value (Melamed 2015; Pulido 2017) but furthermore, as Katharyne Mitchell (2010) suggests, accepting that some life is not even worth the cost of its own reproduction. In the eyes of the dominant system, subprime people deserve, to put it bluntly, to be left homeless and with a debt for life because they have signed a legal (mortgage) contract that must be respected in order to maintain the current political-economic configuration. The findings also point to the complexity of differentially produced capital/life/subject relations and the debt ecologies they generate (Harker 2020). In Spain, the fact that mortgage debt is for life and that many low-income Spaniards and especially all non-European immigrants are obliged to have guarantors, co-borrowers, or crossed guarantors means that creditors attempt to squeeze out mortgage payments even after foreclosure and eviction, as there is always the promise of future payment. Contextualizing and historicizing the specificities of these capital/life/subject relations is critical in order to provide a nuanced understanding of intertwined structural and lived dynamics.

Chapter 4 illustrated, on the one hand, how a Rancierian reading of rupture and politics is useful to theorize how relations of rent that operate in the circulation of capital, in part fueling the production of the built environment, can be disrupted as a political act. In this way, they help take a critical look at how the urban process under capitalism (Harvey 1978) is a political process that can be challenged and subverted. The experiences of compañerxs in the PAH also assist in understanding how creditor-debtor relations of subjection and self-subjection (Lazzarato 2012) can be broken through collective practices, albeit in a nonlinear fashion. Yet Rancière's focus on the event is not enough to understand a deeper and nonlinear process of political subjectivation as it occurs in a living, breathing, and dynamic movement like the PAH because a Rancierian reading ultimately points toward limited and momentary disturbances in the established order. Furthermore, departing from a Marxist framework focusing squarely on class and thus equality, Rancière does not help us advance a racialized or intersectional analysis of political subjectivation. The experiences of/in the PAH do give insight into what happens in between moments of disruption (Hewlett 2007), pointing to an accumulation of collectively learned practices generated by the movement that are both disruptive and propositional. In many ways this is a highly effective interruption in urban politics, as it not only disrupts the current order but also enacts an alternative to the speculative production of the built environment, financialized housing-life relations, and the biopolitics of mortgaged homeownership. The PAH's proposition to turn the hundreds of thousands of units of bank-owned housing into social rental housing managed by the state suggests tenants as temporary possessors of property through inhabitation, with the state managing this housing on behalf of the Spanish population. Yet, since the state does not take this proposition seriously, the enactment of housing equality through occupying these bank-owned properties in many cases becomes a politics of postponement, deferring the legal machinery driving eviction and displacement (Roy 2017).

In this light, as tools of struggle that enact equality for short to medium time frames, it is unclear how the PAH's actions impact deeper structural and long-term housing dynamics, in terms of creating more egalitarian social relations beyond disrupting the circulation of capital into the racialized and gendered production, exchange, and consumption of the built environment. How can a broader equity-based housing politics that cares for intersectional realities be ensured over the long term? How can it be institutionalized? Or rather, can it be institutionalized? Here it becomes clear that other concepts and theoretical tools are needed. The sole guidance to move forward from a Rancierian framing is knowing how the conquest of moments of equality in an unequal world articulates with a new, more equal, and more equitable world—and attempting to follow them through.

Housing Futures in Barcelona, Spain, and Beyond

I learned an enormous amount during my eleven months of research engagement with the PAH, and subsequently as an activist, sometimes activist-researcher, with the PAH during Barcelona's first years of much-lauded and controversial "radical municipalism." This political project, burgeoning around the world, focuses on local-scale action as a lever against austerity and as the site for the transformation of state and capitalist social relations (Thompson 2021). Many important avenues for research related to housing and its life-debt struggles have become visible. These constitute important intellectual explorations in themselves, but can also inform critical political action that has emerged in the Barcelona metropolitan region, Catalonia, the Spanish state, and beyond.

The first has to do with exploring multiple processes of housing dispossession and resistance to it, as renting and squatting have become the core battlefield for access to decent housing. Around 2014–15 the PAHs in Barcelona and Sabadell experienced a shift in the types of cases arriving for collective advising and struggle from majority mortgage related to majority tenant and squatting related. Nearly 85 percent of the almost four thousand evictions annually taking place in the city of Barcelona over the past few years have been rental evictions. Increasing numbers of households are in turn forced to squat in the face of no other housing alternative—be it on their own, after being scammed by organized gangs (Betim 2014; Kassam 2014), with the guidance of the PAH's Obra Social campaign, or with the support of other collectives. Spain's Ministry of Interior reported a significant increase in squatting, with over five thousand registered in the province of Barcelona in 2019. Meanwhile, data from the Catalan Housing Agency in 2020 recorded nearly thirty thousand empty apartments owned by banks and investment funds across Catalonia.

The increases in rental insecurity and in households forced to squat are directly connected to specific legislative developments, speculative investment strategies, and ever more precarious material realities. In terms of the latter, Spanish labor reforms in the early 2010s deepened employment precarity. A study by the UGT union in early 2020 found that 35 percent of employed workers toil in precarious conditions, specifically with temporary full-time or part-time contracts. Women and immigrants are, unsurprisingly, more severely impacted. The Catholic charity Cáritas reports nearly 2.5 million working poor across the country and points to 8 million people facing absolute job insecurity. These figures have only grown with the COVID-19 pandemic. This socioeconomic reality has been made even more unstable through changes to Spain's Rental Law (LAU) in 2012. The revised law reduced the length of rental contracts, removed controls on rent increases, and enabled landlords to initiate eviction proceedings if tenants missed one rental payment. The 2012 LAU combined with Spain's tax-free real estate investment trusts (SOCIMIs) regime have attracted significant speculative investment capital into the rental market. Many vulture funds that bought debt portfolios have seen the opportunity to get a foot into the burgeoning rental market once property underlying the debt is possessed (García-Lamarca 2021; Janoshcka et al. 2020). Crises of all types serve as an opportunity for housing grabs that deepen racialized and class-based inequalities (Graziani et al. 2020). Research into these rental-based dispossession dynamics has begun (Fields 2018; Soederberg 2018; Wijburg, Aalbers, and Heeg 2018; Yrigoy 2021), but more is needed, as is a deeper understanding of lived racialized, gendered, and intersectional experiences of a new speculative housing cycle.

On the other hand, collective organizing to "disrupt" increasing rental precarity and exert squatting as the enactment of the right to housing faces challenges because the legal processes behind both types of evictions have very short turnaround times. In other words, the "right" to home for renters and squatters is virtually unprotected at a legal level in Spain. The precarity of renters and squatters, furthermore, is compounded by their unstable socioeconomic situation. Due to these factors, the practices and processes of political subjectivation the PAH has generated for mortgage struggles are not necessarily as effective—and perhaps not even at all the same—for renters and squatters. This reflection and analysis, also considering racialized and other intersectional dimensions, is a pending task.

Fortunately, since 2016 around a dozen new housing collectives have emerged across Barcelona (Figure C.1), most rooted in their neighborhoods, and these issues are being actively addressed in practice. Some wins are being made. The citywide Sindicat de Llogateres (Tenants Union) has proved successful in beginning to organize renters and achieve change through direct action, negotiation, and legal channels. The Catalan Rental Law was adopted in September 2020, introducing rent controls in cities, largely due to the pressure and lobbying led by the Sindicat de Llogateres alongside other housing movements and organizations. However, the COVID-19 pandemic has made regular forms of in-person organizing and actions more difficult and/or sporadic. While a rent strike was widely adhered to as rental nonpayment rose 380 percent during Spain's state of alarm in early 2020, evictions appeared to have been back to their full barbarity in September 2020 as the six-month freeze on evictions was lifted. And the Catalan Police are increasingly applying the national 2015 Citizen Security Law (popularly known as the Gag Law) to people blocking evictions through hefty fines for disobeying authority or (ironically) obstructing justice. In October 2021 housing movements across Catalonia launched a campaign to pressure the government to cancel the fines—collectively clocking in at over €206,000 for 351 sanctions in Catalonia alone—stop the application of the Gag Law, and ban the use of riot police at evictions (Garcia 2021).

Col·lectius, assemblees i grups d'habitatge

L'HABITATGE, PER LES VEÏNES

les corts

Grup d'Habitatge de les Corts
Ateneu Popular de les Corts
gllescorts@gmail.com

vallcarca

Sindicat d'Habitatge de Vallcarca
Dilluns a les 19:30h
La Fostera, c/Argentera 24
habitatgevallcarca@hotmail.com

eixample

Xarxa d'Habitatge Esquerra de l'Eixample
Dilluns a les 19:00h
Casal Quetic, Rocafort 236
@XhxeixagEE

Fem Sant Antoni
Cada 15 des, dimecres a les 19:30h
Calàbria 66
femsantantoni@gmail.com

Habitatge Eixample Dret
Dimecres a les 20:00h
La Cruilla, C/ Sardenya 256
habitatge.eixample@gmail.com

sants – montjuïc

Sindicat de Barri de Poble Sec
Dilluns a les 18:00h
Ateneu la Base, c/ Hostes 10
poblesec@sindicateixborn.org

Grup d'Habitatge de Sants
Dijous a les 17:30h
Local la Bordeta
C/ Hostafrancs de Sió 1
gruphabitatgesants@gmail.com

barcelona

PAH BCN
Dilluns a les 18:00h
c/Leiva 44
pahbarcelona.org

Sindicat de Llogaters
Consultar horaris del punt de benvinguda
c/ Villarroel 10
sindicatdellogateres@gmail.com

ciutat vella

Sindicat d'Habitatge del Raval
Dimecres a les 18.15h
Casal de Barri Folch i Torres
C/ Vistalegre 15
ravalsindicat@gmail.com

Sindicat d'Habitatge Casc Antic
Dijous a les 18.30h
C/ Rec 27
sindicatcascantic@gmail.com

Resistim al Gòtic
Dilluns a les 18:30h
La Negreta, c/Nou de St Francesc 21
resistimalgotic@gmail.com

Raval Rebel
Dimarts a les 18:00h
Casa de la Solidaritat
C/ Vistalegre 15
+34 608 603 449

Comissió d'Habitatge Barceloneta
Últim dimecres de mes a les 18:00h
Centre Cívic, c/Conreria 1-9
+34 93 256 33 12 / 00

Obra Social Barcelona
obrasocialbarcelona@gmail.com

Difusió Desnonaments Barcelona
Telegram: https://t.me/desnonamentsbcn
Twitter: @Desnonaments Bcn

horta – guinardó

Xarxa d'habitatge Horta Guinardó
@Habitatge_HG
xarxahaguerho@gmail.com

nou barris

Associació 500x20
Dilluns a les 18:00h
Ateneu La Bòbila, c/Estudiants s/n
500x20.prouespeculacio.org

Associació de Veïns i Veïnes de Ciutat Meridiana
Avda. Rasos de Peguera 210bis
avvmeridiana.wordpress.com

sant andreu

Sindicat d'Habitatge de Sant Andreu
Dilluns a les 18:00h
La Cretlla, Rambla Fabra i Puig 32
santandreuhabitatge@gmail.com

Associació 500x20
Dimecres a les 18:00h
Passeig Torres i Bages 101
500x20.prouespeculacio.org

Sindicat d'Habitatge de La Sagrera
Dijous a les 18:00h
La Torre de la Sagrera
C/ Berenguer de Palou 64

gràcia

L'Oficina d'Habitatge Popular de Gràcia
Dimecres 19:00h
Bloc Jardivà, Travessera de Gràcia 156
habitatgegracia@gmail.com

sant martí

Observatori d'Habitatge i Turisme del Clot-Camp de l'Arpa
Dimecres a les 18:00h
AVV Clot-Camp de l'Arpa
C/ Sibelius, 3
habitatgeturismeclot@gmail.com

Comissió d'Habitatge Poblenou
Primer divendres de mes de 18:00 a 20:00h
Rambla del Poblenou, 49
habitatge@elpoblenou.cat

Al Poblenou Ens Plantem
apoblenouensplantem@gmail.com

FIGURE C.1. Housing collectives, groups, and assemblies in Barcelona, 2020.
SOURCE: Maria Conill Hernandez for the *Sindicat de Barri de Poble Sec* (last updated 2019).

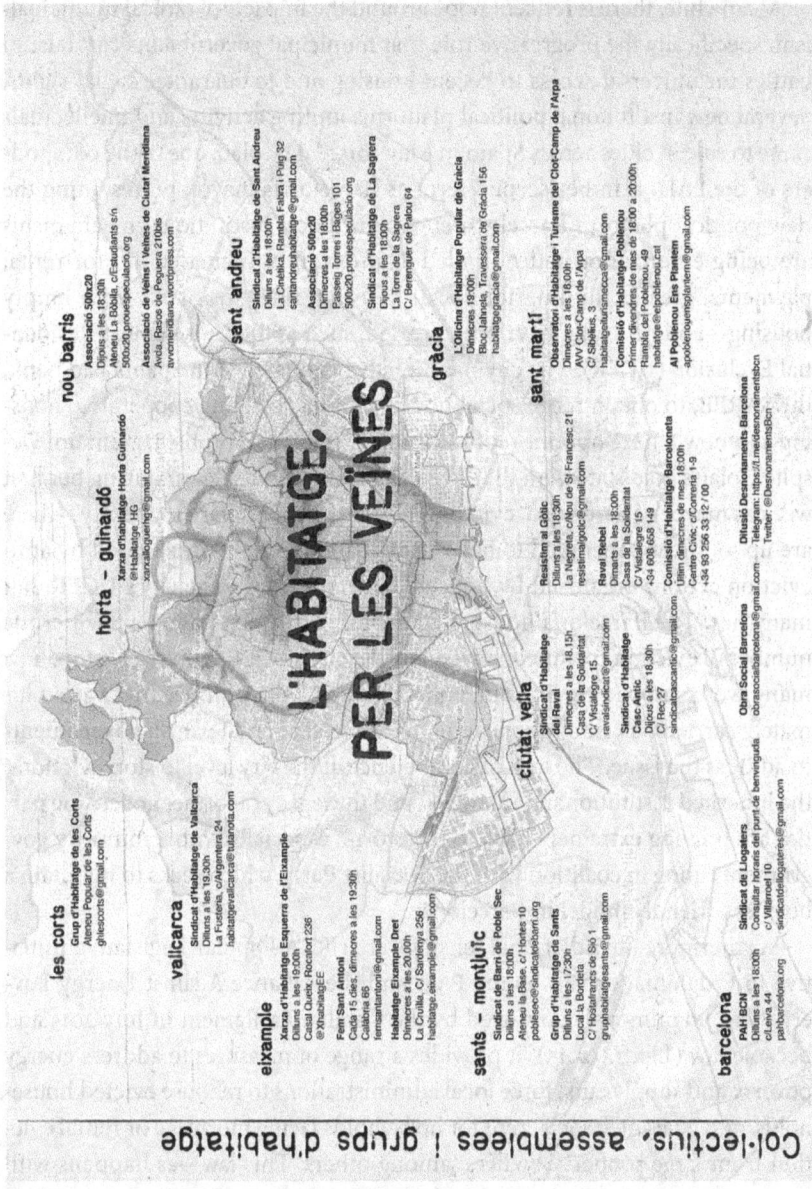

Meanwhile, there is reticent hope around the impacts of radical municipalism, specifically the progressive role that municipal governments can take in battles for universal access to decent housing and to guarantee social rights. Several new institutional political platforms uniting activists and intellectuals came to rule in cities across Spain in May 2015. Ada Colau, one of the cofounders of the PAH, is in her second term as Barcelona's mayor, representing the new political platform Barcelona en Comú. Local institutional mechanisms are being enforced or better funded—for example, increased aid for rental payments, greater funding for social housing, fines for banks with empty housing—and new ones have been created, such as the Unit Against Residential Exclusion (UCER). The city has directly negotiated with Spain's bad bank, the SAREB, to obtain more social housing and is fostering cooperative housing as a new tenure option. Yet fundamental structural problems remain. Despite Colau's bold statement that "we will disobey unjust laws" during her first week as mayor of Barcelona, evictions remain commonplace in the city—there are up to fifteen scheduled to be executed some days, many stopped by antieviction actions organized by housing collectives or by the city's UCER, but many not. The Barcelona housing councilor each week posts on Twitter the number of evictions planned, how many the city's UCER was able to stop, how many were stopped by housing collectives, and the number that were ultimately carried out, finally appealing to the Catalan and Spanish governments to address the issue. The lack of competence at the city level to stop evictions, the inherited institutional framework, and the legacy of former governing parties are proving extremely hard to transform, especially with a minority government ruling in coalition with the Socialist Party, which seeks to maintain a business-friendly model in Barcelona.

Furthermore, jurisdictional tensions are rife. A Popular Legislative Initiative in Catalonia, driven by the PAH and the Alliance Against Energy Poverty, was unanimously approved by the Catalan Parliament in July 2015 and became law (Llei 24/2015). It provides a range of measures to address energy poverty and supply cuts, force local administrations to rehouse evicted households, and guarantee social rent for households facing mortgage or rental eviction from large property owners, among others. This law—as happens with most progressive laws proposed and adopted by autonomous communities in Spain—was challenged through the Constitutional Court and partially overturned, then in 2018 was partially reinstalled thanks to popular pressure. Yet, overall, the rigidity, unwillingness, and/or inability of ruling parties to change national legal frameworks disenable serious structural change at the regional and municipal levels.

Finally, and critically, tensions between the snail's pace of institutional change, the risk of depending on the institutional and legal apparatus in light of the structural realities of capital, and the urgent needs that housing movements confront in their day-to-day experiences are ever present. The way these institutional-movement relations evolve can provide important lessons for how emancipatory struggles in Spain and beyond can interact with and force change in (progressive) institutional structures.

In closing, while the coming battles around housing are multiple, this book provides critical theoretical and political insights related to mortgage debt and its disruption. This is significant because mortgage debt remains extensive in much of the Global North and is growing in reach across the Global South, with mortgaged homeownership enduring as a "wealth generation" strategy for households and governments alike. Despite the particularities of the recent Spanish housing boom-bust cycle, many of the broader processes explored here are inherent in the relation between the production of the built environment and the dynamics of finance capital, pointing to the intimate connections between the reproduction of life, the reproduction of capital, and the production of urban futures. The struggles for mortgage debt liberation in Spain exemplify critical emancipatory processes that have the potential to rupture capital-driven dynamics and the urban forms and relations they create. Either way, the struggles explored in this book undoubtedly provide inspiration for housing and other related mobilizations everywhere.

NOTES

INTRODUCTION. LIFE AND STRUGGLE WITH MORTGAGE DEBT

1. It is important to note that the true number of evictions in the United States might be even higher, as local housing justice groups often point out that Eviction Lab numbers undercount their local movements' figures.

2. The International Tribunal on Evictions (2018) report on Brazil is available online. The Evictions Observatory in São Paulo (2021) provides detailed information about evictions carried out in the city.

3. According to Kutz's (2016) research, Spanish building investments in Morocco exceeded €107 million in 2007, an amount that is nearly double all combined investment over the previous ten years, while in 2008 building investments was almost five times greater than in 2007. Substantial investments followed until 2011. In 2008 and 2010, building investments constituted over 90 percent of Spain's foreign direct investment in Morocco.

CHAPTER 1. GROUNDING SPANISH HOUSING
FINANCIALIZATION AND MORTGAGE BIOPOLITICS

1. While outside the scope of this book, some excellent, critical analyses of the relationship between tourism and the development of Spain's built environment include those by Murray Mas (2015), Observatorio Metropolitano de Madrid (2013), and Charnock, Purcell, and Ribera-Fumaz (2014).

2. Ivan Murray Mas (2015, 102–9) explains how these companies benefited from Spain's housing boom, and Gemma Garcia Fàbrega (2014) uncovers many of the "lords of the boom" in Catalonia. However, this neocolonial dimension deserves further exploration, following the work of Pablo Toral (2001).

3. Especially with the Indignado movement, emerging through the 15 May 2011 (15M) plaza occupations across Spain, the deeper nature of this democratic transition has been put into question.

4. A Catalan Housing Agency employee affirmed, "Housing has been an economic motor. It has been an economic policy, not a social policy" (personal communication, 13 May 2014). A former Catalan parliamentarian in the Socialist Party, currently an aca-

demic, stated that "housing policy has failed," then rectified by saying that it did not succeed as expected (personal communication, 24 April 2014).

CHAPTER 2. THE BIOPOLITICS OF THE 1997–2007 HOUSING BOOM

1. The Mortgage Loan Reference Index (IRPH) was used to calculate interest rates
by several Spanish savings banks instead of the Euro Interbank Offered Rate (Euribor).
The IRPH used a specific and nontransparent interest rate calculation method, whereas
the Euribor is the interest rate at which European-based credit institutions lend money
to each other, where a monthly average over twelve months is used to benchmark mortgages. A court in Spain's Basque region ruled the IRPH illegal in November 2014.

CHAPTER 3. MAINTAINING MORTGAGED LIVES

1. If other indirect or hidden public spending not included in official statistics is considered, such as asset protection schemes and guaranteed state-backed debt, in 2013 the
Citizen Debt Audit Platform calculated the amount to be closer to €1.3 trillion.

2. Most fusions took place from 2010 to 2014. In 2020 CaixaBank bought Bankia, pos-
sibly signaling the end of the cycle. The restructuring process uncovered several significant corruption scandals within many savings banks, particularly regarding excessive
salaries and multimillion-euro pensions disbursed to many high-level savings bank executives before nationalization. Such practices were among many exposed through a Catalan parliamentary commission that investigated the management of nationalized Catalan
savings banks in 2013–14 (see Pellicer 2014).

3. Despite being 45 percent owned by the state, only in 2014 did the SAREB obtain
approval from its board of directors to transfer two thousand housing units to autonomous communities—representing less than 2 percent of the housing stock in their possession—to provide housing under affordable leases. The bad bank stated that this social
housing commitment "represent[s] repaying society for the financial assistance received"
(SAREB 2014, 65). Since SAREB joined the UN Global Compact in September 2013, corporate social responsibility and good governance have appeared in their annual reports,
a complete about-face from their previous position. In October 2013, in response to demands of the Platform for Mortgage-Affected People (PAH) to convert the SAREB's housing into public housing, the SAREB declared, "We don't have a social policy, that is what
the public administration has."

4. Two others wanted grace periods, but the bank would not grant them. María was
told that she would not be able to pay; furthermore, her ex-husband and their guarantors would not sign. Ángela made seven proposals to the bank before she stopped paying: "I've requested a moratorium, a grace period, I asked for the two-month grace period that I am eligible for in my mortgage. I sought an exchange, where the bank takes
my house and gives me another that they have on their website, that is worth less, so they
lower my monthly payments." None of Ángela's proposals were accepted.

5. For those who default on their mortgage loan, the bank cannot seize any percentage of their salary if they earn below €967, an amount 1.5 times less than the minimum
interprofessional salary. This base level increases for those who have children. For peo-

ple who earn between €967 and €1,935, 30 percent of their income can be seized. However, for those who default on a personal loan, the bank can seize 30 percent of their income if they earn between €645 and €1,290. If they earn €1,290 to €1,935, 50 percent can be seized. Furthermore, for Ecuadorian owners of personal loans, unlike with mortgage loans the debt can be reclaimed if the debtor returns to Ecuador.

6. A doubtful loan is classified as one that has fallen into nonpayment for at least ninety days and has a high probability of not being returned, while a substandard loan does not face nonpayment but probably will in the future.

7. It is important to note that these figures *exclude* the €55 billion in non-performing loans transferred to SAREB in December 2012, largely consisting of construction and real estate development credit (Banco de España 2013b).

8. Aside from losing €12 billion in the auction of Caixa Catalunya, the state lost €5.5 billion with Banco de Valencia, €245 million with Banco Gallego, and €8.3 million from NCG Bank (now Abanca) (de Barrón 2014). Bankia was bailed out with a whopping €22 billion. While CaixaBank purchased Bankia in September 2020, it remains to be seen how many billions in public funds will have been permanently privatized.

9. Fortress Group specializes in "investing in distressed debt and beaten-down loans that no one else wants or that are being dumped by sellers under financial duress" (Rose-Smith 2011). In an interview with three high-level executives in *Institutional Investor*, the journalist notes that "even though Fortress's prognosis for the housing market in countries like Spain is not good, Briger [co-CIO] and his team are confident that they can make money given what they paid for the businesses and their experience at servicing similar loans" (Rose-Smith 2011).

10. For further details on the Spanish and Catalan mortgage and housing configuration, see table 1.4.

11. According to the government of Spain's Housing and Land Observatory 2019 annual report, the Bank of Spain stopped collecting data on foreign investment in real estate in 2014, thus this data source is no longer available (Ministerio de Transportes, Movilidad y Agenda Urbana 2020).

12. A report conducted by Observatorio DESC in collaboration with the PAH notes that it is difficult to calculate with certainty the number of people who have taken their lives due to their inability to pay their mortgage. To show the magnitude of the problem, they cite the following cases: "José Miguel Domingo, 54 years old, from Granada, who hung himself on 25 October a few hours before being evicted. Manuel G. B., 53 years old, who threw himself off his balcony in Valencia after a member of the judicial commission arrived to evict him. Amaia Egaña, 53 years old, in the Basque Country, who on 9 November threw herself out of the window of her home on the fourth floor, when the officers of the court arrived to evict her" (Observatorio DESC and PAH 2013, 79).

CHAPTER 4. POLITICAL SUBJECT FORMATION IN STRUGGLES TO DEMORTGAGE LIFE

1. The details of this code (Royal Decree 6/2012) are outlined in chapter 3.

REFERENCES

Aalbers, M. B. 2008. "The Financialization of Home and the Mortgage Market Crisis." *Competition & Change* 12, no. 2: 148–66.

———. 2011. *Place, Exclusion and Mortgage Markets*. Malden, Mass.: Blackwell.

ABC. 1959. "No queremos una España de proletarios, sino de propietarios." May 2, 41–42.

ABC.es. 2013. "Cifuentes acusa a Ada Colau de llevar una 'estrategia radical' con los desahucios." March 25. http://www.abc.es/local-madrid/20130325/abci-cifuentes-desahucios-colau-201303251057.html.

Adell, M., A. Lara, and E. Mármol. 2014. "La PAH: Origen, evolución y rumbo." Betiko .http://fundacionbetiko.org/wp-content/uploads/2014/02/La-PAH.-Origen-evolución-y-rumbo.pdf.

ADICAE. 2010. "Informe Jurídico-Económico de ADICAE en respuesta al informe del Banco de España sobre Clausulas Suelo." Plataforma de afectados de Cláusula Suelo. http://www.afectadosclausulasuelo.org/archivos/InformeclausulasueloADICAE.pdf.

Adkins, L. 2018. *The Time of Money*. Stanford, Calif.: Stanford University Press.

AEAT. 2007. "Asalariados, percepciones salariales y salarios por nacionalidad, tramos de salario, edad y sexo." Agencia Tributaria, Gobierno de España. https://www.agencia tributaria.es/AEAT.

Aguilar Fernández, S., and A. Fernández Gibaja. 2010. "El movimiento por la vivienda digna en España o el porqué del fracaso de una protesta con amplia base social." *Revista Internacional de Sociología* 68, no. 3: 679–704.

Aitken, R. 2007. *Performing Capital: Toward a Cultural Economy of Popular and Global Finance*. New York: Palgrave Macmillan.

Alberdi, B. 1997. "Recent Mortgage Market Development in Spain." *Housing Finance International* 11: 23–30.

Allon, F. 2014. "The Feminisation of Finance." *Australian Feminist Studies* 29, no. 79: 12–30.

Allon, F., and G. Redden. 2012. "The Global Financial Crisis and the Culture of Continual Growth." *Journal of Cultural Economy* 5, no. 4: 375–90.

Altuzarra, A., J. Ferriero, C. Gálvez, C. Gómez, A. González, P. Peinado, C. Rodríguez, and F. Serrano. 2013. "Report on the Spanish Financial System." FESSUD Studies in Financial Systems No. 6. http://fessud.wpengine.com/wp-content/uploads/2012/08/the-spain-financial-system.pdf.

Álvarez Chillida, G. 2014. "Epígono de la Hispanidad: La españolización de la colonia Guinea durante el primer franquismo." In *Imaginarios y representaciones de España durante el franquismo*, edited by S. Michonneau and X. M. Núñez-Seixas, 103–25. Madrid: Casa de Velazquez.

Álvarez Peláez, R. 1998. "Eugenesia y fascismo en la España de los años 30." In *Ciencia y fascismo*, edited by R. Huertas and C. Ortiz, 77–96. Madrid: Ediciones Doce Calles.

Anguren Martín, R., J. M. Marqués Sevillano, and L. Romo González. 2013. "Covered Bonds: The Renaissance of an Old Acquaintance." http://www.bde.es/webbde /GAP/Secciones/Publicaciones/InformesBoletinesRevistas/RevistaEstabilidad Financiera/13/Mayo/Fic/ref2013244.pdf.

Arrighi, G. 1994. *The Long Twentieth Century: Money, Power, and the Origin of Our Times*. London: Verso.

Artola Blanco, M. 2012. "La transformación del mercado de alquiler de fincas urbanas en España (1920–1960)." *Biblio 3W: Revista Bibliográfica de Geografía y Ciencias Sociales* 17, no. 988: 1–15.

Ashton, P. 2009. "An Appetite for Yield: The Anatomy of the Subprime Mortgage Crisis." *Environment and Planning A* 41: 1420–41.

Autonomous Geographies Collective. 2010. "Beyond Scholar Activism: Making Strategic Interventions Inside and Outside the Neoliberal University." *ACME: An International E-Journal for Critical Geographies* 9, no. 2: 245–75.

Avesani, R., A. Garcia Pascual, and E. Ribakova. 2007. "The Use of Mortgage Covered Bonds." *IMF Working Paper, Monetary and Capital Markets* 7: 1–20.

Ayuso, M. 2011. "La hipoteca impagada y la responsabilidad del deudor en el Decreto Ley de 1 de julio de 2011." *Expansión*, July 11. http://www.expansion.com/blogs/de-leyes -que/2011/07/11/la-hipoteca-impagada-y-la.html.

Baklanoff, E. 1996. "Spain's Economic Strategy toward the 'Nations of Its Historical Community': The 'Reconquest' of Latin America?" *Journal of Interamerican Studies and World Affairs* 38, no. 1: 105–27.

Balibar, É. 2013. "Politics of the Debt." *Postmodern Culture* 23, no. 3: n.p.

Banco de España. 2007. "Informe anual 2006." http://www.bde.es/f/webbde/Secciones /Publicaciones/PublicacionesAnuales/InformesAnuales/06/inf2006.pdf.

———. 2010. "Informe del Banco de España sobre derminadas cláusulas presentes en los préstamos hipotecarios." *Boletín Oficial de las Cortes Generales* 9, no. 457. http:// www.senado.es/legis9/publicaciones/pdf/senado/bocg/I0457.PDF.

———. 2013a. "Comunicación sobre refinanciaciones." http://www.bde.es/f/webbde /GAP/Secciones/SalaPrensa/NotasInformativas/13/Arc/fic/presbe2013_33.pdf.

———. 2013b. "Informe de Estabilidad Financiera." http://www.bde.es/f/webbde /Secciones/Publicaciones/InformesBoletinesRevistas/InformesEstabilidadFinancera /13/IEF-Mayo2013.pdf.

———. 2014. "Financial Stability Report." http://www.bde.es/f/webbde/Secciones /Publicaciones/InformesBoletinesRevistas/InformesEstabilidadFinancera/14/IEF -Ing-Mayo2014.pdf.

BBVA. 2007. "Situación Inmobiliaria." https://www.bbvaresearch.com/KETD/fbin/mult /SIES_0706_SituacionInmobiliaria_21_tcm346-176831.pdf.

Bellamy Foster, J. 2006. "The Household Debt Bubble." *Monthly Review* 58, no. 1. http://monthlyreview.org/2006/05/01/the-household-debt-bubble/.

Bernardos Domínguez, G. 2009. "Creación y destrucción de la burbuja inmobiliaria en España." *ICE*, no. 850: 23–40.

Betim, F. 2014. "Se vende piso ocupado por 1.000 euros." *El País*, January 22. http://ccaa.elpais.com/ccaa/2014/01/22/madrid/1390420420_296720.html.

Betrán Abadía, R. 2002. "De aquellos barros, estos lodos. La política de vivienda y post-franquista." *Acciones e Investigaciones Sociales* 16: 25–67.

Bhattacharyya, G. 2018. *Rethinking Racial Capitalism: Questions of Reproduction and Survival*. London: Rowman & Littlefield.

Blackburn, R. 2008. "The Subprime Crisis." *New Left Review* 50: 63–106.

Blanchar, C. 2014. "Sí, pudieron." *El País*, February 21. http://politica.elpais.com/politica/2014/02/21/actualidad/1393010178_488272.html.

Blázquez, P. 2013. "Cómo se alimentan los fondos buitre de los créditos basura de la banca española." *elDiario.es*, September 21. http://www.eldiario.es/economia/fondos_buitre-banca_0_177432630.html.

Blomley, N. 2004. *Unsettling the City: Urban Land and the Politics of Property*. New York: Routledge.

Bookchin, N., P. Brown, S. Ebrahimian, Colectivo Enmedio, A. Juhsaz, L. Martin, MTL, N. Mirzoeff, A. Ross, A. JoanSaab, and M. Sitrin. 2013. *The Militant Research Handbook*. http://www.visualculturenow.org/wp-content/uploads/2013/09/MRH_Web.pdf.

Brat, I., and C. Bjork. 2013. "Spain's Banks Boost Books by Refinancing Loans to Home-owners." *Wall Street Journal*, November 6. http://www.wsj.com/articles/SB10001424052702303843104579172191864835708.

Bryan, D., R. Martin, M. and Rafferty. 2009. "Financialization and Marx: Giving Labor and Capital a Financial Makeover." *Review of Radical Political Economics* 41, no. 4: 458–72.

Bustelo, M. 2009. "Spain: Intersectionality Faces the Strong Gender Norm." *International Feminist Journal of Politics* 11, no. 4: 530–46.

Byrne, M. 2015. "Bad Banks: The Urban Implications of Asset Management Companies." *Urban Research & Practice* 8, no. 2: 255–66.

———. 2016. "From Puerto Rico to the Dublin Docklands: Vulture Funds and Debt in Ireland and the Global South." Dublin: Debt and Development Coalition Ireland. https://www.financialjustice.ie/download/pdf/ddci_vulture_funds_report.pdf.

Cabré, A., and J. A. Módenes. 2004. "Homeownership and Social Inequality in Spain." In *Home Ownership and Social Inequality in a Comparative Perspective*, edited by K. Kurz and H.-P. Blossfeld, 233–54. Stanford, Calif.: Stanford University Press.

Calleja, A. 2008. "Ahora llegan las prisas en España." *La Vanguardia*, October 26, 7.

Campos, R. 2016. "Authoritarianism and Punitive Eugenics: Racial Hygiene and National Catholicism during Francoism, 1936–1945." *História, Ciências, Saúde—Manguinhos* 23: 1–16.

Capel, H. 1975. *Capitalism y morfología urbana en España*. Barcelona: Los Libros De La Frontera.

Carpintero, O., S. Sastre, and P. Lomas. 2015. "'Del todo a las partes': Una visión general del metabolismo de las Comunidades Autónomas, 1996–2010." In *El metabolismo económico regional español*, edited by O. Carpintero et al., 75–166. Madrid: FUHEM Ecosocial.

Casas-Cortés, M. I., M. Osterweil, and D. E. Powell. 2008. "Blurring Boundaries: Recognizing Knowledge Practices in the Study of Social Movements." *Anthropological Quarterly* 81, no. 1: 17–58.

———. 2013. "Transformations in Engaged Ethnography: Knowledge, Networks, and Social Movements." In *Insurgent Encounters: Transnational Activism, Ethnography, and the Political*, edited by J. S. Juris and A. Khasnabish, 199–228. Durham, N.C.: Duke University Press.

Chakravartty, P., and D. F. da Silva. 2012. "Accumulation, Dispossession, and Debt: The Racial Logic of Global Capitalism—An Introduction." *American Quarterly* 64, no. 3: 361–85.

Charnock, G., T. Purcell, and R. Ribera-Fumaz. 2014. *The Limits to Capital in Spain: Crisis and Revolt in the European South*. London: Palgrave Macmillan.

Charusheela, S. 2013. "Intersectionality." In *Handbook of Research on Gender and Economic Life*, edited by D. M. Figart and T. L. Warnecke, 32–45. Cheltenham: Edward Elgar.

Chislett, W. 2008. *Spain Going Places: Economic, Political and Social Progress 1975–2008*. Madrid: Telefónica.

Christophers, B. 2015. "The Limits to Financialization." *Dialogues in Human Geography* 5, no. 2: 183–200.

Colau, A., and A. Alemany. 2012. *Vidas hipotecadas: De la burbuja immobiliaria al derecho a la vivienda*. Barcelona: Cuadrilátero de Libros.

———. 2013. *¡Sí se puede!* Barcelona: Ediciones Destino.

Cox, J. 2012. "'Buying Opportunity' All over Europe, Even Greece: Trump." *CNBC*, June 19. http://www.cnbc.com/id/47871682.

Crawford, L. 2003. "Franco's Slaves." *Financial Times*, July 5, 22–27.

Crenshaw, K. 1989. "Demarginalizing the Intersectionality of Race and Sex: A Black Feminist Critique of Antidiscrimination Doctrine, Feminist Theory, and Antiracist Politics." *University of Chicago Legal Forum* 1: 139–67.

Davidoff, S. 2012. "Profits in G.M.A.C. Bailout to Benefit Financiers, Not U.S." *New York Times*, August 21. http://dealbook.nytimes.com/2012/08/21/profits-in-g-m-a-c-bailout-to-benefit-financiers-not-u-s/.

Davidson, M., and K. Iveson. 2014. "Recovering the Politics of the City: From the 'Post-Political City' to a 'Method of Equality' for Critical Urban Geography." *Progress in Human Geography* 38, no. 3: 1–17.

Davies, W., M. Montgomerie, and S. Wallin. 2015. "Financial Melancholia: Mental Health and Indebtedness." London: Political Economy Research Centre. http://www.perc.org.uk/perc/wp-content/uploads/2015/07/FinancialMelancholiaMentalHealthand Indebtedness-1.pdf.

Dawney, L., S. Kirwan, and R. Walker. 2020. "The Intimate Spaces of Debt: Love, Freedom and Entanglement in Indebted Lives." *Geoforum* 110: 191–99.

Dean, J. 2012. *The Communist Horizon*. London: Verso.

———. 2014. "After Post-Politics: Occupation and the Return of Communism." In *The Post-Political and Its Discontents: Spaces of Depoliticization, Spectres of Radical Politics*, edited by J. Wilson and E. Swyngedouw, 261–78. Edinburgh: Edinburgh University Press.

De Andres Creus, L. 2011. *Barraques: La lluita dels invisibles*. Badalona: Ara Llibres.

de Barrón, Í. 2014. "¿Cuánto dinero se ha inyectado en la banca? ¿cuánto se ha perdido?" *El País*, November 21. http://economia.elpais.com/economia/2014/11/21/actualidad/1416599768_030102.html.

de Castro Rodríguez, M. 2013. "TVE perpetúa el poso racista del colonización en Guinea." *El Salto (Hemeroteca Diagonal)*, May 23. https://www.elsaltodiario.com/hemeroteca-diagonal/tve-perpetua-el-poso-racista-del-colonialismo-en-guinea.

Deville, J. 2015. *Lived Economies of Default: Consumer Credit, Debt Collection and the Capture of Affect*. Abingdon: Routledge.

Díaz Molinaro, M. 2010. "L'ocupació, la construcció i la vida a les barraques." In *Barraques: La Barcelona informal del segle XX*, edited by M. Tatjer and C. Larrea, 83–106. Barcelona: Ajuntament de Barcelona.

Díez, L. 2017. "Franco encargó a Vallejo-Náguera un plan para crear 'la nueva raza española.'" *Cuarto Poder*, January 11. https://www.cuartopoder.es/new/espana/2016/07/17/el-diseno-de-la-nueva-raza-espanola-objetivo-prioritario-del-mando-golpista/.

Dikeç, M. 2005. "Space, Politics and the Political." *Environment and Planning D: Society and Space* 23, no. 2: 171–88.

———. 2012. "Space as a Mode of Political Thinking." *Geoforum* 43, no. 4: 669–76.

Dillon, M. 2007. "Governing through Contingency: The Security of Biopolitical Governance." *Political Geography* 26, no. 1: 41–47.

Dillon, M., and L. Lobo-Guerrero. 2008. "Biopolitics of Security in the 21st Century: An Introduction." *Review of International Studies* 34, no. 2: 265–92.

Durham Community Research Team. 2011. "Community-Based Participatory Research: Ethical Challenges." Durham: Durham University. http://www.dur.ac.uk/resources/beacon/CCDiscussionPapertemplateCBPRBanksetal7Nov2011.pdf.

Dymski, G. 2009. "Racial Exclusion and the Political Economy of the Subprime Crisis." *Historical Materialism* 17, no. 2: 149–79.

Dymski, G., J. Hernandez, and L. Mohanty. 2013. "Race, Gender, Power, and the U.S. Subprime Mortgage and Foreclosure Crisis: A Meso Analysis." *Feminist Economics* 19, no. 3: 124–51.

Ealham, C. 2004. *Class, Culture and Conflict in Barcelona, 1898–1937*. London: Routledge.

El Confidencial. 2008. "Zapatero en Nueva York: 'El sistema financiero español es el más sólido del mundo.'" September 24. http://www.elconfidencial.com/espana/2008-09-24/zapatero-en-nueva-york-el-sistema-financiero-espanol-es-el-mas-solido-del-mundo_205463/.

Elmundo.es. 2007. "Zapatero afirma que España juega en la 'Champions League' económica." *El Mundo*, September 11. www.elmundo.es/mundodinero/2007/09/11/economia/1189506158.html.

England, K. V. L. 1994. "Getting Personal: Reflexivity, Positionality, and Feminist Research." *Professional Geographer* 46, no. 1: 80–89.

Europa Press. 2012. "Martín (AEB) dice que los desahucios son consecuencia de la crisis y no de la ley hipotecaria." December 3. http://www.europapress.es/economia /finanzas-00340/noticia-economia-finanzas-martin-aeb-dice-desahucios-son -consecuencia-crisis-no-ley-hipotecaria-20121203100740.html.

European Mortgage Federation. 2011. "Hypostat 2010: A Review of Europe's Mortgage and Housing Markets." http://www.hypo.org/Content/default.asp?pageId=578.

———. 2012. "Study on Mortgage Interest Rates in the EU." http://www.hypo.org /content/default.asp?PageID=527.

———. 2020. "Hypostat 2019: A Review of Europe's Mortgage and Housing Markets." https://hypo.org/app/uploads/sites/2/2020/10/HYPOSTAT-2019_web.pdf.

Eurostate. 2014. "Sareb, Europe's Largest Property Fund Manager Starts Liquidation Process." http://www.eurostate.com/Eurostate_Spanish Bad Bank_ENG.pdf.

Evictions Observatory in São Paulo. 2021. "Mapeamento Colaborativo RMSP." http:// www.labcidade.fau.usp.br/mapa-denuncias/

Ezcurra Pérez, M. 2012. "Análisis del impacto de la titulización hipotecaria española en la concesión de préstamos subprime y en la estabilidad financiera bancaria." PhD dissertation, Universidad de Santiago de Compostela.

Ezquerra, S. 2014. "Spain, Economic Crisis, and the New Enclosure of the Reproductive Commons." *Monthly Review* 65, no. 11. https://monthlyreview.org/2014/04/01/spain -economic-crisis-new-enclosure-reproductive-commons/.

Fernández, R. 2004. "Proposta de decàleg pel dret a l'habitatge." *Nous Horitzons* 176: 3–12.

Fernández Durán, R. 2006. "El Tsunami urbanizador español y mundial." *Boletín CF+ S* 38/39: 1–43.

Fernández Navarrete, D. 2005. "La política económica exterior del Franquismo: del aislamiento a la apertura." *Historia Contemporánea* 30: 47–78.

Fernández Rincón, A. R. 2013. "Publicitando la burbuja: Una aproximación metodológica para el análisis del discurso publicitario en el sector hipotecario." *Signos do Consumo* 5, no. 1: 88–116.

Ferrer, A. 2010. "Barraques i polígons d'habitatges en la Barcelona del segle XX." In *Barraques: La Barcelona informal del segle XX*, edited by M. Tatjer and C. Larrea, 61–79. Barcelona: Ajuntament de Barcelona.

Fields, D. 2018. "Constructing a New Asset Class: Property-Led Financial Accumulation after the Crisis." *Economic Geography* 94, no. 2: 118–40.

Fields, D., R. Kohli, and A. Schafran. 2016. "The Emerging Economic Geography of Single-Family Rental Securitization." Federal Reserve Bank of San Francisco Working Paper 2016-02. https://www.frbsf.org/community-development/files/wp2016-02.pdf

Fields, D., K. Libman, and S. Saegert. 2010. "Turning Everywhere, Getting Nowhere: Experiences of Seeking Help for Mortgage Delinquency and Their Implications for Foreclosure Prevention." *Housing Policy Debate* 20, no. 4: 647–86.

Fields, D., and E. L. Raymond. 2021. "Racialized Geographies of Housing Financialization." *Progress in Human Geography* 45, no. 6: 1625–45.

Financial Times. 2013. "Spanish 'Bad Bank' Starts Home Sales." February 4. http://www .ft.com/cms/s/0/853de444-6f02-11e2-9ded-00144feab49a.html#ixzz2QAisZtyT.

Fine, B. 2010. "Locating Financialisation." *Historical Materialism* 18, no. 2: 97–116.

Flyvbjerg, B. 2006. "Five Misunderstandings about Case-Study Research." *Qualitative Inquiry* 12, no. 2: 219–45.

Foucault, M. 1978. *The History of Sexuality Volume 1: An Introduction*. Translated by H. Robert. New York: Pantheon.

———. 1991. *Discipline and Punish: The Birth of the Prison*. Translated by A. Sheridan. New York: Vintage.

———. 2003. *Society Must Be Defended: Lectures at the Collège de France, 1975–76*. Translated by D. Macey. New York: Picador.

———. 2007. *Security, Territory, Population: Lectures at the Collège de France, 1977–78*. Translated by G. Burchell. London: Palgrave Macmillan.

———. 2008. *The Birth of Biopolitics: Lectures at the Collège de France 1978–1979*. Translated by Graham Burchell. Hampshire: Palgrave Macmillan.

Freire, P. 2005a. *Education for Critical Consciousness*. London: Continuum.

———. 2005b. *Pedagogy of the Oppressed*. Translated by M. Bergman Ramos. London: Continuum.

French, S., and J. Kneale. 2009. "Excessive Financialisation: Insuring Lifestyles, Enlivening Subjects, and Everyday Spaces of Biosocial Excess." *Environment and Planning D: Society and Space* 27: 1030–53.

———. 2012. "Speculating on Careless Lives: Annuitising the Biofinancial Subject." *Journal of Cultural Economy* 5, no. 4: 391–406.

Fuentes Egusquiza, I. 2007. "La titulización en España: principales características." Boletín Económico del Banco de España. http://www.bde.es/f/webbde/SES/Secciones/Publicaciones/InformesBoletinesRevistas/BoletinEconomico/07/Dic/Fich/art5.pdf.

Fullilove, M. T. 2001. "Root Shock: The Consequences of African American Dispossession." *Journal of Urban Health* 78, no. 1: 72–80.

Garcia, G. 2021. "Més de 206.000 euros en sancions per llei mordassa per intentar aturar desnonaments." *La Directa*, October 13 https://directa.cat/mes-de-206-000-euros-en-sancions-per-llei-mordassa-per-intentar-aturar-desnonaments/.

García, M. 2010. "The Breakdown of the Spanish Urban Growth Model: Social and Territorial Effects of the Global Crisis." *International Journal of Urban and Regional Research* 34, no. 4: 978–80.

Garcia Fàbrega, G. 2014. *Els senyors del boom*. Barcelona: Edicions Saldonar.

García-Lamarca, M. 2017. "From Occupying Plazas to Recuperating Housing: Insurgent Practices in Spain." *International Journal for Urban and Regional Research* 41, no. 1: 37–53.

———. 2021. "Real Estate Crisis Resolution Regimes and Residential REITs: Emerging Socio-spatial Impacts in Barcelona." *Housing Studies* 36, no. 9: 1407–26.

García-Lamarca, M., and M. Kaika. 2016. "'Mortgaged Lives': The Biopolitics of Debt and Homeownership in Spain." *Transactions of the Institute of British Geographers* 41, no. 3: 313–27.

García Montalvo, J. 2003. "La vivienda en España: desgravaciones, burbujas y otras historias." *Perspectivas del sistema financiero* 78: 1–43.

———. 2007. "Créditos de alto riesgo 'a la española.'" *Expansión*, April 16. http://www.econ.upf.edu/~montalvo/columnas/alto%20riesgo%20expansion001.pdf.

———. 2008. *De la quimera inmobiliaria al colapso financiero: crónica de un desenlace anunciado.* Barcelona: Antoni Bosch.

———. 2010. "RIP: Ministerio de Vivienda." *La Vanguardia*, June 22, 58.

———. 2014. "Crisis financiera, reacción regulatoria y el futuro de la banca en España." *Estudios de Economía Aplicada* 32, no. 2: 497–528.

———. 2015. "Situación y perspectivas del saneamiento inmobiliario del sector financiero español." *Cuadernos de Información Económica* 248: 71–87.

García Montalvo, J., and J. M. Raya Vilchez. 2012. "What Is the Right Price of Spanish Residential Real Estate?" *Spanish Economic and Financial Outlook* 1, no. 3: 22–28.

Gessamí, F. 2020. "El precio por intentar frenar un desahucio en Barcelona: 18.030 euros en multas 'mordaza.'" *elDiario.es*, November 10. https://www.elsaltodiario.com /cataluna/precio-intentar-frenar-desahucio-barcelona-18.030-euros-en-multas-ley -mordaza.

Gilmore, R. W. 2007. *Golden Gulag: Prisons, Surplus, Crisis, and Opposition in Globalizing California.* Berkeley: University of California Press.

Gobierno de España. 2012. "Real Decreto-ley 6/2012, de 9 de marzo, de medidas urgentes de protección de deudores hipotecarios sin recursos." *Boletín Oficial del Estado*, March 10. https://www.boe.es/boe/dias/2012/03/10/pdfs/BOE-A-2012-3394.pdf.

———. 2013. "Ley 1/2013, de 14 de mayo, de medidas para reforzar la protección a los deudores hipotecarios, reestructuración de deuda y alquiler social." *Boletín Oficial del Estado*, May 15. https://www.boe.es/boe/dias/2013/05/15/pdfs/BOE-A-2013-5073 .pdf.

Goldstein, A. 2014. "Finance and Foreclosure in the Colonial Present." *Radical History Review* 118: 42–63.

Goldstein, M. 2015. "As Banks Retreat, Private Equity Rushes to Buy Troubled Home Mortgages." *New York Times*, September 28. https://www.nytimes.com/2015/09/29 /business/dealbook/as-banks-retreat-private-equity-rushes-to-buy-troubled-home -mortgages.html.

Gonick, S. 2016. "From Occupation to Recuperation: Property, Politics and Provincialization in Contemporary Madrid." *International Journal of Urban and Regional Research* 40, no. 4: 833–48.

———. 2021. *Dispossession and Dissent: Immigrants and the Struggle for Housing in Madrid.* Stanford, Calif.: Stanford University Press.

González Pérez, J. M. 2010. "The Real Estate and Economic Crisis: An Opportunity for Urban Return and Rehabilitation Policies in Spain." *Sustainability* 2: 1571–1601.

Gordon, C. 1991. "Governmental Rationality: An Introduction." In *The Foucault Effect: Studies in Governmentality*, edited by G. Burchell, C. Gordon, and P. Miller, 1–51. Chicago: University of Chicago Press.

Gotham, K, F. 2006. "The Secondary Circuit of Capital Reconsidered: Globalization and the U.S. Real Estate Sector." *American Journal of Sociology* 112, no. 1: 231–75.

———. 2009. "Creating Liquidity Out of Spatial Fixity: The Secondary Circuit of Capital and the Subprime Mortgage Crisis." *International Journal of Urban and Regional Research* 33, no. 2: 355–71.

Graziani, T., J. Montano, A. Roy, and P. Stephens. 2020. "Who Profits from Crisis? Housing Grabs in Times of Recovery." Los Angeles: UCLA Luskin Institute for Inequality and Democracy. https://escholarship.org/uc/item/5pw706tf.

Gurney, C. M. 1999. "Pride and Prejudice: Discourses of Normalisation in Public and Private Accounts of Home Ownership." *Housing Studies* 14, no. 2: 163–83.

Halawa, M. 2015. "In New Warsaw." *Cultural Studies* 29, nos. 5–6: 707–32.

Hale, C. R. 2006. "Activist Research v. Cultural Critique: Indigenous Land Rights and the Contradictions of Politically Engaged Anthropology." *Cultural Anthropology* 21, no. 1: 96–120.

Hall, S. 2012. "Geographies of Money and Finance II: Financialization and Financial Subjects." *Progress in Human Geography* 36, no. 3: 403–11.

———. 2016. "Everyday Family Experiences of the Financial Crisis: Getting By in the Recent Economic Recession." *Journal of Economic Geography* 16, no. 2: 305–30.

———. 2020. "The Personal Is Political: Feminist Geographies of/in Austerity." *Geoforum* 110: 242–51.

Han, C. 2012. *Life in Debt: Times of Care and Violence in Neoliberal Chile*. Berkeley: University of California Press.

Haraway, D. 1991. *Simians, Cyborgs, and Women: The Reinvention of Nature*. New York: Routledge.

———. 1995. "Nature, Politics, and Possibilities: A Debate and Discussion with David Harvey and Donna Haraway." *Environment and Planning D: Society and Space* 13: 507–27.

Hardt, M., and A. Negri. 2012. *Declaration*. New York: Argo Navis.

Harker, C. 2020. *Spacing Debt: Obligations, Violence, and Endurance in Ramallah, Palestine*. Durham, N.C.: Duke University Press.

Harker, C., and S. Kirwan. 2019. "Introduction: Geographies of Debt and Indebtedness." *Geoforum* 100: 236–38.

Harker, C., D. Sayyad, and R. Shebeitah. 2019. "The Gender of Debt and Space: Notes from Ramallah-Al Bireh, Palestine." *Geoforum* 98: 277–85.

Harvey, D. 1978. "The Urban Process under Capitalism: A Framework for Analysis." *International Journal of Urban and Regional Research* 2, nos. 1–4: 101–31.

———. 1982. *The Limits to Capital*. London: Verso.

———. 1998. "The Body as an Accumulation Strategy." *Environment and Planning D: Society and Space* 16, no. 4: 401–21.

———. 2012. *Rebel Cities: From the Right to the City to the Urban Revolution*. London: Verso.

Herbert, S. 2000. "For Ethnography." *Progress in Human Geography* 24, no. 4: 550–68.

Hernanz, C. 2009. "Fortress entra en el negocio de deuda 'subprime' española." *El Confidencial*, December 30. https://www.elconfidencial.com/economia/2009-12-30/fortress-entra-en-el-negocio-de-deuda-subprime-espanola_249538/.

Hesse, B. 2007. "Racialized Modernity: An Analytics of White Mythologies." *Ethnic and Racial Studies* 30, no. 4: 643–63.

Hewlett, N. 2007. *Badiou, Balibar, Rancière: Re-thinking Emancipation*. London: Continuum.

Hoekstra, J., I. Heras Saizarbitoria, and A. Etxezarreta Etxarri. 2010. "Recent Changes in

Spanish Housing Policies: Subsidized Owner-Occupancy Dwellings as a New Tenure Sector?" *Journal of Housing and the Built Environment* 25, no. 1: 125–38.

Holman, O. 1996. *Integrating Southern Europe: EC Expansion and the Transnationalisation of Spain.* London: Routledge.

Illueca, M., L. Norden, and G. F. Udell. 2014. "Liberalization and Risk-Taking: Evidence from Government-Controlled Banks." *Review of Finance* 14, no. 4: 1217–57.

INE. 2013. *Censos de Población y Viviendas 2011. Edificios y viviendas. Datos provisionales.* Madrid: Instituto Nacional de Estadística. http://www.ine.es/prensa/np775.pdf.

———. 2014a. *Encuesta de Población Activa. Tasas de paro por nacionalidad, sexo y comunidad autónoma.* Madrid: Instituto Nacional de Estadística.

———. 2014b. *INE Base. Hipotecas Estadísticas financieras y monetarias.* Madrid: Instituto Nacional de Estadística. http://www.ine.es/jaxi/menu.do?L=0&type=pcaxis &path=/t30/p149&file=inebase.

———. 2020a. *Ganancia media anual por trabajador, sexo y nacionalidad, 2008.* Madrid: Instituto Nacional de Estadística. https://www.ine.es/jaxiT3/Tabla.htm?t=28202&L=0

———. 2020b. *Estadística de variaciones residenciales. Serie 1998–2019. Altas por país de procedencia y sexo.* Madrid: Instituto Nacional de Estadística. https://www.ine.es/jaxi /Datos.htm?path=/t20/p307/serie/l0/&file=2_7.px#!tabs-tabla.

———. 2021. *Tasas de paro por nacionalidad, sexo y comunidad autónoma.* Madrid: Instituto Nacional de Estadística. https://www.ine.es/jaxiT3/Tabla.htm?t=4249&L=0.

International Monetary Fund. 2014. "Spain. Financial Sector Reform: Final Progress Report." Washington, D.C.: IMF. http://www.imf.org/external/pubs/ft/scr/2014/cr1459 .pdf.

International Tribunal on Evictions. 2018. "Brasil: Casos e Recomendaços." www .tribunal-evictions.org.

Izquierdo, L., and C. del Riego. 2013. "Cospedal: 'Los votantes del PP son los que pagan la hipoteca.'" *La Vanguardia*, April 17. http://www.lavanguardia.com/politica /20130417/54372496568/cospedal-votantes-dejan-comer-antes-hipoteca.html.

James, D. 2014. *Money from Nothing: Indebtedness and Aspiration in South Africa.* Stanford, Calif.: Stanford University Press

Janoshcka, M., G. Alexandri, H. Orozco Ramos, and S. Vives-Miró. 2020. "Tracing the Socio-spatial Logics of Transnational Landlords' Real Estate Investment: Blackstone in Madrid." *European Urban and Regional Studies* 27, no. 2: 125–41.

Jiménez, A. 2013a. *¿La PAH, es de derechas o de izquierdas? ¿Importa?* Rotekeil. http:// rotekeil.com/2013/06/07/la-pah-es-de-derechas-o-de-izquierdas-importa/#more-132.

———. 2013b. *La PAH o el sueño de Gramsci.* Rotekeil. http://rotekeil.com/2013/04/12 /la-pah-o-el-sueno-de-gramsci/.

Jiménez, G., A. Mian, J. L. Peydró, and J. Saurina. 2010. "Estimating the Aggregate Impact of Credit Supply Channel: Evidence from Securitization in Spain." Bank of Spain.

Joseph, M. 2014. *Debt to Society: Accounting for Life under Capitalism.* Minneapolis: University of Minnesota Press.

Jones, D. 2015. *Money from Nothing: Indebtedness and Aspiration in South Africa.* Stanford, Calif.: Stanford University Press.

Jordá, Ò., M. Schularick, and A. M. Taylor. 2014. "The Great Mortgaging: Housing Finance, Crises, and Business Cycles." Federal Reserve Bank of San Francisco Working

Paper Series. http://www.frbsf.org/economic-research/publications/working-papers
/wp2014-23.pdf.

Juris, J. S., and A. Khasnabish. 2013. "Introduction: Ethnography and Activism within
Networked Spaces of Transnational Encounter." In *Insurgent Encounters: Transnational Activism, Ethnography, and the Political*, edited by J. S. Juris and A. Khasnabish,
1–36. Durham, N.C.: Duke University Press.

Kaika, M. 2004. "Interrogating the Geographies of the Familiar: Domesticating Nature
and Constructing the Autonomy of the Modern Home." *International Journal of Urban and Regional Research* 28, no. 2: 265–86.

Kassam, A. 2014. "Spain's Crash Landlords: Empty Homes Spawn Black Housing Market." *Guardian*, February 23. http://www.theguardian.com/society/2014/feb/23/spain
-property-black-market-housing-madrid.

Katz, C. 1994. "Playing the Field: Questions of Fieldwork in Geography." *Professional Geographer* 46, no. 1: 67–72.

Kear, M. 2013. "Governing Homo Subprimicus : Beyond Financial Citizenship, Exclusion, and Rights." *Antipode* 45, no. 4: 926–46.

KPMG. 2013. "Global Debt Sales." Portfolio Solutions Group, KPMG International
https://www.kpmg.com/NL/nl/IssuesAndInsights/ArticlesPublications/Documents
/PDF/Transactions-Restructuring/Global-Debt-Sales-2013.pdf.

Keynes, J. 1933. "National Self-Sufficiency." *Yale Review* 22: 755–69.

Kish, Z., and J. Leroy. 2015. "Bonded Life: Technologies of Racial Finance from Salve Insurance to Philanthrocapital." *Cultural Studies* 29, no. 5–6: 630–51.

Krippner, G. R. 2012. *Capitalizing on Crisis: The Political Origins of the Rise of Finance.*
Cambridge, Mass.: Harvard University Press.

———. 2015. "Possessive Collectivism: Ownership and the Politics of Credit Access in
Late Twentieth-Century America." Unpublished manuscript.

Kutz, W. 2016. "The Eurozone Crisis and Emerging-Market Expansion: Capital Switch-
ing and the Uneven Geographies of Spanish Urbanization." *International Journal of
Urban and Regional Research* 40, no. 6: 1075–93.

Kutz, W., and J. Lenhardt. 2016. "'Where to Put the Spare Cash?' Subprime Urbanization
and the Geographies of the Financial Crisis in the Global South." *Urban Geography*
37, no. 6: 926–48.

Lafraya, C. 2019. "Sabadell vende la promotora Solvia por 882 millones." *La Vanguardia*,
August 5. https://www.lavanguardia.com/economia/20190805/463861354229/sabadell
-vende-promotora-solvia-882-millones.html.

Lancione, M. 2020. "Radical Housing: On the Politics of Dwelling as Difference." *International Journal of Housing Policy* 20(2): 273–89.

Langley, P. 2006. "Securitising Suburbia: The Transformation of Anglo-American Mortgage Finance." *Competition & Change* 10, no. 3: 283–99.

———. 2007. "Uncertain Subjects of Anglo-American Financialization." *Cultural Critique* 65, no. 1: 67–91.

———. 2008. *The Everyday Life of Global Finance: Saving and Borrowing in Anglo-
America.* Oxford: Oxford University Press.

Lapavitsas, C. 2013. *Profiting without Producing: How Finance Exploits Us All.* London:
Verso.

Lazzarato, M. 2012. *The Making of the Indebted Man: An Essay on the Neoliberal Condition*. Los Angeles: Semiotext(e).

Leal, J. 2005. "La política de vivienda en España." *Documentación social* 138: 63–80.

LeBaron, G. 2010. "The Political Economy of the Household: Neoliberal Restructuring, Enclosures, and Daily Life." *Review of International Political Economy* 17, no. 5: 889–912.

LeBaron, G., and A. Roberts. 2012. "Confining Social Insecurity: Neoliberalism and the Rise of the 21st Century Debtors' Prison." *Politics & Gender* 8, no. 1: 25–49.

Lefebvre, H. 1968. *The Sociology of Marx*. Translated by Norbert Guterman. London: Penguin.

Lemke, T. 2001. "'The Birth of Bio-politics': Michel Foucault's Lecture at the Collège de France on Neo-liberal Governmentality." *Economy and Society* 30, no. 2: 190–207.

lisahunter, E. Emerald, and G. Martin. 2003. *Participatory Activist Research in the Globalised World*. London: Springer.

Llonch, P. 2013. "La PAH com a eina contra el capitalisme. Virtuts i riscos." *Espai Fàbrica*, October 27. http://espaifabrica.cat/index.php/perspectives/item/698-la-pah-com-a-eina-contra-el-capitalisme-virtuts-i-riscos.

Llordén Miñambres, M. 2003. "La política de vivienda del régimen franquista: nacimiento y despegue de los grandes constructores y promotores inmobiliarios de España, 1939–1960." In *Los Empresarios de Franco. Política y economía en España (1936–1957)*, edited by G. Sánchez Recio and L. J. Tascón Fernández, 145–70. Barcelona: Crítica.

Lombardo, E. 2017. "Austerity Politics and Feminist Struggles in Spain: Reconfiguring the Gender Regime?" In *Gender and the Economic Crisis in Europe: Politics, Institutions and Intersectionality*, edited by J. Kantola and E. Lombardo, 209–30. Basingstoke: Palgrave Macmillan.

López, I., and E. Rodríguez. 2010. *Fin de ciclo: Financiarización, territorio y sociedad de propietarios en la onda larga del capitalismo hispano (1959–2010)*. Madrid: Traficantes de Sueños.

———. 2011. "The Spanish Model." *New Left Review* 69 (May–June): 5–29.

López Díaz, J. 2003. "Vivienda social y Falange: ideario y construcciones en la década de los 40." *Scripta Nova* 7, no. 146(024): 1–13.

Macías, C. 2013. "Del empoderamiento a la autotutela de derechos: El caso de la PAH." *El Viejo Topo* 306–7: 44–48.

Maestrojuán, F. J. 1997. "'Ni un hogar sin lumbre ni un español sin hogar' José Luis de Arrese y el simbolismo ideológico en la política del Ministerio de la Vivienda." *Príncipe de Viana Pamplona* 210: 171–87.

Mahmud, T. 2012. "Debt and Discipline." *American Quarterly* 64, no. 3: 469–94.

Maixé-Altés, J. C. 2010. "Competition and Choice: Banks and Savings Banks in Spain." *Journal of Management History* 16, no. 1: 29–43.

Malo, M. 2004. *Nociones comunes. Experiencias y ensayos entre investigación y militancia*. Madrid: Traficantes de Sueños.

Manetto, F. 2013 "Cospedal tilda los escraches de 'nazismo puro' propio de antes de la Guerra Civil." *El País*, April 13. http://politica.elpais.com/politica/2013/04/13/actualidad/1365848717_144600.html.

Marchart, O. 2007. *Post-foundational Political Thought—Political Difference in Nancy, Lefort, Badiou and Laclau*. Edinburgh: Edinburgh University Press.

Marcilhacy, D. 2014. "La Hispanidad bajo el franquismo: El americanismo al servicio de un proyecto nacionalista" In *Imaginarios y representaciones de España durante el franquismo*, edited by S. Michonneau and X. M. Núñez-Seixas, 73–102. Madrid: Casa de Velazquez.

Martin, R. 2002. *Financialization of Daily Life*. Philadelphia: Temple University Press.

Martín Corrales, E. 2017. "La esclavitud negra en Cataluña entre los siglos XVI y XIX." In *Negreros y esclavos: Barcelona y la esclavitud atlántica (siglos XVI–XIX)*, edited by Martín Rodrígo y Alharilla and Lisbeth Chaviano Pérez, 17–45. Barcelona: Icaria, 2017.

Martinez, M. 2017. "BBVA vende a Cerberus el 80% de su cartera inmobiliaria por 4.000 millones." *Expansión*, November 29. https://www.expansion.com/empresas/banca/2017/11/29/5a1e5c73268e3e104d8b465c.html.

Masjuan, E. 2010. *Les coves de Sant Oleguer. La perifèria de la ciutat industrial durant el franquisme*. Ajuntament de Sabadell. http://ca.sabadell.cat/Coves/p/portada_cat.asp.

———. 2015. "Abocats a viure a la llera del riu: el problema de l'infrahabitatge a Sabadell, 1939–1970. De l'habitatge protegit al negoci immobiliari." *Documents d'Anàlisi Geogràfica* 61, no. 1: 135–58.

Massad, T. G. 2012. "INFOGRAPHIC: Overall $182 Billion Committed to Stabilize AIG during the Financial Crisis Is Now Fully Recovered." U.S. Department of the Treasury, September 11. http://www.treasury.gov/connect/blog/Pages/aig-182-billion.aspx.

May, T. 2008. *The Political Thought of Jacques Rancière: Creating Equality*. Edinburgh: Edinburgh University Press.

McDowell, L. 1992. "Doing Gender: Feminism, Feminists and Research Methods in Human Geography." *Transactions of the Institute of British Geographers* 17, no. 4: 399–416.

McKinsey Global Institute. 2015. "Debt and (Not Much) Deleveraging." https://www.mckinsey.com/featured-insights/employment-and-growth/debt-and-not-much-deleveraging.

McVeigh, P. 2005. "Embedding Neoliberalism in Spain: From Franquismo to Neoliberalism." In *Internalizing Globalization: The Rise of Neoliberalism and the Decline of National Varieties of Capitalism*, edited by S. Soederberg, G. Menz, and P. G. Cerny, 90–105. Basingstoke: Palgrave MacMillan.

Melamed, J. 2015. "Racial Capitalism." *Critical Ethnic Studies* 1, no. 1: 76–85.

Méndez, R. 2013. "Los despojos de la burbuja." *El País*, May 26. http://economia.elpais.com/economia/2013/05/24/actualidad/1369425866_941056.html.

Méndez, R., and L. Pellicer. 2013. "¿Quién compra España?" *El País*, September 13. http://economia.elpais.com/economia/2013/09/13/actualidad/1379103316_384990.html.

Mendiola Gonzalo, F. 2011. "Forced Labour in Franco's Spain: Workforce Supply, Profits and Productivity." *European Historical Economics Society Working Paper* 4: 1–29.

Mestre, A. 2014. "Vallejo-Nágera, el Mengele de Franco, y la estirpe desigual de Rajoy." *La Marea*, March 2. https://www.lamarea.com/2014/03/02/vallejo-nagera-el-mengele-de-franco-y-la-estirpe-desigual-de-rajoy/.

Ministerio de Fomento. 2014. "Observatorio de Vivienda y Suelo. Boletín Anual 2014."

http://www.fomento.gob.es/MFOM.CP.Web/handlers/pdfhandler.ashx?idpub
=BAW029.

Ministerio de Transportes, Movilidad y Agenda Urbana. 2020. "Observatorio de Vivienda y Suelo, Boletin Anual 2019." https://apps.fomento.gob.es/CVP/handlers/pdfhandler.ashx?idpub=BAW069.

Miraftab, F., and S. Wills. 2005. "Insurgency and Spaces of Active Citizenship: The Story of Western Cape Anti-Eviction Campaign in South Africa." *Journal of Planning Education and Research* 25: 200–217.

Mir García, J., J. França, C. Macías, and P. Veciana. 2013. "Fundamentos de la Plataforma de Afectados por la Hipoteca: activismo, asesoramiento colectivo y desobediencia civil no violenta." *Educación Social: Revista de Intervención Socioeducativa* 55: 52–61.

Mitchell, K. 2010. "Pre-Black Futures." *Antipode* 41, no. s1: 239–61.

Montgomerie, J., and M. Büdenbender. 2015. "Round the Houses: Homeownership and Failures of Asset-Based Welfare in the United Kingdom." *New Political Economy* 20, no. 3: 386–405.

Montgomerie, J., and D. Tepe-Belfrage. 2017. "Caring for Debts: How the Household Economy Exposes the Limits of Financialisation." *Critical Sociology* 43, nos. 4–5: 653–68.

MUHBA. 2010. "Exposició: Barraques. La ciutat informal." In *Barraques: La Barcelona informal del segle XX*, edited by Mercè Tatjer and Cristina Larrea, 179–281. Barcelona: Ajuntament de Barcelona.

Munoz, M. 2014. "Blackstone Buys CatalunyaCaixa Mortgages for EU3.6 Billion." *Bloomberg*, July 16. http://www.bloomberg.com/news/articles/2014-07-16/blackstone-said-to-buy-catalunya-banc-s-distressed-mortgages.

Muriel, E. 2012. "'Las hipotecas son la versión contemporánea de la esclavitud." *Público.es*, May 1. http://www.publico.es/espana/431543/las-hipotecas-son-la-version-contemporanea-de-la-esclavitud.

Murray Mas, I. 2015. *Turismo y capitalismo en España. Del "milagro económico" a la "gran crisis."* Barcelona: Alba Sud.

Naredo, J. M. 2004. "Perspectivas de la vivienda." *Revistas ICE*, May–June, 143–54.

———. 2009. "La cara oculta de la crisis. El fin del boom inmobiliario y sus consecuencias." *Revista de Economía Crítica* 7: 118–33.

———. 2010. "El modelo inmobiliario español y sus consecuencias." *Boletín CF+ S*, 44: 13–27.

Naredo, J. M., Ó. Carpintero, and C. Marcos. 2007. "Boom inmobiliario, ahorro y patrimonio de los hogares: evolución reciente y comparación internacional." *Cuadernos de Información Económica* 200 (September/October): 71–91.

———. 2008. *Patrimonio inmobiliario y balance national de la economía española (1995–2007).* Madrid: Fundación de las Cajas de Ahorros.

Narváez Baena, I. 2013. "El fracaso del desarrollismo urbanístico en la Costa del Sol Occidental. Otras prácticas de producción de ciudad." In *Paisajes devastados. Después del ciclo inmobiliario: impactos regionales y urbanos de la crisis*, edited by Observatorio Metropolitano de Madrid, 431–52. Madrid: Traficantes de Sueños.

Nasarre-Aznar, S. 2002. "The Funding of the Mortgage Loans in Spain by the Issue of

Mortgage Securities. Their Legal Structure." In *Housing Construction: An Interdisciplinary Task*, 1–8. IAHS World Congress on Housing.

Neill, A. 2000. "Buccaneer Ethnography: Nature, Culture, and Nation in the Journals of William Dampier." *Eighteenth-Century Studies* 33, no. 2: 165–80.

Nettleton, S., and R. Burrows. 2000. "When a Capital Investment Becomes an Emotional Loss: The Health Consequences of the Experience of Mortgage Possession in England." *Housing Studies* 15, no. 3: 463–78.

Neumann, J. 2014. "Spain's Bad Bank Picks Apollo, TPG and Cerberus to Sell Assets." *Wall Street Journal*, December 4. http://www.wsj.com/articles/spains-bad-bank -picks-apollo-tpg-and-cerberus-to-sell-real-estate-assets-1417708826.

Observatorio DESC and PAH. 2013. "Emergencia habitacional en el estado español: La crisis de las ejecuciones hipotecarias y los desalojos desde una perspectivea de derechos humanos." http://afectadosporlahipoteca.com/wp-content/uploads/2013/12 /2013-Informe_habtitatge-17Dic.pdf.

Observatorio Metropolitano de Madrid. 2013. "Competitividad territorial y circuito secundario de acumulación." In *Paisajes devastados Después del ciclo inmobiliario: impactos regionales y urbanos de la crisis*, edited by Observatorio Metropolitano de Madrid, 25–76. Madrid: Traficantes de Sueños.

Ochotorena, J. C. 2019. *Del pisito a la burbuja inmobiliaria: La herencia cultural falangista de la vivienda en propiedad, 1939–1959*. Valencia: Universitat de València.

Oliver Wyman. 2012. "Bank of Spain Stress Testing Exercise." http://www.bde.es/f /webbde/GAP/Secciones/SalaPrensa/InformacionInteres/ReestructuracionSector Financiero/Ficheros/en/informe_oliverwymane.pdf.

Ollero, D. 2013. "Los fondos de inversión 'colonizan' las inmobiliarias de la banca." *El Mundo*, November 25. http://www.elmundo.es/economia/2013/11/25/52938ff661fd3d1 03b8b457f.html.

Otero-González, L., M. Ezcurra-Pérez, R. Lado-Sestayo, and P. Durán-Santomil. 2015. "The Main Determinants of Subprime Securitization in the Spanish RMBS Securities." *Applied Economics* 47, no. 58: 6301–16.

Oyón, J. L., and B. Iglesias. 2010. "Les barraques i l'infrahabitatge en la construcció de Barcelona, 1914–1950." In *Barraques: La Barcelona informal del segle XX*, edited by M. Tatjer and C. Larrea, 23–36. Barcelona: Ajuntament de Barcelona.

PAH. 2014. "Libro Verde de la PAH: Una guía básica sobre la PAH." Barcelona. http:// afectadosporlahipoteca.com/wp-content/uploads/2014/01/LibroVerde-PAH-32.pdf.

———. 2019. "Informe Blackstone." https://pahbarcelona.org/wp-content/uploads /2019/06/Dossier-BlackStone-PAH-2019.pdf.

PAHC Sabadell. 2014. "Estadístiques del 2014." Plataforma d'Afectades per la Hipoteca i la crisi de Sabadell. http://www.afectatscrisisabadell.cat/2015/01/estadistiques-del-2014/.

Pain, R., and P. Francis. 2013. "Reflections on Participatory Research." *Area* 35, no. 1: 46–54.

Palomera, J. 2014. "How Did Finance Capital Infiltrate the World of the Urban Poor? Homeownership and Social Fragmentation in a Spanish Neighborhood." *International Journal of Urban and Regional Research* 38, no. 1: 218–35.

Pareja Eastaway, M., and I. San Martin. 1999. "General Trends in Financing Social Housing in Spain." *Urban Studies* 36, no. 4: 699–714.

Pareja Eastaway, M., and I. San Martin Varo. 2002. "The Tenure Imbalance in Spain: The Need for Social Housing Policy." *Urban Studies* 39, no. 2: 283–95.

Pellandini-Simányi, L., F. Hammer, and Z. Vargha. 2015. "The Financialization of Everyday life or the Domestication of Finance?" *Cultural Studies* 29, nos. 5–6: 733–59.

Pellicer, L. 2014. "Las cajas actuaron sin transparencia ni ética, acusa la comisión del Parlament." *El País*, June 4. http://ccaa.elpais.com/ccaa/2014/06/03/catalunya/1401824820_875285.html.

Pérez, C. 2007. "Solbes avisa de malas prácticas en la concesión de hipotecas." *El País*, October 31. https://elpais.com/diario/2007/10/31/economia/1193785205_850215.html.

Ponce de León, R. 2020. "La fusión de Bankia y CaixaBank eleva los riesgos de reducir la competencia en el sistema financiero español." *elDiario.es*, 4 September. https://www.eldiario.es/economia/fusion-bankia-caixabank-eleva-riesgos-reducir-competencia-sistema-financiero-espanol_1_6201814.html.

Portelli, S. 2015. *La ciudad horizontal: Urbanismo y resistencia en un barrio de casas baratas de Barcelona*. Manresa: Bellaterra Edicions.

Porteous, J. D., and S. E. Smith. 2001. *Domicide: The Global Destruction of Home*. Montreal: McGill-Queen's University Press.

Pou, V. 2007. "En profundidad: El impacto del mercado inmobiliario en las finanzas públicas." Madrid: BBVA https://www.bbvaresearch.com/KETD/fbin/mult/SIES_0706_SituacionInmobiliaria_21_tcm346-176831.pdf.

Predmore, S. 2020. "Feminist and Gender Studies Approaches to Financialization." In *The Routledge International Handbook of Financialization*, edited by P. Mader, D. Mertens, and N. van der Zwan, 102–12. London: Routledge.

PricewaterhouseCoopers and Urban Land Institute. 2015. "Emerging Trends in Real Estate: A Balancing Act." http://www.pwc.com/en_IM/IM/publications/assets/emerging-trends-in-real-estate-europe—2015.pdf.

Prieto Serrano, D. 2014. "Producción del espacio urbano y participación ciudadana. El 'habitar' la ciudad de los movimientos sociales en Madrid." In *15MP2P: Una mirada transdisciplinar del 15M*, edited by E. Serrano, A. Calleja-López, A. Monterde, and J. Toret, 255–72. Barcelona: INE/UOC.

Público.es. 2013. "Aguirre compara los escraches con el 'matonismo de ETA' y con los 'peores totalitarismos.'" April 14. https://www.publico.es/politica/aguirre-compara-escraches-matonismo-eta.html.

Puig Gómez, A. 2011. "El modelo productivo español en el período expansivo de 1997–2007: insostenibilidad y ausencia de politicas de cambio." *Revista de Economía Crítica* 12: 64–81.

Pulido, L. 2002. "Race, Class, and Political Activism: Black, Chicana/o, and Japanese-American Leftists in Southern California, 1968–1978." *Antipode* 34, no. 4: 762–88.

———. 2008. "FAQs: 'Frequently (Un)Asked Questions about Being a Scholar Activist." In *Engaging Contradictions Theory, Politics, and Methods of Activist Scholarship*, edited by C. R. Hale, 341–65. Berkeley: University of California Press.

———. 2017. "Geographies of Race and Ethnicity II: Environmental Racism, Racial Capitalism and State-Sanctioned Violence." *Progress in Human Geography* 41, no. 4: 524–33.

Purcell, M. 2014. "Rancière and Revolution." *Space and Polity* 18, no. 2: 168–81.

Quelart, R. 2013. "Aumentan las reclamaciones por las hipotecas multidivisa." *La Vanguardia*, June 19. http://www.lavanguardia.com/economia/20130619/54376090180/aumentan-reclamaciones-hipotecas-multidivisas.html.

Rancière, J. 1989. *The Nights of Labor: The Worker's Dream in Nineteenth-Century France*. Translated by John Drury. Philadelphia: Temple University Press.

——. 1992. "Politics, Identification, and Subjectivization." *October*, 61: 58–64.

——. 1999. *Disagreement: Politics and Philosophy*. Translated by Julie Rose. Minneapolis: University of Minnesota Press.

——. 2001. "Ten Theses on Politics." *Theory and Event* 5, no. 3.

——. 2004a. *The Politics of Aesthetics: The Distribution of the Sensible*. Translated with an introduction by Gabriel Rockhill. London: Continuum.

——. 2004b. "Who Is the Subject of the Rights of Man?" *South Atlantic Quarterly* 2/3: 297–310.

——. 2008. *The Politics of Aesthetics: The Distribution of the Sensible*. Translated by Gabriel Rockhill. London: Continuum.

Rancière, J., and D. Panagia. 2000. "Dissenting Words: A Conversation with Jacques Rancière." *Diacritics* 30, no. 2: 113–26.

Roberts, A. 2013. "Financing Social Reproduction : The Gendered Relations of Debt and Mortgage Finance in Twenty-First-Century America." *New Political Economy* 18, no. 1: 21–42.

Robinson, C. 1983. *Black Marxism: The Making of the Black Radical Tradition*. Chapel Hill: University of North Carolina Press.

Robinson, J. N. 2020. "Making Markets on the Margins: Housing Finance Agencies and the Racial Politics of Credit Expansion." *American Journal of Sociology* 124, no. 4: 974–1029.

Roca Cladera, J., and M. C. Burns. 2000. "The Liberalization of the Land Market in Spain: The 1998 Reform of Urban Planning Legislation." *European Planning Studies* 8, no. 5: 547–64.

Rodríguez Alonso, R. 2004. "Infrautilización del parque de viviendas en España: aparición de viviendas vacías y secundarias." *Boletín CF+ S* 29/30: n.p.

——. 2009. "La política de vivienda en España en el contexto europeo. Deudas y Retos." *Boletín CF+ S* 47/48: 125–72.

Rodríguez-Castellanos, A., M. A. Peña-Cerezo, F. J. Ibáñez-Hernández, and M. A. Pérez-Martínez. 2013. "Análisis del mercado del rating de las emisiones de titulación en España (1993–2011)." *Análisis Financiero* 121: 17–34.

Rolnik, R. 2013. "Late Neoliberalism: The Financialization of Homeownership and Housing Rights." *International Journal of Urban and Regional Research* 37, no. 3: 1058–66.

——. 2019. *Urban Warfare: Housing under the Empire of Finance*. London: Verso.

Romero, J., F. Jiménez, and M. Villoria. 2012. "(Un)sustainable Territories: Causes of the Speculative Bubble in Spain (1996–2010) and Its Territorial, Environmental, and Sociopolitical Consequences." *Environment and Planning C: Government and Policy* 30, no. 3: 467–86.

Ronald, R. 2008. *The Ideology of Home Ownership: Homeowner Societies and the Role of Housing*. Hampshire: Palgrave Macmillan.

Rose, N. 2007. *The Politics of Life Itself: Biomedicine, Power, and Subjectivity in the Twenty-First Century.* Princeton, N.J.: Princeton University Press.

Rose-Smith, I. 2011. "Fortress Investment Group's Junkyard Dogs." *Institutional Investor,* November 21. http://www.institutionalinvestor.com/Article/2930321/Fortress-Investment-Groups-Junkyard-Dogs.html#/.Vsyt6Bg9Vro.

Ross, A. 2017. "Calculating the Debt Gap." *Antipode* 49, no. S1: 19–33.

Rossi, U. 2013. "On Life as a Fictitious Commodity: Cities and the Biopolitics of Late Neoliberalism." *International Journal of Urban and Regional Research* 37, no. 3: 1067–74.

Roy, A. 2016. "Who's Afraid of Postcolonial Theory?" *International Journal of Urban and Regional Research* 41, no. 1: 200–209.

———. 2017. "Dis/possessive Collectivism: Property and Personhood at City's End." *Geoforum* 80: A1–A11.

Rullan, O. 1999. "La nueva Ley del Suelo de 1998 en el contexto del neoliberalismo post-moderno." *Investigaciones Geográficas* 22: 5–21.

Rusiñol, P. 2015. "Si protestas, te desahuciamos." *elDiario.es,* January 18. http://www.eldiario.es/alternativaseconomicas/protestas-desahuciamos_6_347225282.html.

Salmon, K. 2010. "Boom to Bust—Reconstructing the Spanish Economy. Part Two: Policy Responses to the Economic Crisis." *International Journal of Iberian Studies* 23, no. 2: 83–91.

Salo, K. E. 2015. "Local Practices and Trans-local Solidarities: Reflections on Anti-eviction Practices on the Cape Flats, South Africa, and in South Side Chicago." In *Cities and Inequalities in a Global and Neoliberal World,* edited by F. Miraftab, D. Wilson, and K. E. Salo, 217–26. London: Routledge.

Sánchez Martínez, M. T. 2008. "The Spanish Financial System: Facing Up to the Real Estate Crisis and Credit Crunch." *European Journal of Housing Policy* 8, no. 2: 181–96.

Santos, F. G. 2020. "Social Movements and the Politics of Care: Empathy, Solidarity and Eviction Blockades." *Social Movement Studies* 19, no. 2: 125–43.

SAREB. 2014. "Annual Report 2014." https://www.sareb.es/wp-content/uploads/2021/04/2014-sareb-annual-activity-report.pdf.

Scheper-Hughes, N. 1995. "The Primacy the Ethical: Propositions for a Militant Anthropology." *Current Anthropology* 36, no. 3: 409–20.

Segovia, E. 2014. "Los 10 males del banco malo." *El Confidencial,* January 26. http://www.elconfidencial.com/empresas/2014-01-26/los-10-males-del-banco-malo_80317/.

Seigworth, G. J. 2016. "Wearing the World Like a Debt Garment: Interface, Affect, and Gesture." *Ephemera* 16, no. 4: 15–31.

Selmeczi, A. 2012. "Abahlali's Vocal Politics of Proximity: Speaking, Suffering and Political Subjectivization." *Journal of Asian and African Studies* 47, no. 5: 498–515.

Serra Ramoneda, A. 2011. *Los errores de las cajas: adiós al modelo de las cajas de ahorro.* Barcelona: Ediciones Invisibles.

Sharp, J. P. 2009. *Geographies of Postcolonialism: Spaces of Power and Representation.* London: SAGE.

Smith, S. J. 2008. "Owner-Occupation: At Home with a Hybrid of Money and Materials." *Environment and Planning A* 40: 520–36.

Smyth, S., and R. Urban. 2013. "Spanish Banks Cut Developers as Zombies Dying: Mortgages." *Bloomberg*, March 20. https://www.bloomberg.com/news/articles/2013-03-19/spanish-banks-cut-developers-as-zombies-dying-mortgages.

Soederberg, S. 2014. *Debtfare States and the Poverty Industry: Money, Discipline and the Surplus Population*. London: Routledge.

———. 2018. "The Rental Housing Question: Exploitation, Eviction and Erasures." *Geoforum* 89: 114–23.

Sorinas, B. 2015. "Recuperar derechos entre cadáveres de la especulación." *elDiario.es*, July 5. http://www.eldiario.es/catalunya/opinions/Recuperar-derechos-cadaveres-especulacion_6_406019409.html.

Sorinas, B., and E. Giné. 2017. "Tranquilos, podéis iros de vacaciones." *El Salto*, April 5. https://www.elsaltodiario.com/ocupacion/tranquilos-podeis-iros-de-vacaciones

Suarez, M. 2017. "Debt Revolts: Ecuadorian Foreclosed Families at the PAH in Barcelona." *Dialectical Anthropology* 41: 263–77.

TAIFA. 2005. "La situación actual de la economía española." http://seminaritaifa.org/pdf/Informe_01_ES.pdf.

———. 2007. "Hay pobres porque hay muy, muy ricos." http://seminaritaifa.org/pdf/Informe_04_ES.pdf.

———. 2008. "Auge y crisis de la vivienda en España." http://informes.seminaritaifa.org/informe-05/.

Tascón, J. 2003. "Capital internacional antes de la 'internacionalización del capital' en España, 1936–1959." In *Los Empresarios de Franco. Política y economía en España (1936–1957)*, edited by G. Sánchez Recio and L. J. Tascón Fernández, 281–306. Barcelona: Crítica.

Tassin, E. 2012. "De la subjetivación política. Althusser/Rancière/Foucault/Arendt/Deleuze." *Revista de Estudios Sociales* 43: 36–49.

Tatjer, M. 2005. "La vivienda obrera en España de los siglos XIX y XX: de la promoción privada a la promoción pública (1853–1975)." *Scripta Nova* 9, no. 194(23): n.p.

———. 2008. "La Vivienda en Cataluña desde una perspective histórica: El siglo XX." In *Vivienda y sociedad: nuevas demandas, nuevos instrumentos*, edited by C. Bellet, J. Ganau Casa, and J. M. Llop, 379–402. Lleida: Milenio.

Thompson, M. 2021. "What's So New about New Municipalism?" *Progress in Human Geography* 45, no. 2: 317–42.

Toral, P. 2001. *The Reconquest of the New World: Multinational Enterprises and Spain's Direct Investment in Latin America*. Aldershot: Ashgate.

Trilla, C. 2014. "Desigualdad y vivienda." *ACE: Architecture, City and Environment = Arquitectura, Ciudad y Entorno* 9, no. 26: 95–126.

Tuhiwai Smith, L. 1999. *Decolonizing Methodologies: Research and Indigenous Peoples*. London: Zed Books.

van Gent, W. P. C. 2010. "Housing Policy as a Lever for Change? The Politics of Welfare, Assets and Tenure." *Housing Studies* 25, no. 5: 735–53.

Venteo, D. 2012. *La Barceloneta: guia d'història urbana*. Barcelona: Ajuntament de Barcelona.

Vilarós, T. M. 2003. "The Passing of the Xarnego-Immigrant: Post-Nationalism and the Ideologies of Assimilation in Catalonia." *Arizona Journal of Hispanic Cultural Studies* 7: 229–46.

Wijburg, G., M. B. Aalbers, and S. Heeg. 2018. "The Financialisation of Rental Housing 2.0: Releasing Housing into the Privatised Mainstream of Capital Accumulation." *Antipode* 50, no. 4: 1098–119.

Wöhl, S. 2017. "The Gender Dynamics of Financialization and Austerity in the European Union: The Irish Case." In *Gender and the Economic Crisis in Europe: Politics, Institutions and Intersectionality*, edited by J. Kantola and E. Lombardo, 139–60. Basingstoke: Palgrave Macmillan.

Wyly, E., M. Atia, H. Foxcroft, D. J. Hammel, and K. Phillips-Watts. 2006. "American Home: Predatory Mortgage Capital and Neighbourhood Spaces of Race and Class Exploitation in the United States." *Geografiska Annaler. Series B, Human Geography* 88, no. 1: 105–32.

Wyly, E., M. Moos, D. Hammel, and E. Kabahizi. 2009. "Cartographies of Race and Class: Mapping the Class-Monopoly Rents of American Subprime Mortgage Capital." *International Journal of Urban and Regional Research* 33, no. 2: 332–54.

Wyly, E., and C. S. Ponder. 2011. "Gender, Age, and Race in Subprime America." *Housing Policy Debate* 21, no. 4: 529–64.

Ximénez de Sandoval, P. 2010. "Vivienda la ruina del gran tinglado 'subprime.'" *El País*, December 12. https://elpais.com/diario/2010/12/12/domingo/1292129555_850215.html.

Youngman, T., and L. Barrio. 2021. "Housing Is Not a Crime: Madrid's Post-crisis Squatters' Movement Tell Our Story through Activist Research." *Radical Housing Journal* 3, no. 1: 207–28.

Yrigoy, I. 2021. "The Political Economy of Rental Housing in Spain: The Dialectics of Exploitation(s) and Regulations." *New Political Economy* 26, no. 1: 186–202.

INDEX

Africa, 10, 51, 73, 81, 143
Arrese, José Luis, 45–46, 101
autonomous communities, 29, 52–53, 58, 190, 194n3

bailouts, 11, 94, 103–4, 165, 178
Bancaja, 5, 89. *See also* Bankia
Bankia, 5–6, 111, 115–17, 121, 194n2, 195n8
banking legislation, 50, 62, 124, 166
Bank of Spain: annual report, 72; Cirbe and, 91; compañerxs and, 95; debt collection, 80; European Union and, 181; experiences with, 90; home appraisals, 61; mortgage applications and, 2, 89, 120; mortgage debt and, 120; real estate and, 195n11; refinancing and, 116, 118; securitization, 9; Spanish Fund for Orderly Bank Restructuring (FROB) and, 109
bankruptcy: Fadesa, Martinsa, 108; law, 81; personal, 3, 11, 53, 71, 142
Barcelona: activism, 144; *barracas*, 40–41; Cathedral, 73; class breakdown, 18; compañerxs, 79, 85, 91, 181; evictions, 155, 160, 190; experiences in, 1, 168–71, 178; Good Practices Code, 158; housing boom, 71, 34, 37, 103, 112, 171, 175; housing collectives, 188–89; housing conditions, 45; housing futures, 186–87, 190; housing rights movement, 33, 139, 190; international banks, 160; *La Vanguardia*, 51; living conditions, 40; metropolitan region, 18, 29, 71, 93, 99; migration to, 47; mortgage debt, 15, 28, 80, 88, 136; mortgaged lives, 139; municipal

politics, 36; National Housing Plan, 43; 1992 Olympics, 55; overcrowding, 40; PAH, 5, 12, 16, 30, 35, 121–22, 138, 140–43, 145, 168, 173; peripheries of, 132; shantytowns, 126; Social Urgency Plan, 38
barracas, 39–41, 47
biopolitics: assistentialism and, 167; definition of, 22; Foucault and, 26; housing booms and, 70, 99; of mortgage debt, 14, 16–18, 22, 24–25, 34, 37, 139, 172, 175–76, 179, 181–82, 184, 186; norms and, 24; security functions and, 180
Blackstone, 117, 124–25
buccaneer, 87–88, 98

CaixaBank (La Caixa), 75, 77, 90, 93–94, 107; Bankia, 194n2, 195n8; foreign investment funds, 117; mortgage credit, 72; postcrisis, 121; SAREB, 111
Caixa Catalunya: auction of, 195n8; BBVA, 121; CatalunyaBanc, 124; experiences with, 88, 91, 94, 114, 129; foreign investment funds, 117; mortgage debt, 113–14, 129
Caixa Penedès, 120
capitalism, 12, 15, 19, 132; exploitation and, 33; Foucault and, 22; inequality and, 22, 33; proletarianization and, 21; racial, 167, 175, 182; Spanish, 37; urban process and, 185
Cáritas, 187
Catalan Rental Law, 188
Catalonia: activism, 187–88; autonomous community, 29; bank branches, 92; Catalan Housing Agency, 187; evictions, 30, 155;

GEOGRAPHIES OF JUSTICE AND SOCIAL TRANSFORMATION